SEX FACTS

FOR THE FAMILY

CLIFFORD & JOYCE PENNER

WORD PUBLISHING
Dallas·London·Vancouver·Melbourne

SEX FACTS FOR THE FAMILY

Library of Congress Cataloging-in-Publication Data

Penner, Clifford.
     Sex facts for the family / Clifford and Joyce Penner.
        p.   cm.
     Rev. ed. of : A gift for all ages. 1986.
     Includes bibliographical references (p.) and index.
     ISBN 0–8499–3287–4
     1. Sex. 2. Sex instruction. 3. Sex—Religious aspects—
Christianity. I. Penner, Joyce. II. Penner, Clifford. Gift for all
ages. III. Title.
     HQ31.P4466   1992
     306.7—dc20   91-43251
                                                                CIP

Printed in the United States of America

2 3 4 5 9   LB   9 8 7 6 5 4 3 2 1

We dedicate this to our family

Julene Maree

Gregory Boyd

Kristine Renée

For further information regarding seminars
or other speaking engagements,
please write or call:

Clifford and Joyce Penner
2 North Lake Avenue, Suite 610
Pasadena, Calif. 91101
818–449–2525

Contents

Part 5 Handling Adult Sexuality in Special Situations

Part 6 Tough Sexual Issues

Acknowledgments

For the first edition, published in 1986 as *A Gift for All Ages,* we expressed our gratitude to our dear friends, Peb Jackson and Roland Hinz, for their extensive support and criticism, to Dr. Larry Majovski for providing access to computerized research files, to Carla Schuler, our research assistant, for organizing and summarizing the research information, to Ava Klein-Selski for her expertise on birth control methods, to sister Milli Penner for her long hours at the word processor and her many helpful suggestions, and for all the assistance from Christy Claxton-Brink, Heidi Carter, Julie Rathbun, Shannon Thyne, and Lori Young. To all those who shared themselves so openly with us, we are especially grateful!

For this second edition, we would like to add a special word of appreciation to Sue Ann Jones for her great editing and her wonderful spirit.

Introduction: Sex Versus Sexuality

Sex is powerful! In the act of sex, two people become one, losing themselves in each other. Sex can take us to the highest peaks of ecstasy or to the deepest pits of despair and degradation. It is part of God's design for us.

Our sexuality is much broader than mere sexual intercourse, however. It is a vital part of who we are as human beings created in the image of God. It is that intense, personal dimension that makes us a whole person, male or female. Our sexuality is with us for life—from before birth until death. It includes all the characteristics and feelings that make each of us unique.

We associate sexuality with the roles we play as boys and girls (or as men and women) and with the way we relate to people of the same sex and the opposite sex. The feelings and thoughts that stir inside us are part of those relationships.

Our vitality—our sexual drive—is the basis for getting things done in life and the basis for sexual arousal and release. In addition, sexuality includes *all* sexual behavior, from hand-holding and kissing to sexual intercourse. And all of this is in God's image!

Even though our sexuality is basic to who we are as human beings, we may harbor unexpressed issues of sexuality inside ourselves. These issues can be our most private secrets. We have difficulty sharing them and thus revealing what we really think and feel. We lack knowledge, and feel inadequate and unsure of ourselves. When these feelings are exposed, how easily we feel ashamed and embarrassed!

Sexuality develops in our family of origin. Every family sends messages about sexuality to its members. Some of these messages are spoken, but the loudest ones are *lived*. They are silently communicated through actions and attitudes about the sexual issues that concern and confront all families. These issues can be avoided or distorted, but they won't go away.

Our culture also influences our sexuality. Modern-day culture saturates us with sex. Part of this overexposure is caused by the media. But our conversations, jokes, dramas, and literature all contribute, too. Sex is woven into the very fabric of our existence. There is no escape. We cannot protect our children from it, and we cannot pretend it doesn't exist. So the only choice is to be knowledgeable about it. We need to have the best information to help ourselves and to help our children. Knowledge can make a positive difference in our lives and influence the development and adjustment of our children. That is what this book is all about; that is its intention and purpose.

We have been working together in this field since we joined our professional lives in 1975. Until that time, Joyce had been teaching nursing at California State University in Los Angeles; she also coordinated development of the curriculum for the new school of nursing at Azusa Pacific University in Azusa, California. Cliff had a private practice as a clinical psychologist. He had trained lay counselors in churches and trained and supervised volunteers for operating a suicide hotline in Los Angeles.

Our work together actually began when Cliff was asked to teach a ten-week class on sexuality to seminary wives. Confronted by the challenge of talking about sex with sixty women, he coerced Joyce into joining him. The result was a combining of Cliff's psychological and theological expertise with Joyce's physiological-psychosomatic awareness.

We studied diligently and presented ten, two-hour sessions on sexuality. Being clinicians, we never really expected knowledge to make a difference in people's sexual experience—but to our delight it did! The success of that experience led us to teach seminars on sexual adjustment for couples in churches throughout the country. The content of the seminars developed into our first book, *The Gift of Sex*.

Becoming known as experts on the subject of sex, we began teaching sexuality to all age groups. Joyce developed a sex-education program for our own school district. We began giving human-sexuality lectures on college campuses and teaching sex education to junior-high and high-school students, and to singles and premarital couples. Joyce was asked to teach nurses and nursing students to deal with sex and illness. Cliff started groups for women who had been sexually abused as children. And thus, our second book, *A Gift for All Ages* evolved.

In the years since then, our approaches to many of the issues addressed in *A Gift for All Ages* have been modified to incorporate medical and sociological developments. New birth-control methods, advancements in the treatment of infertility and menopause, the effects of AIDS, and other information needed to be incorporated into a new version; thus, *A Gift for All Ages* has been revised to become *Sex Facts for the Family*.

In our home, sex has been such a common topic that we sometimes worried that we would miss sharing some developmentally necessary communication with our children. The worry came because we realized we might take for granted that they were well informed because of our familiarity with the topic.

We will be referring to our children throughout this book because they have taught us much of what we know about teaching kids about sex. We are convinced that, as parents, we can learn much of what we need to know about parenting our children if we take time to listen to them.

Julene, our graduate-student adult, has always been a question asker. She has dated throughout her adolescence and young adulthood, and has been very open with us in the process of learning about her sexuality. Her ability to struggle with life's major decisions keeps us assured that she will not make impulsive mistakes.

Greg is our college-aged young adult who is very serious about his life decisions, while keeping us in stitches with his wry humor. He reads avidly and thinks through who he wants to be and how he is going to behave. His deliberateness is comforting. His solitude often makes us wonder what's going on inside.

Kristine is no longer our twerp. She is a high-school adolescent, seven years younger than Greg, and has always seemed like a little adult. She is the one who has grown up with sex being so familiar that she has not asked the typical age-appropriate questions, so we sometimes wonder what all she has assimilated in that alert mind of hers.

We tend to be very involved parents, loving and giving but with high expectations, probably even a little overanxious. Our family is a vital part of who we are. We thank God; we have been very blessed.

Sex Facts for the Family is a family handbook on sexuality. It deals with all *informative* issues on sexuality without attempting to resolve the theoretical issues. It is oriented to the practical needs of the family. Every home needs some portion of this book. It is designed to be a resource book, a family's first-aid kit for sexual issues. Parents may want to read some chapters with their children. Other chapters will give them guidance in dealing with their children, and still others are for the parents, themselves. Adults will find some sections beneficial in making major life decisions or for helping a friend in trouble. Adolescents will benefit from reading several of the chapters. There is information for the single person, children of all ages, the childless couple, parents, and the elderly. Since our sexuality is with us from birth to death, it is still true that sex is a gift for all ages.

For Further Study

Masters, William H., Virginia E. Johnson, and Robert C. Kolodny. *Masters and Johnson on Sex and Human Loving*. Boston: Little, Brown and Co., 1986.

Penner, Clifford L., and Joyce J. Penner. *The Gift of Sex*. Waco, Tex.: Word, 1981.

————. *Counseling for Sexual Disorders*. Dallas: Word, 1990.

Part 1

Family Planning

1

To Baby or Not to Baby

The only absolutely irreversible relationship decision you will ever make is the choice to bring a life into this world. That may sound dramatic. It may tie your stomach in knots or leave you in a real quandary about how to decide. But it remains a fact. If you buy a house, choose a career, even choose a husband or wife, those decisions are reversible—as difficult, unpleasant, or immoral as they may be. But with the decision to have a child, you have no recourse. To whatever degree you assume or relinquish responsibility for that child, the child is yours! Isn't it incredible that millions of children are born each year, when the decision is this fateful? And it is even more surprising that many modern, educated, enlightened couples never give a thought as to whether their having children is a wise decision.

Not only is having a child an irreversible decision, but it also involves long-term commitment. The initial commitment to parenting is from birth through adolescence. But there are additional financial and certainly emotional commitments that go far beyond the exciting yet turbulent years of adolescence. Parents whose children have long ago left home report that the sense of being the concerned parent never leaves. So not only is it impossible to reverse the decision, but you are left to live with the consequences throughout your life. Death and giving up the child for adoption are the only forces that break that commitment and responsibility. Giving a child up for adoption may free the parent technically, but many times not emotionally.

The awesomeness of this decision, its irreversibility and the resulting long-term commitment, all increase the significance of the choice to have children. To bring a life into the world is a serious responsibility. You take on the feeding, clothing, and sheltering of that life, as well as the shaping, the influencing, and the educating of that person. Your children come to you with what they inherit through their genes, but their lives are like empty slates. You, as the parent, bear the responsibility for filling that slate. You help to shape these undeveloped beings into unique persons of special worth in society.

When we consider all the forces at work in the world—the threat of overpopulation, the high divorce rate, the increase in single-parent families, pollution and the depletion of our natural resources, the uncertain inflation level and cost of living, the millions of uncared for and unwanted children—the importance of deciding to have a child becomes obvious. Children deserve the right to be born into a world where they are wanted, where they will be loved and cherished. Not only do they have basic physical needs, but they have emotional and spiritual needs as well. They need a home where they will receive loving care and warm acceptance.

The Rewards

Now let's look at the other side of the coin: the rewards of having children. The decision to have a child is the decision to bring into our lives that wonderful, soft, dependent bundle of joy who can fulfill us as parents. Babies evoke an instinctive response in their parents. A child also offers us the opportunity to give ourselves totally to someone else. We can share our values and our faith more completely with our children than with anyone. In addition to the dependence of an infant, and the joy of all the stages of development, some parents have children so that they will be cared for in their old age. There are many specific rewards that push couples to have children besides the unexplainable, indefinable urge toward procreation. The drive for self-perpetuation—that is, making sure you have offspring to survive you—is a major force behind baby-making.

Most couples have the capacity to procreate. To make a decision *against* what is your potential, against what or how you were created, takes a great deal of struggle and conscious effort.

Cultural Expectations

The process usually goes like this: Fun comments about children are made during the engagement time and during the early years of marriage, and relatively little pressure is felt. After several years of marriage, the couple may notice the comments are increasing both in frequency and expectation. "When should we be expecting our first grandchild?" they may be asked, or, "How is everything going between you and Steve?"

The pressure may be even more demanding. Family members and friends may ask directly if the woman is pregnant or if the couple is planning to start their family soon. Others *assume* that the couple wants children, sending the spouses an unspoken message: *You will not live up to our expectations if you do not have a child and don't have one soon!* For the couple who is planning on having children, this can easily become a mild irritant because parents or friends are not letting them do what they want to do when they want to do it. This desire isn't coming from inside them. For those couples who are *not* planning on having children (or are unsure or unable), this pressure can be incredible.

As the years pass and still there are no children, the pressure may become unbearable. When the woman reaches her thirtieth birthday or gets a raise or promotion on the job, the nervousness of her "directors" heightens. As time goes on, the pressure can increase to the point of being obnoxious.

We have known couples whose out-of-town relatives have sent them letters with suggestions for assuring fertility. Other couples have been told that friends or relatives were praying for their pregnancy—when the couple wasn't even trying to conceive (and, in fact, was using birth control). Too often, the couple will hear, "What is the matter with you? Have you been checked out by a doctor? There are all kinds of modern ways that you can be helped these days."

All this may occur before the couple has even decided they want to have a child. It expresses a cultural expectation or anticipation that the choice for children will be made. Some people think that society is violated or the couple is being selfish if they choose not to have children. Having a family is not considered an option, but an expectation. The assumption is, *Of course you'll be having children!* It's as expected as the assumption that, *Of course, now that you're married, you'll be living together.*

At the same time that couples are experiencing the pressure to have children, they may be observing a most contradictory message about being parents. Before having children, they get this message: *Children are wonderful. They fulfill your life; they provide you with one of life's happiest experiences. If you don't have children you will be missing out on something vitally important.* This is a clear and strong message that says, *to have children is not only expected, but very fulfilling.*

Once the couple has children, however, the message changes. The new message is that one should get this parenting business over with as quickly as possible. The wonderfulness somehow seems to disappear in these messages, and being a parent is portrayed as being a real drag. Parenting is not held in high esteem as a full-time job. Mothers often express their frustration with their children, rather than their delight and pride. When delight and pride *are* expressed, parents are made to feel that they are being inappropriately boastful.

Our culture seems to give conflicting messages: that babies are something you should look forward to—but then not expect to enjoy.

Split Decision

A major source of stress in a marriage relationship can be disagreement between husband and wife about when or whether to have a baby.

There are many reasons why either the husband or wife might not be ready for a child: A woman may feel she needs more security in her career, or she may have difficulty interrupting her career to start a family. Emotionally, she may feel she is not ready to give herself so totally to another person. Her relationship with her husband may not be stable enough to warrant bringing a child into the family. Finances also can be a major issue. She may fear that without her income the family could not survive. In such a situation a child would cause severe stress or a major change in lifestyle. She may not be ready for the impact of these changes. It's wise to consider all these feelings and possibilities before becoming pregnant.

From the man's perspective, the reasons could be very similar. He may have financial concerns, anxiety about timing, or conflict in the marriage relationship. Most frequently, when the man is resistant, he is not ready to take on the role of being the responsible father. He senses that this new role is going to dramatically alter his lifestyle. He is right! Bringing a baby into the family will change life drastically! It is most reasonable that a husband consider those issues *before* deciding to become a parent.

For both spouses, there may be the fear of the unknown. Even as marriage brings about radical changes and requires adjustments, so does having a child. The effects of these changes are never completely predictable. For some, it is surprisingly jarring. For others, parenthood is a natural, easy adjustment and the couple falls into their roles as if they had always been parents.

Mary and Fred had been married five years. He was just completing an advanced degree. She had already completed her education. Both had strong professional careers. They were very responsible people who had every reason to believe that life with a child would flow smoothly because of how they had adjusted to other changes.

But in spite of their positive history together, Fred had a deep-seated fear that even though he was twenty-six years old, he was not competent to become a father. He worried that this new role was going to demand more from him than he could deliver. Nevertheless, he decided to go along with his wife's desire to have children. Fortunately, once he became a father, he naturally accepted his role and has functioned most adequately as a parent with all three of his children.

Diane and Jerry started having children early in their married life, mainly because Diane wanted them. While Jerry was hesitant, Diane had been trained in childcare and was eager for the children to be born. The unpredictable happened. Diane found being a mother extremely stressful. Often she became overwhelmed with the care of the children and left them in day care as long as possible each day. Jerry, on the other hand, gave of himself in a free and loving way. He was able to be a most involved father, quite in contrast to what he had expected.

What if one of you definitely does not want a child at all? This is a real dilemma. Obviously, such a conflict should have been discussed before marriage and usually has been if you have had premarital counseling. What sometimes happens is this: The man tells his bride-to-be that he doesn't think he ever wants to have children, but she assumes that she can talk him into it. She thinks she can change his mind and then is severely disappointed and distraught when she discovers two or three years later that he's even more adamant about not having children than he was before.

It is always dangerous to go into a marriage assuming that you can change your spouse's viewpoint on a major issue. There are good reasons why some people might not want to have children. The passage of time or a new relationship does not necessarily reverse those reasons.

Should you find that the two of you cannot come to an agreement on whether or not you want children, we would strongly encourage you first to talk about it as openly as you can.

Second, do some reading on the subject. One book written for this exact purpose is *A Baby? Maybe: A Guide to the Most Fateful Decision in Your Life* by Elizabeth M. Whelan. This book will help you think through your decision about having children. It will guide you in defining the ramifications of this vital decision.

If the two of you cannot reach agreement regarding parenthood, you should seek professional help. It is important, though, that you not expect the professional to make your decision for you. Rather, seek someone who can help you define your differences, negotiate those differences, and make decisions that will be acceptable to both of you.

Some marriages end in divorce because the issue of whether or not to have children is irreconcilable.

The Impact of Babies on the Marriage

The expectation that children will resolve stress in a marriage is, for the most part, unfounded. However, as we have interacted with various couples, we have discovered that for some, having children *has* improved their relationship. A certain kind of bond or connection begins when a child is born. Up until that point the marriage may have been in jeopardy. But having a child together may be the "cement" that binds some couples together. Unfortunately, there are many more cases where the opposite is true. Couples who count on children saving their marriage usually end up divorced. Their children did not help resolve their marital difficulties; instead, the stress of the new responsibilities accentuated the conflict that was already present. The following examples illustrate how children can affect a marriage.

At the time of Eric and Nancy's marriage, Nancy's parents had strongly opposed the relationship. The couple had gone through continual stress in their dating, breaking up and getting back together many times. Finally, somewhat on an impulse, they decided to marry. When they found that married life was not really much better than the dating life had been, they agreed that perhaps they needed children. So they brought two children into the world. Two and a half years later they separated and were finally divorced. Having children only made a bad situation worse.

Sometimes, however, just the opposite happens.

Glen and Linda had been married about four years. Linda married Glen on the rebound after the man she really wanted to marry had broken off their engagement. Throughout the first four years of their married life, Linda's mind continually returned to her first love and the joy she believed would have been hers in that marriage. Glen didn't offer the warmth, intensity, and excitement she had known with her previous boyfriend.

Linda became pregnant without planning for it, and a change began immediately. Glen became much more involved in the relationship. His care for Linda was intense as they anticipated the arrival of their first child. When the baby arrived, Glen became a most caring, loving, and devoted husband and father. It was as if something new had happened to him as a result of his child being born.

We tell these actual, real-life stories to illustrate that there is no easy way to predict a couple's response to having a child. We can say very emphatically, however: It should never be assumed that a child is going to improve a relationship. That may be the outcome, but it should not be the expectation. Many children are brought into the world because they are desired for the purpose of improving a marriage. That is a most inadequate and potentially dangerous basis for having children.

Eyes Wide Open to the Delights and the Dilemmas

In choosing to have children, it is crucial to get a realistic perspective on parenting. Spend time with couples who have children of all ages. Babysit for children of various ages. Read about children.

We are struck by the fact that as a couple prepares for their first child, all of their energy seems to be going toward preparing a room oriented around a baby. All of the investment goes toward what is needed for the first twelve months. Many come to parenting with this "baby-care" attitude. They see themselves parenting this wonderful, warm, soft, cuddly little baby.

They disregard the fact that they are going to be up nights, that the baby is going to have messy diapers and at some stage is going to smear that mess all over the lovely, newly decorated walls. The baby is going to have croup, and not only will it keep them up at night but it will have them worried about whether he or she is going to survive.

Once babies reach that first stage of independence, they are going to want their own way. They are going to enjoy taking a dish of rice and turning it upside down on their heads. It's fun to have those little granules go showering down all around them. Often the fun is accentuated by watching Mother bounce off the walls. This provides a great deal of entertainment for the little two-year-old.

Some babies are going to want to be rocked; but others prefer to be put into the crib, so you won't get to hold them as much as you want.

They will grow and change. At each stage of development, you will need to flex and adjust to their ever-changing need for you as parents. You are going to have to be ready to give and give and give.

On the other hand, there is nothing that can compare with the joy of watching a growing child. Your own little children running after you and calling you "Mommy" or "Daddy," asking to be comforted when there has been a scratch or a fall, and wanting to be held when they are sick are all examples of the incredible warmth children bring. They love to play games. They run to hide as you walk into the room or they make some new discovery about the world around them. Nothing can compare with the rewards of these experiences.

As you move toward the decision to have children, it is absolutely crucial that you face realistically the joys on the one hand and the burdens and stress on the other. It is important that you know yourselves and your reactions to the responsibility of children. The more you have to give, the more you receive. Loved children are clearly easier to parent than deprived children.

Stewardship and Responsibility

We hear much about stewardship, about the need to be good stewards of that with which we have been entrusted. In society, we talk about being stewards of the natural resources, not wasting

water or trees, and not polluting the air, soil, or rivers. Stewardship is important. But we hear relatively little about being good
stewards of children who have been entrusted to us.

Parenting is society's way of perpetuating itself. We are entrusted with the full responsibility to nurture the development of
our children's potential as long as they are in our care. So much
human potential is wasted because it was never developed by
those who were responsible for nurturing it. The responsibility
of being good stewards of the natural resources that are present
in our children includes training them to be good members of
society, assisting them in learning effective decision-making skills,
and helping them to fully develop their natural gifts. We are also
responsible to teach them to respect themselves and those around
them, to help them recognize their dependence on God, the
Creator and giver of life.

It is our strong feeling that society's encouragement to have
children must be accompanied with the encouragement to accept
the serious responsibilities of parenting. We see this as the only
way to break into the dilemma of negative or inadequate
parenting being passed from one generation to the next.
Parenting education and consultation are needed to reverse
negative parenting patterns.

Choosing to Be Childless

Most of us grew up assuming that we would someday have
children. Parents usually want their children to have children.
You can count on all of your friends who are having children to
want you to have children, too. So deciding to be childless is a
daring move. It counters the natural expectations.

If you choose not to have children, the most automatic response
from others will be to label this as a selfish decision. Yet whether
you are thinking about that choice for yourselves or you have
friends who are thinking about remaining childless, it is vital that
you hear and understand why that choice is being made.

There are many reasons why couples decide not to have children.
The most common reason for deciding against having children
is age. Either one or both spouses feel they are emotionally or

physically too old or inadequate. This is especially true for second marriages in which one partner already has a child. In some instances, a couple may fear that they have experienced too much stress in their relationship. Bringing children into their world would only add to that stress, and they don't think their relationship could survive. This seems like a mature, head-out-of-the-sand kind of decision. Others believe they would be inadequate parents because they were inadequately parented, themselves. We've known people who were so committed to serving others that they felt a child would interrupt that commitment. In still other instances, some have chosen to be childless for medical reasons or because of concern about one or the other partner not being able to be a responsible parent.

Richard and Martha were struggling with whether to have children. Richard had had a severe problem with impulsively exposing his genitals within the extended family and in public. He still struggled with this at times. They had reached the decision that with his sexual insecurities and a very unstable employment history, it was important not to bring a child into their home. Martha knew she would be in constant fear of both sexual exploitation and financial insecurity.

Even though childlessness is an option in today's world, it is important to note that only about 2 or 3 percent of the population ever make this choice. Couples choosing to remain childless are clearly in the minority. There is a need to be very gentle with those who are making the choice to be childless. It is their personal choice and they must be free to make it.

A word from the authors might be in order here. We are both delighted with the fact that we have three children. They are an *important* part of our lives. The whole experience of parenting has been very positive for us. So our stressing both sides of parenting should not be construed as an indication that somehow we think choosing to be parents is a bad idea. However, we do believe it is a serious decision that is often taken too lightly, so we are emphasizing the seriousness of bringing children into the world.

Naturally, there are questions about remaining childless. Some people believe that bright, healthy couples with strong genetic histories have a responsibility to supply the world with as many offspring as they can physically, emotionally, and spiritually manage. Other people ask, "Is it not my Christian responsibility, my moral responsibility to have children? Did not God command Adam and Eve to subdue and replenish the earth? Was it not part of the Hebrew culture to perpetuate life? Is it not a natural, God-given instinct to be a parent?" It seems that all those questions can be answered in the affirmative. However, it's important to remember that people today have not chosen to live their lives in the most natural, creative way. If they did, they would begin producing children at age thirteen, fourteen, or whenever they are physically capable. And women would keep on having children until menopause, which might be ten, twenty, or thirty children later!

Once a couple has decided not to have as many children as physically possible, they have decided to go against what is natural. Then the obvious option is available: They can choose to have one child, or two, or five, or none at all. Let us repeat again—we are not advocating that couples choose not to have children. We are advocating that people make a *conscious choice.*

Getting Pregnant: A New Reason for Lovemaking

In most people there seems to be the urge to show the ability to impregnate or be impregnated and bear children. It is part of human beings' vitality as men and women. When couples have decided they want children, their sexual experiences take on special meaning.

When you reach this decision and you are ready to conceive, we'd recommend that you make it a very special time, somewhat like your wedding night. The attitude with which you start a life will, at least subtly, be transmitted to your child. If at some point you can say to your child, "When we decided that we wanted to have you, we went off to the seashore for a weekend and we spent our time talking and walking and loving one another in a most special and close way. You are the product of love. We didn't get pregnant that weekend, but a few months later we were pregnant and you were starting to grow. That time of love and closeness is how you began. You are very special!"

Some couples find a new freedom in their lovemaking as a result of not having the concern about birth control. If you had been using birth-control pills, there may have been anxiety about its effect on the woman. If you were using a barrier method such as a condom or a diaphragm, you may have had an ongoing concern as to whether it would do its work. If you were using some variation of the rhythm method, you may have had concern as to whether you were making love on a safe day. So now, without the fears about pregnancy—in fact, with the desire for pregnancy—you experience new freedom. This can be especially true for the woman when she finds herself able to let go and be as intensely sexual as she is able, because she has the great urge to become pregnant.

For the husband, there may be a new feeling of potency that says, *Now I am able to make love for all of the right reasons. Not only for the joy and pleasure but also for the possibility of impregnation.* When these feelings are shared, they can serve to bring the two of you closer to one another.

Timing the Arrival of Children

The question is often asked, "When is the right time to get pregnant?" There rarely is a perfect time. For most couples it is best to wait until they have connected deeply and adjusted to each other's uniqueness. But beyond this point, there are so many variables that it is hard to say when is the right time.

Even though many women are successfully producing and enjoying their first babies in their late thirties or early forties, we do know that, physically, the twenties are the best child-bearing years for a woman. But there are other issues: how children fit into your education and career goals, your finances, and other family responsibilities. If you wait to reach perfection in your jobs, your marriage, or your finances, you will likely never have children, so forget that goal! You can plan for parenthood, choose wisely, and set goals. If you have fears or hesitations, these should be confronted. Sometimes one or both spouses keep delaying because of some anxiety about the possibility of having a child. When that is the case, it is important to face and define those fears.

We have a seven-year gap between our second and third children because of such a delay. Joyce had German measles during the twelfth week of her second pregnancy, incurring a 90 percent chance of having a defective child. There was no way to know until he was born that Greg would be totally normal and healthy. So we lived with five months of concern. From that point, we connected pregnancy with anxiety about producing a normal child. Since we already had a healthy girl and boy, we were hesitant to go for a third. We finally had the courage six years and three months later, and what a special treat that third child, Kristine, has been.

Facing the Decision

In conclusion, to baby or not to baby is a decision every couple will face. In the complexity of today's world, to have children is not as natural an outcome of marriage as was true during the past, when lifestyles were simpler and more family-oriented. This is a decision that needs to be made between the two of you, with the sense of God's blessing.

For parents of married-but-childless children, we encourage you to "set them free"! Let them make their own decision in their own time. Nothing is a greater delight to parents or grandparents than the arrival of a child freely chosen. Children are a beautiful gift from God, but they bring with them a lifetime commitment of responsible parenting. Those who choose to be without children need your ongoing love and support, even though you may be disappointed in their decision. Those unable to conceive need your most special love and care.

For Further Study

*Elvenstar, Diane C. *Children: To Have or Not Have—A Guide to Making and Living with Your Decision*. San Francisco: Harbor Publishing, 1982.

Whelan, Elizabeth M. *A Baby? Maybe: A Guide to the Most Fateful Decision in Your Life*. New York: Macmillan, 1980.

*This book is no longer in print but is still available in many libraries.

2

Choosing and Using Birth Control

Family planning is the process of setting up a reproductive life program. It is thinking, praying, and talking with each other about whether to have children, when to have children, and how to regulate those choices with an effective birth-control measure.

Once a couple decides that they are not going to allow themselves to get pregnant any time that would happen naturally, they have chosen to use birth control. It is estimated that if women decided to let nature take its course for their reproductive life spans, most women would produce between ten and thirty babies! That would not only create an incredible personal and financial burden, but also a world overpopulation problem of monumental dimensions! The command God gave to be fruitful, multiply, and fill the earth has already been completed. The current world concern is how we are going to responsibly care for the children already in the world. This has led couples to approach reproduction by choice, rather than by chance. When choice fails, either because of inability to reproduce (see chapter 4) or because of an unwanted pregnancy, both individuals and the family unit are strongly impacted.

Moral and Religious Issues

Over the years, the church has struggled with the issue of birth control. The concern has been that taking reproduction into our own hands is interfering with God's plan for our lives. In other words, we are in some way interrupting the work of the Master Creator. The Mormon church takes a position of not interfering with reproduction in any way. In fact, the more children the better!

Other religious leaders recommend that responsible choices need to be made, but that no "unnatural" methods of controlling conception be used. In 1984, Pope John Paul II took a bold stand on birth control. He proclaimed that the practice and attitude of contraception were "harmful to man's interior spiritual culture" (*Time,* 3 December 1984). The challenge from Pope John Paul VI to the members of the Roman Catholic Church was to be available for motherhood and fatherhood. The Roman Catholic Church has held that abstinence during the woman's fertile time is the only acceptable means of preventing conception. The belief is that sexual union and procreation are inseparable in the plan of God. These pronouncements are based on "natural law" rather than direct biblical teaching. Natural law promotes the concept of a moral order or reasonable principle of humanity that fits with creation as determined by the Roman Catholic Church.

Still others would put no restrictions on birth control; instead, they see it as a personal choice. The belief is that God created us as intelligent human beings. He gave us dominion over the earth. His primary message is how He wants to relate to us as His people—how we can come to Him, be forgiven by Him, and become members of His family. He gave us free choice and expects us to use that freedom wisely. The primary goals for His people are that we love Him and each other.

Each person must come to grips with the religious and moral issues of birth control. Next, those issues have to be worked through within the marriage relationship. It is best if the birth-control issue is settled before marriage. Ask yourselves, "How does our reproductive plan fit with our religious beliefs? Would we like to have children? How old would we like to be when we have children? How would we feel if we couldn't have children? How would we feel if we got pregnant without planning for it? What are our life goals? How do children fit into those goals?"

Each spouse comes to the marriage with attitudes regarding childbearing. The purpose of birth control is to conceive only when that is desired and planned. Attitudes about childbearing will affect each individual's feelings about using birth control. These need to be cleared with each other before the two people decide to marry.

We have an acquaintance who married a man older than she. *After* marriage, she discovered that he was violently opposed to having children. They are now divorced. The opposite can also happen: One spouse may be totally against using birth control, and the other not ready to allow babies to arrive at random.

Agreement concerning the spouses' attitudes and feelings about birth control is vital to family planning. If a choice is made that birth control will be used, then the method needs to be selected.

Definitions and History

Birth control includes all methods of limiting the birth of children. Contraception is one of these. Contraception prevents the man's sperm from uniting with the egg cell from the woman. Contraception is used to prevent pregnancy, not to interrupt it once conception has taken place. That is an important moral and religious distinction. We are not talking about *taking* life, we are talking about *preventing* a new life from beginning. Even though many texts include abortion in the chapter with birth control, and many times abortion is the method used to prevent childbearing, we believe in birth control as a means of preventing conception, not interrupting pregnancy once conception has occurred.

There is no perfect method of contraception. There are many that work, but what works well for one couple may not work well for another. All methods currently practiced have both advantages and disadvantages. The method of choice will be as effective as the couple using it.

The rhythm method of avoiding intercourse during the woman's fertile time and the withdrawal method of Onan in the Old Testament have always been with us, and contraceptives have been used since the 1500s. Crude forms of condoms were used at that time. Rubber condoms and diaphragms were first used in the 1840s. Providing barriers between the sperm and the egg were the only methods of birth control until the 1930s. About that time, Dr. Ernst Graffenburg, the discoverer of the G-spot in the woman's vagina, developed the first IUD from silkworm gut. Oral contraceptives (the pill), which came onto the scene in the late 1950s, actually resulted from the search for a method to increase fertility.

Today a variety of reliable methods are available. However, there is no one perfect method. Choosing a proper birth control method is a serious matter. It is not the woman's decision. It is the couple's decision that needs to be made with thought and care. Help is available to make that decision.

Making the Choice

In choosing a birth-control method, four issues need to be considered:

- Safety
- Effectiveness
- Convenience
- Personal preference

The fourth consideration, personal preference, may be based on the other three: safety, effectiveness, or convenience. Or it may be connected with choices that have nothing to do with the facts. It may be based on something you've heard or some past experience. If a method is not going to be used faithfully because of who you are, it will not be "effective," even if it is, by definition, safe, effective, and convenient. Your personal preference may depend on how a method interferes with your sexual relations; this preference needs to be discussed by the two of you. In the following discussions of the various contraceptive methods, we will provide information on the other three considerations.

Abstinence

Refraining totally from sexual intercourse as a method of birth control is 100 percent effective. Even though it may seem to be convenient and risk-free as well, it certainly isn't much fun.

Divorce would be the risk. We believe abstinence is the method of choice before marriage, but clearly against biblical teaching after marriage. First Corinthians 7:3–5 says that we are not to withhold ourselves from one another except by agreement for a season of prayer and then we're to come together again quickly lest we be tempted. Nowhere does the Bible state that we should abstain to prevent pregnancy.

Withdrawal

Having intercourse (entry of the penis into the vagina), but removing the penis from the vagina before the man ejaculates (releases seminal fluid containing sperm) is a frequently practiced method of birth control. It has many drawbacks, however. First, it can be emotionally and physically upsetting. Two people have united themselves intensely; then (and at the height of openness and vulnerability) they pull apart. Second, many men do not have fine control over when they ejaculate, so accidents are most likely to happen. A man has five to ten seconds warning before he is about to ejaculate. Once he is about to ejaculate, he cannot stop it. He may not get out and get far enough away from the vagina in those five to ten seconds. Also, the higher the degree of arousal, the less self-control he has. So even if he started with the best intentions of withdrawing at the peak of arousal, he may not do so. Third, for many men, seminal fluid containing sperm is released before ejaculation. Thus, the withdrawal method is not effective or convenient.

Douching

Using some means to flush the seminal fluid containing sperm out of the vagina has been attempted for ages. Unfortunately, this method is neither effective nor safe. The ineffectiveness stems from the fact that those tenacious little sperm are fast and determined. They get into the uterus and go looking for the egg in the uterine tube long before the woman can get to her douche bag and solution. In addition to being ineffective, douching is not recommended because it upsets the natural environment of the vagina and makes a woman more susceptible to infection.

One of the most dangerous douching methods is practiced by teenagers who use cola drinks. Yes, the colas are spermicidal, so they kill any sperm that haven't already found their way into the uterus. However, the bubbles of the pressurized carbonated soda may be forced into the uterus where they might be absorbed into the bloodstream as an embolus and cause sudden death.

Douching is *not* a method of birth control, even though it is thought to be.

Barrier Method

Barrier methods of birth control prevent the sperm from meeting the egg. The barrier contraceptives we will discuss are condoms, the sponge, diaphragms, cervical caps, and vaginal spermicides.

Condoms

A condom is commonly referred to as a rubber, prophylactic, safety, or sheath. It is a rubber (latex) device shaped like the finger of a glove that is placed over the erect penis before entry into the vagina. For people who are allergic to rubber products, natural, animal-skin condoms can be purchased.

Besides their use as a birth-control method, condoms provide a barrier to protect against sexually transmitted diseases. This helps explain their increased use in the United States during recent years, as a result of the AIDS epidemic. The spermicide nonoxynol-9 is recommended for use on and inside the condom to kill both sperm and disease-producing viruses. Another reason for condoms' popularity is their advantage of being easy to purchase without a physician's prescription. There are no side effects from the use of condoms, so they are safe.

Their effectiveness depends on how they are used. The statistics for effectiveness vary from a 2 percent failure rate to a 25 percent failure rate. The most common failure is failure to use the condom! To use condoms successfully, you must be certain the condom is new and free of holes or tears. It is important that the condom be rolled over the erect penis leaving one-half inch slack to catch semen. The woman's vagina needs to be lubricated before entry with a condom. A dry vagina may cause the condom to be removed during thrusting. If vaginal lubricant is not adequate, saliva or other water-based lubricants can be used. Petroleum-based products such as Vaseline, lotions, Albolene, and some oils, should not be used with rubber condoms because petroleum breaks down rubber. After the man ejaculates, he must hold the condom in place as he withdraws from the vagina so that no seminal fluid containing sperm will seep out.

Condoms are sexually inconvenient: Love play must be interrupted to put them on and the man must keep an erection until withdrawal from the vagina. That can cause considerable anxiety for some men and, thus, interfere with their sexual response. For others, it is just a nuisance. Repeated experiences with condoms and incorporating the application of the condom as part of the love play can reduce the inconvenience and enhance their use.

The Sponge

The contraceptive sponge has been referred to as the female condom because of its easy availability and use. It can be purchased by anyone without prescription and does not require a fitting. It is a two-inch-round, soft, pillow-shaped polyurethane sponge that is permeated with spermicide (one gram of nonoxynol-9). An advantage over the condom is that it is inserted before sexual play. While the manufacturers say it can be left in place for twenty-four hours with equal effectiveness for repeated intercourse, recent findings are questioning that claim. It is 76–83 percent effective in preventing pregnancy but must be left in place for at least six hours after intercourse. Insertion is easy. After wetting it, the woman folds it and places it deep in the vagina with a finger. The pressure of the vaginal wall holds the sponge in place against the opening of the cervix.

Although there is no evidence of significant health risks for women using the sponge, allergic reactions to the spermicide and chronic vaginal irritation have been reported. Toxic shock syndrome has occurred in a few cases when the sponge was forgotten and left in for more than thirty hours. Even though a woman can purchase and use a sponge without professional assistance, it is recommended that she seek help to learn to find her cervix and properly place and remove the sponge. The position of her uterus may be such that the sponge cannot adequately protect her cervix.

The Diaphragm

This barrier method has been used effectively for well over one hundred years. The vaginal diaphragm is made of soft rubber and is shaped like a bowl, with a flexible spring at the outer edge. A spermicidal jelly or cream must be used with a diaphragm to ensure effectiveness, since the diaphragm, itself, cannot prevent all sperm from reaching the cervix. To insert the diaphragm, the woman puts a small amount of spermicidal jelly or cream in the bowl and around the edge of the diaphragm. She then pinches the opposite sides of the rim together so that the diaphragm folds in the middle. The flattened shape can then be inserted into the vagina. Once inserted, the flexible rim resumes its original shape. The woman can then properly position the diaphragm to completely cover the cervix. It should fit securely and comfortably between the rear wall of the vagina and the upper edge of the pubic bone.

The diaphragm is 82 percent effective in preventing pregnancy. That means eighteen out of one hundred women per year using the diaphragm get pregnant. That risk is reduced to about 2.4 percent with experienced insertion and 100 percent usage among women over thirty years old who have intercourse fewer than four times per week. Likewise, a woman's risk of pregnancy increases to more than 18 percent if she is 25 or younger and has intercourse four or more times weekly.

The diaphragm has the advantage of having no side effects. Also it is usually inserted before intercourse, and thus does not interfere with scheduled love play. The diaphragm must be prescribed and fitted by a physician. The fit should be checked after pregnancy, pelvic surgery, or a weight change of ten pounds or more. The position of the diaphragm should be checked every time you have intercourse.

Some women cannot use a diaphragm because of poor vaginal muscle tone, a sagging uterus, or vaginal obstructions. A regular diaphragm will not stay in place for women with these conditions, so an arcing, or bow-bend, diaphragm may be needed.

For all women, the diaphragm must be left in place for at least six hours after intercourse and the woman should not douche during this time. After removal, the diaphragm is to be washed with soap and water, rinsed, dried carefully, checked for holes by holding it up against the light, powdered lightly with corn or potato flour, and placed in its special container. When using a rubber diaphragm it is important not to use petroleum-based vaginal lubricants because they interfere with the effectiveness.

Cervical Cap

This method is similar to the diaphragm in function and effectiveness. It is made of thick rubber or plastic, is thimble-shaped, has a rim, and fits over the cervix. Just like the diaphragm, the cap needs to be fitted by a professional on a healthy cervix. It comes in four sizes. The cap is inserted in a similar way as is the vaginal diaphragm, but insertion can be difficult. The cap is pressed together and pushed along the back wall of the vagina until it comes to rest against the back of the cervix. Then the cap is allowed to open and is pushed up to cover the cervix. Its placement over the cervix needs to be checked.

The same guidelines for using spermicidal gel or cream apply to the cervical cap as well as the vaginal diaphragm.

Caps have the advantage of staying in place for several days. Once in place, they are less likely to dislodge than the diaphragm. The only cervical cap currently available in the United States is the Prentif Cavity Rim. Your physician or clinic may be willing to fit it for you and order it from Cervical Cap Ltd., P.O. Box 38003-292, Los Gatos, Calif. 95031.

Vaginal Spermicides

Spermicidal creams, jellies, and tablets inserted into the vagina block the cervical opening and immobilize and kill the sperm. They must be inserted at designated times before intercourse. Foam is the most effective of this group, but all of these products increase their effectiveness when used in combination with another barrier method. They are increasing in popularity because they can reduce sexually transmitted disease transmission rates.

IUD (Intrauterine Device)

The IUD is a device that is inserted into the uterus by a physician to prevent pregnancy. The devices have been made of various shapes and materials, including silver, copper, and plastic. A string is attached to the device to allow the woman to check that the IUD is still in place and to allow the physician to remove it.

In the 1970s, 10 percent of contraception use in the United States was by the IUD. Today that use is less than 1 percent. The history, detailed in the book, *Contraceptive Technology, 1990-1992*, involves bankruptcy of the companies producing the IUDs due to tens of thousands of lawsuits by women who believed they were not sufficiently warned by the companies of potential serious pelvic inflammatory infection (PID), which can result in sterility.

Because of this concern, women should not use an IUD if they have a history of PID or sexually transmitted disease or if they are sexually active with more than one partner or with a partner who has multiple sexual partners. Women who have an IUD inserted should be very alert to any signs of infections (fever, pelvic pain or tenderness, and unusual cramping or bleeding) and seek medical help immediately if those symptoms occur.

Other possible complications while using the IUD are abnormal bleeding, cramping and pain, partial or complete expulsion of the IUD, or problems with the string. Any of these merit medical attention.

What about effectiveness? It depends upon the skill of the medical person who inserts the IUD and the woman's checking to make sure it is still in place. Expulsion is the biggest hazard in the IUD's effectiveness.

Convenience is the IUD's advantage. A physician can insert it at any time, even ten minutes after delivering a baby. It remains in place; thus, it does not require insertion and removal by the user when intercourse is pursued. Nor does the woman have to remember to take a pill.

How does the IUD prevent pregnancy? The mechanism of action is not certain. For some time, the belief was that the IUD caused abortion by expelling the fertilized egg. This is currently in doubt because of a study that collected released eggs from women using the IUD and from women using no form of contraception. Half of the eggs from the women not using contraception had been fertilized, while none of the eggs from the IUD users showed signs of fertilization, according to *Contraceptive Technology 1990-1992,* page 356. IUDs *may* affect the sperm, the egg, the fertilization process, implantation, or the endometrium as the means to interrupting pregnancy.

If you are considering using an IUD for contraception, get thorough and recent information. Work with a medical person who has inserted many IUDs and has had few complications. Be sure you are taught how to check the string and follow those instructions consistently. Be alert to infections or other complications and seek medical help immediately if they occur. Never attempt to remove the IUD yourself.

Hormonal Pregnancy Prevention

Various forms of "the pill" have been researched and debated since their arrival on the market in the late 1950s. Their convenience and effectiveness make them more desirable. When the pill is taken consistently, it has a track record of 99.7–100 percent effectiveness. Yet the possibility of health complications for pill users has alerted everyone's attention.

The pill is a combination of synthetic estrogen and progesterone hormones that, when given to a woman, shuts off the natural production of these hormones so that she no longer ovulates (produces an egg). It also inhibits other processes of impregnation. There are various types and brands of pills; the ratio and amount of the chemical replacement of progesterone and estrogen vary with the different types. Each person's body has to be evaluated to determine which pill will be most effective with the fewest side effects. Unfortunately, some women try one pill, have side effects, and decide that this method is not for them. Instead, they may need to change to a lower level dosage or a pill that has a different proportion of progesterone to estrogen. *The Oral Contraceptive User Guide* by Dr. Richard P. Dickey has a helpful chart on pages 34–35 to help you choose the correct pill for you.

Even though about twenty-eight different pills are available in the United States, they all fit into one of three types:

The Combined Pill

This is the most common type of birth-control pill. It is taken daily for twenty-one days, starting with the fifth day of the cycle. Then it is discontinued, and bleeding starts on the twenty-eighth day. The name refers to this type's having any dosage combination of estrogen and progesterone.

The Triphasic Pill

This type contains a higher dose of estrogen, yet the total amount of hormones is lower than the combined pill. Twenty-one pills are taken, but they have varying levels of estrogen and progesterone in each of three phases to try to reproduce more directly the normal female hormonal cycle. There are six of one kind, five of another, and ten of another. They need to be taken in the order prescribed to be effective. Side effects are reduced with this system.

The Mini Pill

This pill comes with progesterone only. It is taken daily without a break. Unlike the other oral contraceptives, it prevents the sperm from getting through, rather than stopping ovulation. It is not as effective as the other two types of pills.

All pills contain powerful chemicals that are absorbed into the circulation and affect the total body. One report suggests that there are over fifty metabolic side effects associated with taking oral contraceptives. So even though some women tolerate the pill very well, their body chemistry is being affected.

Since liver function and metabolism of carbohydrates, fats, and proteins are all affected, vitamin and mineral absorption is reduced. Therefore, women on the pill should take a vitamin-mineral supplement that is high in vitamin B6, folic acid, vitamin C, calcium, phosphorus, magnesium, and zinc. High doses of vitamin A should not be taken because it is fat soluble, and fat metabolism is not as effective when on the pill.

Increase in body weight occurs for some women because of retention of fluid. An increase of ten pounds or more is a sign that the birth-control pills should be changed or discontinued.

Some women experience minor discomfort when they first start taking the pill. These symptoms of breast tenderness, nausea, vomiting, and spotting between periods usually go away after two to three months of use.

Cancer, heart problems, circulatory disease, and liver impairment have all been fears associated with taking the pill. Couples deciding whether or not to use the pill need to know if the woman's health is likely to be jeopardized. Although there are conflicting reports, there is also consistent evidence regarding the safety of the pill for many women. The risk of serious problems occurs primarily in women who are over thirty-five years of age, who smoke more than fifteen cigarettes per day, who have high blood pressure, who are diabetic or have high blood-fat levels, or who are one-third above their ideal weight. Long-term, steady use of oral contraceptives for more than five years *may* increase the risk of circulatory disease.

What does this mean? Young women in their twenties and thirties who have had regular periods for at least one year, who are not smokers, overweight, diabetic, or do not have high blood pressure, jaundice, mononucleosis, or other liver disorders will probably be able to take the pill without complication. They are usually advised to periodically go off the pill and use another method. Pill use is ruled out for women who have had blood clots, inflammation in the veins, serious liver disease, unexplained bleeding from the vagina, or suspicion or history of cancer. Young girls who are still growing and whose hormonal functioning is not yet mature should not take the pill because it will slow or stop normal growth and development.

Women should be aware that certain medications will interfere with the effectiveness of the pill. Some antibiotics, antihistamines, sedatives, tranquilizers, Dilatin, Phenobarbital, and others may interfere with the pill's purpose of preventing pregnancy. This was demonstrated when a granny-to-be wrote a well-known advice columnist saying that her son and daughter-in-law were about to have their first baby. She said the pregnancy was due to the daughter-in-law's ear infection that was treated with antibiotics while she was trusting the pill for pregnancy protection. Check with your physician about any medication you are to take. Ask how it interacts with and changes the effectiveness of your hormonal contraceptives.

There are other benefits from the pill besides birth control. Premenstrual tension lessens, cramps at the time of menstruation decrease, the number of days and the amount of blood loss is lessened, the time of menstruation is totally predictable, sometimes acne declines, protection against pelvic inflammatory disease is provided, the risk of ovarian and endometrial cancer is lessened, breast cysts and noncancerous breast tumors are less likely, and ovarian cysts are reduced by up to 90 percent. For many women, these benefits far outweigh the risks.

The pill also can affect a woman's sexuality. Some find the physical changes with their periods and the reduction of acne enhances their sexuality and body image. About equal numbers of women report an increase or decrease in sexual desire. Just as some women experience positive side effects, others report negative changes such as actual increase in acne, chronic vaginitis, breast tenderness, and so on. These complications lead to decreased sexual desire and responsiveness. Many women using oral contraceptives do not experience any significant change in sexual behavior, sexual interest, or sexual enjoyment.

If you are experiencing side effects from the oral contraception you are taking, determine with your physician if those problems are due to estrogen increase or decrease or progesterone increase or decrease. Each pill will vary in its estrogen, progesterone, testosterone, and endometrial activity. The symptoms you are experiencing may be relieved by changing to a pill with more or less of one of the hormonal activities. A helpful guide to give you information to enable you to talk more intelligently with your physician is Dr. Dickey's book, *Oral Contraceptive User Guide*.

Norplant

A new hormonal contraceptive is Norplant, a progesterone-only implant that provides five years of protection. It was approved in December 1990 by the Food and Drug Administration for use in the United States.

This is a much-needed new option for women. In one minor surgical procedure, six rubber-like capsules the size of small matchsticks are inserted under the skin of the inner, upper arm in a fan-shaped configuration. Within twenty-four hours of insertion the woman has virtually 100 percent protection from pregnancy for up to five years. Norplant failures are extremely rare; failures after the second year have occurred in women who are significantly overweight. Of course, this is a new product that does not have the benefit of long-term studies, as some of the other products do.

The six match-sized capsules contain thirty-six milligrams of levonorgestrel (a progesterone that is released at a slow, steady rate over the five-year period). Effectiveness is decreased after that time.

Norplant is ideal for women who desire long-term protection from pregnancy, who cannot tolerate estrogen, or who have not been reliable in using other birth-control measures. Norplant is *not* recommended for women with liver disease, unexplained vaginal bleeding, blood clots, or breast cancer.

The possible side effects and benefits of Norplant are similar to those of other hormonal contraceptives.

Although the five-year cost to use the pill would be significantly more than the cost of Norplant, the $500 to $600 one-time fee for implanting Norplant is prohibitive for many women. It is this cost that may limit its use despite its safety, convenience, and effectiveness.

The Morning-After Pill

What about the morning-after pill, or postcoital contraception? Large doses of progesterone, estrogen, or a combination of the two have traditionally been given within twelve to twenty-four hours after rape or unintended intercourse to prevent impregnation.

There is current, legitimate concern, however, that the result may actually be an abortion of a fetus. What are the facts? The sperm can live in the uterus up to five days after ejaculation. For impregnation to occur, the egg must unite with the sperm within twelve to twenty-four hours after it is released from the ovary. Thus the union of the egg and sperm could occur inside the woman any time from minutes to five days after intercourse. Initially, the sperm attaches itself to the egg until implantation, which occurs four to seven days after the sperm and egg have found each other. At the time of implantation, the sperm penetrates the egg, forming a new creation, which attaches itself to the uterine wall; then the fetus begins to grow. Thus, it is unlikely that postcoital contraceptives taken twelve to twenty-four hours after intercourse would cause abortion of a newly formed baby, but rather would prevent pregnancy. Still, this is an issue yet to be resolved and definitely should be reserved for emergency situations.

Are there hormonal contraceptives for men? No, there are not.

Hormonal methods of birth control are constantly being researched. Family-planning services and your physician usually have up-to-date reports. Keep yourself informed so that your choice is based on fact rather than fear.

"Natural" Methods

More and more couples today are considering "natural" methods of birth control because they fear the potential risks of many contraceptives. The various natural methods are based on the principle of avoiding sexual intercourse during the woman's fertile phase of the menstrual cycle. The "rhythm," or "Billings," method may be the terms you've heard in reference to natural family planning. The Roman Catholic Church has helpers trained to teach natural methods.

Most family services offer a thorough program of training. Other excellent resources also are available. *The Ovulation Method of Natural Family Planning* details every dimension of planning pregnancies without using contraceptives or sterilization. While we cannot provide enough details here to train you to be able to effectively practice natural family planning, we will summarize the key ingredients to help you determine if this is the method you would prefer.

The traditional "rhythm" method is based purely on calculation—which always offers an element of risk because a woman's cycle can vary. Effective, natural family planning requires mucus charting, tabulating the temperature of the body at rest upon awakening, and inspection of the cervix to determine the woman's fertile days. There are four days of the menstrual cycle, during menstruation, when the woman is absolutely infertile. After that she is considered 97–99 percent infertile until she sees that her vaginal mucus is stretchy, thicker, and yellower.

At that time, she can start checking her cervix to detect a change. After menstruation, the cervix feels hard and the opening into the vagina is closed. As the cycle moves toward ovulation, the cervix loosens up and softens, so that at about the time of ovulation it feels soft and the opening actually gapes slightly. After ovulation it returns to its firm, closed state. To prevent pregnancy, total abstinence is necessary from the time of seeing the mucus and noting the softened, open cervix until the woman's temperature has been elevated for three days.

Elevation of the temperature for three days will ensure that the egg is no longer fertilizable. The egg lives twelve to twenty-four hours, but sperm live three to five days.

This is the process that must be learned to practice the rhythm method. Much more training is required than what we have given you here, so do not expect to safely use natural family planning by following this information alone.

For disciplined, determined, well-trained couples, natural family planning has been successful and enjoyable. Couples can enhance their sexual relationship by exploring total body pleasure without intercourse during their fertile or questionable days.

Surgical Methods

The opposite extreme of natural family planning is sterilization, a final form of birth control. It ends the capacity of the man or woman to reproduce. Even though a man's sterilization may be reversed in many cases (75 percent), it needs to be thought of as a final, not temporary, method of birth control.

For the woman, sterilization is referred to as tubal ligation. Simple tubal ligation, the tying of the fallopian tubes to prevent the sperm and egg from meeting, is rarely done today because of its ineffectiveness. In addition to the tubes being tied, they need to be either crushed, divided and buried, have a section removed, or have a combination of the last two procedures to ensure sterilization. These procedures do not require major abdominal surgery. An instrument can be used that passes through the abdominal wall, the vagina, or the uterus. Many times hospitalization is not necessary.

Reversible methods of tubal ligation are being explored with high effectiveness. Clips or bands have been used to shut the tubes, and plugs have been inserted to block the end of the tubes. An Italian gynecologist, Igno Tergi, M.D., uses a procedure that moves the tubes. He detaches the tubes from the ovary, makes incisions into the peritoneum (the lining of the abdominal cavity), and sews the fallopian tubes into this lining. When the woman wants to get pregnant, he surgically disconnects the tubes and moves them back to their original position.

When tubal methods fail, which is only 1 percent of the time, it is because the procedure itself failed due to the surgeon's misjudgment. There are some surgical risks involved. Even though reversibility has been successfully performed, women should think of the tubal methods as permanent. If you are a woman pursuing sterilization, gather all the data you can about the specific method your physician will use, the success rate, and any complications and possible aftereffects. Some methods are thought to interfere with pelvic blood flow and produce symptoms of premenstrual tension. Ask questions. It's your body!

Vasectomy for the man is the simplest and safest form of surgical sterilization. The live sperm are prevented from reaching the penis. The sperm normally travel from the testes, where they are produced, through the vas deferens, a tube that leads through the prostate gland to the urethra. During a vasectomy, a small portion of the vas deferens is removed and the cut ends are tied off and sometimes cauterized. This procedure interrupts the sperm's journey, so that sperm will not be released when a man ejaculates during a sexual experience. He will still produce seminal fluid, since some of that is produced in the portion of the duct system above the cut. One caution: A man may have to ejaculate twenty-five times or more before all live sperm are cleared from the duct system above the cut. Several seminal fluid specimens should be taken to the laboratory for confirmation that the sterilization process is finalized.

Sterilization should not be taken lightly. Even though the results bring incredible freedom to the couple or individual who is definitely finished with childbearing, the unforeseen can happen. A child may die, a spouse can be lost through death or divorce, or other great tragedies can wipe out a family except for the one parent. That is why we recommend that the person who is absolutely certain he or she does not want any more children, no matter what the circumstances, is the one who is sterilized. If both spouses are certain, then the vasectomy is the recommended choice because of its ease and safety.

Neither male nor female sterilization changes the sexuality of the person in any way. The woman will still produce eggs and the man will still produce sperm. These disintegrate and are absorbed. The woman continues to menstruate. Hormonal production remains normal for both. Sexual responsiveness and behavior are unaffected. More freedom may result.

Birth control is a very personal matter. Personal feelings, as well as the technical facts, are important parts of the couple's choice of birth control. It is not an easy decision because no method is perfect in both effectiveness and safety. Yet everything has risk, including life, itself. It is important to remember that no known contraceptive has a death rate as high as pregnancy. And the death rate for pregnancy is very low.

For Further Study

Close, Sylvia. *Sex During Pregnancy and After Childbirth*. San Bernardino, Calif.: Borgo Press, 1986.

Dickey, Richard P., M.D., Ph.D. *Managing Contraceptive Pill Patients*. 6th ed. Durant, Okla.: Essential Medical Information Systems, 1991.

————. *Oral Contraceptive User Guide*. Durant, Okla.: Creative Infomatics, 1987. 34–35.

Hatcher, Robert A., et al. *Contraceptive Technology, 1990–1992.* 15th rev. ed. New York: Irvington Publishers, 1990.

*Keith, Louis G., ed. *The Safety of Fertility Control.* New York: Springer Publishing Co., 1980.

*Kolodny, Robert C., et al. "Sex and Family Planning." In *Textbook of Human Sexuality for Nurses.* Boston: Little, Brown, and Co., 1979.

*Kolodny, Robert C., William H. Masters, Virginia E. Johnson. "Sex and Family Planning." In *Textbook of Sexual Medicine.* Boston: Little, Brown, and Co., 1979.

McIlhaney, Joe S., Jr., M.D. *1250 Health-Care Questions Women Ask.* Grand Rapids: Baker Book House, 1988. Pages 555–602.

Wilger, Thomas, M.D. *The Ovulation Method of Natural Family Planning* 2d ed. Omaha: Pope Paul VI Institute for the Study of Human Reproduction, 1983.

*This book is no longer in print but is still available in many public or medical libraries.

3

Sex and Infertility

A True Story

Gail and Paul's sexual experience took on new meaning when they decided to start their family. They were eager to conceive. Their sexual life together was fun and fulfilling. Both were vitally interested, highly arousable, and orgasmic. Yes, they had their share of the normal stresses of life. But sexually, they were both finding fulfillment and joy in their sexual relationship.

The edge of their eagerness to conceive disappeared, though, as slight disappointment crept in. Each month when Gail's menstrual period began there was the letdown that "it hasn't happened yet." But, as is true for most couples, they began each month with new hope.

As time went on, that small feeling of doubt and concern built to the point of panic. At first neither of them said anything to the other about it. Gail's excitement when her period didn't come the morning it was expected turned to despair when it did show up. Both thought, What if we're unable to have kids? and then tried to push the thought away.

Paul and Gail began their four- to five-year struggle with infertility, the problem that affects 10 to 15 percent of all couples during their reproductive years. A couple is not considered to be experiencing a fertility problem until they have attempted to conceive for at least a year. On the average, most couples conceive in about six months, with about 25 percent conceiving after one month of trying, around 60 percent by the end of six months, and about 80 to 85 percent after one year.

After a year, Paul and Gail pursued medical help. The exploration for the source of the problem began. Blame for their failure to conceive became an issue of tension.

It is natural to want to blame one another or at least to pinpoint who is responsible for a couple's failure to conceive. In our society, there is still a tendency to assume that the woman is the one with the difficulty since she is the one who is unable to get pregnant. Yet, equally as often, it is the man who is unable to impregnate. Regardless of which spouse is responsible for the infertility, both suffer from the impact of being unable to conceive.

Infertility balances out rather evenly between men and women. About two-fifths of the time it is the woman's problem and about two-fifths of the time it is the man's problem. About one-fifth of the time it is impossible to diagnose the source of the problem—or both partners contribute to the cause. It is never predictable as to whether the man or the woman is hindering the process of impregnation. Therefore, when a couple is unable to conceive, both spouses should be medically evaluated.

First, basic assumptions of the impregnation process are validated by the physician. For example, the doctor might begin by asking if the husband is able to ejaculate inside the woman. Some men experience what is called "retarded ejaculation." They find themselves fully aroused with a complete erection, able to experience intercourse, but unable to ejaculate when inside the woman. This is an emotional, rather than a physical, dilemma; it can be reversed through sexual therapy. Still other men ejaculate so prematurely that it takes place outside the vagina. If this were the case, the sperm would have less opportunity to travel through the vagina into the cervix and on up to meet the ovum (egg) inside the fallopian tubes.

Paul's affirmative answers to questions about these possibilities indicated that his and Gail's difficulty was not caused by his mechanical inability to deposit the sperm where it needed to be placed. So other assumptions necessary for the impregnation process were evaluated.

Sexual functioning must be mechanically adequate. Several couples with whom we have worked have experienced difficulties with impregnation because of either severe impotence or vaginismus. Impotence has to do with the inability to achieve or maintain an erection. When there is an inability to maintain an erection long enough for vaginal entry, impregnation is highly unlikely. A couple may not have been able to culminate their marriage in sexual intercourse because of impotence on the part of the man.

The inability to have sexual intercourse can also be caused by vaginismus, that is, an involuntary closing of the vagina by the woman (see chapter 14). Unconsummated marriages are treatable situations. In dealing with either of these conditions, a couple should seek help first from a physician and then from a sexual therapist.

For Gail and Paul, sexual functioning was not the problem. So the next step in their evaluation was to eliminate more superficial, technical difficulties. The doctor wanted to know whether Gail was using a lubricant that might be killing the sperm. He also wanted to know whether she was douching, and, thus, altering the natural vaginal environment or washing out a large portion of seminal fluid containing sperm. This could be making it difficult for the sperm to survive or reach the egg.

The doctor discouraged Gail from using any aspirin-containing products during her ovulation time. He also recommended that Paul wear boxer-type underwear rather than tight-fitting briefs that kept his testicles close to the body and increased their temperature. When the testicles are kept cooler, optimum sperm production is encouraged. Cigarette smoking and alcohol consumption were discouraged.

The positions used during intercourse were questioned. When the doctor discovered that part of the dilemma was Paul's low sperm count, he suggested a position that would bring the ejaculate in direct contact with the opening of the cervix. This was to increase the likelihood of a healthy sperm traveling into and surviving within the uterine passage. The suggested position was with Gail on her back, buttocks slightly elevated with a pillow, and knees pulled up toward the chest, allowing Paul to penetrate as deeply as possible (an exaggerated "missionary" position).

When the difficulty in conceiving is due to the position of the cervix and uterus, the woman may need to assume a certain position for an extended period of time after intercourse. With some problems, it is necessary for the woman to stay on her back with her buttocks slightly elevated by a pillow and her legs up to help the sperm arrive right at the opening of the cervix.

If the gynecologist discovers that the woman has a retroverted or tipped uterus, he or she may suggest entry from the rear with the woman staying in what is called the "knee-chest position," that is, on her knees with her chest on the bed for an extended period after ejaculation. This is an uncomfortable position to maintain for a long period of time, but it can certainly help with conception.

Gail and Paul's frequency of sexual intercourse also were evaluated. In many cases, the plan for scheduling intercourse and the timing between ejaculations to increase the possibility of impregnation needs to be managed by an infertility specialist. The doctor noted that recent stress in the couple's life together could also hinder conception by blocking ovulation. Thus, severe illness, death, financial trauma, vocational upheaval, marital difficulties, or even extended travel are all stresses that could hinder conception.

After these technical, mechanical reasons for infertility had been eliminated, the doctor explored possible physical reasons. Many intrusive medical procedures are necessary in the diagnosis of infertility. The woman's vaginal secretions have to be receptive to the man's sperm for impregnation to occur. If the sperm are destroyed by her allergic reaction, impregnation will be interrupted.

A certain concentration, or count, of active sperm per cubic centimeter of ejaculate is needed for impregnation to be likely. When the count gets below twenty or thirty million per cubic centimeter there is a much lower chance of impregnation. A count of forty to sixty million live sperm per cubic centimeter would be ideal. The count of active sperm also is compared with the count of sluggish sperm.

If the man contracted mumps in adulthood, with subsequent damage to the testicles, he may have a low sperm count. A varicocele, or varicose vein, on the testicle increases the temperature in the testicles and thus reduces the number of vigorous sperm produced. Sometimes an underdeveloped testicle has lasted throughout puberty, causing damage to the part of the testicles that produces the sperm. There are other temporary and long-term causes for low sperm count. Whatever the source of the difficulty, if there are not enough active, healthy sperm, the likelihood of pregnancy is lessened. In Paul's situation, it was discovered that he did have a varicocele that was lowering his sperm count.

Medical procedures revealed that Gail had physical interruptions of her reproductive cycle that contributed to their infertility as well. She was not ovulating on a regular basis. Gail had never regained a consistent ovulation cycle after going off the birth-control pill she had been using to delay having children. After medical treatment to "fire" the ovaries, Gail and Paul succeeded in conceiving. Then Gail experienced a miscarriage, a huge disappointment!

After Gail recovered from the miscarriage, they resumed their efforts to conceive. The monthly expectation for pregnancy returned. Yet at the end of each month they discovered that she had not even ovulated. There was incredible disappointment! For eight months they were taking temperatures, checking vaginal mucus, ingesting medication to induce ovulation, and calling Paul home in the middle of the day for intercourse. The physician recommended frequent sexual activity around the time of ovulation and then little the rest of the month. Sex was by prescription, not desire.

Finally, after this eight-month period, there was an ovulation. Gail did become pregnant and a healthy baby boy was born. Eager to have another child, they shortened the breastfeeding period to allow ovulation to resume.

Again, they struggled. Gail went in for minor exploratory surgery—a laparoscopy, to examine the reproductive system. Paul had his varicocele repaired, which helped raise his sperm count. Every other part of him was also reviewed, evaluated, and repaired if needed.

Getting pregnant the second time was even more difficult than the first. Artificial insemination was attempted at Gail's peak ovulation time. Paul would hurry home, ejaculate into a bottle, and Gail would then rush across town on a forty-five-minute drive to their doctor. The doctor would artificially implant the sperm at the ideal spot for impregnation. After six monthly attempts, they conceived and Gail gave birth to a beautiful little girl.

By this time, sex had become associated with such a demand to produce at a certain time and in a certain way that they no longer desired each other for the purpose of sexual pleasure. With Paul's quick trips home when Gail called, his ejaculating into a bottle, the artificial insemination, and their focus on temperatures, mucus, and sperm counts, they had become so clinically oriented that they no longer had a capacity to connect to each other with feeling. All romance was gone from their relationship.

For the first nine months after their second child was born, they had no sexual experience whatsoever. They avoided each other. Sex felt like a burden, rather than a joy. By this time, Paul was thinking, *There's something wrong with me. I'm not interested anymore. I couldn't care less about this. Life is fine without sex. If I'm a sexual being I certainly don't know where that part of me is. I probably couldn't even function if I tried.*

Gail was having many of the same thoughts. After sharing their doubts with each other, they sought our counsel. They were excited about their two children. But now they lacked desire for one another sexually and it seemed impossible to imagine getting back together.

Whether the problem is low sperm count or some kind of testicular problem for the man, or ovulation problems, cervical problems, endometriosis, or the position of the uterus for the woman, it is likely to bring emotional stress and distance to the relationship.

Sexual Problems That Occur As a Result of Infertility

By now it is obvious why a couple might have difficulty maintaining sexual intimacy through all the gyrations of trying to conceive. Infertility produces a state of crisis. In addition, many of the necessary procedures interfere with free sexual closeness.

So the demand to produce sexually comes from outside rather than from the spouses' own internal urges or feelings that grow between them as they take and give to enjoy each other. The possibility for intimacy is obviously decreased if the woman is on her knees and chest for an hour after the sexual experience or if the man is having to run home at 11:42 in the morning to ejaculate into a bottle. These "command performances" do little to enhance sexual pleasure and enjoyment.

Only an unusual couple can avoid the negative impact of an extended effort at conception. When sexual intercourse becomes a means to an end—even the very natural goal of conceiving a child—it is likely to lose the spontaneity, the joy, and the enthusiasm that may have been there previously. In fact, this is true any time we find ourselves focused on sexual goals rather than on sexual pleasure. We deal with this problem extensively in our book, *The Gift of Sex.*

Let's review the scene. The couple begins by anticipating that pregnancy will be easy and natural. After an extended period of trying, the internal pressure and anxiety build as the lack of conception is prolonged. It's at this point that the first blaming begins and the desperate mood sets in. By now, it is almost impossible for the couple to have a natural sex life because sex has become an effort to produce a result. The natural flow of pleasure and intimacy diminishes. The man wonders about himself and whether he is "really a man"—and the woman doubts her sexuality and femininity.

Opposite forces are at work. On the one hand is the drive to conceive, which brings a couple together. On the opposite side is the sexual demand that produces a noticeable decrease in sexual desire as pressure reduces sexual enjoyment. A chronic depression may set in—not the depression that would send a person to a hospital ward, but an ongoing state of despondency. Spontaneity is lost. Hopelessness overwhelms expectancy. The demanding, programmed sexual performances destroy the romantic dimension.

The procedures the couple goes through elevate the stress. The continual pelvic examinations by the physician have a detrimental effect. The woman repeatedly experiences her genitals as "the doctor's" to examine, rather than her and her husband's source of sexual pleasure. Producing sperm samples into a bottle leaves the husband with little desire for normal sexual arousal and release. This is especially true if he has to produce at the physician's office. The artificial insemination leaves the woman feeling that she is on the soft end of a probing syringe. The man may feel he is inadequate because he can't even impregnate his own wife. He feels he can't be much of a man if he's "shooting blanks."

All of these factors reduce the couple's self-esteem and, naturally, affect their sexual life. It should also be noted that many times, as in the case of Paul and Gail, the whole procedure (from starting the attempt to conceive to coming to the sexual counselor's office) can be a five-year process. Through all of this, high levels of anger, frustration, and tension can cause other marital difficulties.

Any time a sexual experience becomes goal-oriented rather than pleasure-oriented, any time sex is by demand rather than by desire, any time sexual experience is directed from outside of us rather than in response to our inner urges, it will significantly disrupt the sexual relationship. The woman's orgasmic response will inevitably diminish. The husband may have difficulty getting or keeping an erection because he has become anxious about having to produce at a certain time under unarousing conditions. Both may have lost their desire for sexual intimacy.

Fulfillment in Spite of Pressure

Togetherness can be maintained when both spouses are committed and helped to focus on the intimacy of lovemaking in spite of the pressure to conceive. Whether the consequences of trying bring about loss of orgasm for the woman, impotence for the man, or diminished sexual desire, there are certain steps that couples can take to help reduce the negative consequences of infertility. We suggest six areas for your attention. These steps are not to be taken in any particular order, but should happen simultaneously.

1. Know that you are not the first couple to experience this difficulty. Faced with the problems of infertility, couples often feel terribly alone in their experience. They ask the questions, "Why us? Is God punishing us? Is it because we were sexually involved before we were married? What is wrong with us?" It helps to be aware that infertility is experienced by 10 to 15 percent of couples. In most cases, help is available to assist you in having the child you so dearly desire. Most problems are treatable and can be remedied. Sometimes just knowing that you are not alone helps. Part of the problem is that most people don't talk about their infertility difficulties because it makes them feel less adequate than others. Hence, you may have friends who may have struggled with infertility—but did not tell you.

2. Continue living a life that's as normal as possible. Just because you are struggling to get pregnant doesn't mean you need to withdraw from society, stop enjoying your hobby, give up your participation in community or church activities, or quit playing on the local softball team. Yes, you may need to lessen a high-pressure schedule to have time for each other, but it is crucial to continue to be involved with those activities that have brought joy into your individual lives. In your marital life, pay close attention to doing those special things you have always done. By all means, continue to get away for weekends, whether you enjoy camping or staying at a downtown hotel. Keep up those positive aspects of life.

3. Communication must take place on at least three levels. First of all, during this stressful time it is vital that you continue, or even increase, the patterns of communication that have been important for your relationship. When self-esteem is being tested, hope is fading, and depression is setting in, pay special attention to the effective communication skills that have maintained your healthy marriage. If you have not established an ongoing system for communication, with time set aside for just the two of you, this is an important time to begin the habit.

A second absolutely essential focus of communication is sharing your thoughts, feelings, and reactions to the problem of infertility. Much benefit can come from expressing those anxieties as they occur: the hopelessness as it creeps in, the despair as it is felt, the fluctuations in the feelings that are inevitable, the impact on your masculinity and femininity as it is experienced, and the way your attitude toward the future is altered. Anything that can get your feelings out in the open will help you survive.

Recognize that this is a dilemma you share. You are in it together. If you have never learned to talk openly with each other, this would be an ideal time for the two of you to begin a learning experience that increases your communication skills and helps you develop more intimacy in your relationship. Marriage Encounter programs or other seminars, classes, or retreats that teach effective communication in marriage can be beneficial in helping you learn to share your feelings without attacking or blaming each other. And once you've learned these communication skills, find some way to *keep* sharing the feelings and reactions as they occur—without pushing each other away. These emotions might include the first feelings of surprise and anger, the sense of isolation or separateness that you may feel from all your friends who are conceiving, or the grief experienced as the waiting persists.

A third essential level of communication is with someone, apart from each other, with whom you can talk freely and openly about your dilemma. This may be family members—parents, brothers and sisters, aunts, uncles. It may be a special couple who are deep and close friends and with whom your privacy can be assured. Or it may be that you would deal with this best in a professional situation, with a minister, a marriage and family counselor, or a psychologist.

Organizations exist to provide help and support for those with fertility problems. One such organization that operates at a national level to provide support and information on fertility questions is Resolve, Inc., Post Office Box 474, Belmont, Mass. 02178-0474. The American Fertility Society, 1608 13th Avenue South, Suite 101, Birmingham, Ala. 35205, will have helpful information and resources. Young Couples International, 216 Calhoun Street, Charleston, S.C. 29401, is an organization that also offers guidance for those struggling with infertility. A crucial source of encouragement will be the knowledge that you have support and care, both from each other and from a few important, concerned people.

4. Educate yourselves. Get as much information as possible so that you have clear knowledge of what is happening to you. Begin by asking your physician for information on the subject of infertility. Ask questions as they occur to you. Find an up-to-date book at your local bookstore or library that will enlighten you about the causes of and remedies for infertility. Attend a lecture at the local hospital. Pay attention to magazine articles written by knowledgeable professionals who explain the current understanding of infertility. Much more information is available on infertility than we can cover here. Our focus in this chapter is to help you deal with your relationship and sexual effects of infertility, rather than providing an exhaustive statement on its possible causes and treatments.

   5. Continue the pleasure and intimacy of the sexual experience even when trying to conceive. This will not be possible for all sexual experiences. When lovemaking is a rushed event because the temperature charts or the mucous secretions indicate that this is the right time for impregnation, the sexual act will become more functional and perhaps less pleasurable. Try to separate that type of "impregnation sex" from "pleasure sex" if necessary.

   When possible, create a special atmosphere to add spark to the rushed, daytime experiences. For a noon attempt at conception, use your private patio in the summertime or a cozy area in front of the fireplace in the winter. Move to a bedroom that you usually don't use for sleeping or find a place with a view if the woman is going to have to stay in a certain position. The newness of the atmosphere can distract from the demand to produce.

   Make a plan for physical intimacy in your less rushed, scheduled times to conceive. Go the extra mile in setting up an atmosphere that will bring excitement. For example, if the experience is going to be at night, prepare the room by lighting candles or making a love nest on the floor. Turn on your favorite lovemaking music. Get out those satin sheets and make the event special.

   In addition to setting the atmosphere, a focus on bodily pleasure can make most sexual experiences special. Enjoying the pleasure of each other's bodies is affirming and brings connection for the couple. Many books have been written on this subject; we have outlined step-by-step experiences in *The Gift of Sex*.

When possible, take extended time for body caressing to increase sexual pleasure, heighten the arousal, and maintain some of the vitality, even when you are getting together on the doctor's schedule for the purpose of impregnation.

Another important ingredient for keeping intimacy and pleasure alive during the months or years of pursuing impregnation is to make a concerted effort to get together at times other than when you are striving to conceive. Have sex for fun and no other purpose! We are aware that you may need to limit sexual ejaculation at times. But even during these times sexual play without ejaculation adds fun and variety. During the rest of the month, when sexual experiences are your choice, plan for relaxed sexual enjoyment without any demands. If sex has never been fun, this would be a good time to learn to have sexual fun together. Read a book or attend a seminar on sexual enhancement to learn ways to add new variety to your experiences. Do the sexual-enhancement exercises in the order listed in the table of contents of *The Gift of Sex*.

6. Maintain or develop ongoing, nonsexual affection. Not only is sharing feelings and sexual intimacy important, but so is sharing affection, including hugs and kisses. Take time to affirm each other. Remind yourselves of your love. Take time to go out to dinner, to a movie, for a walk. Plan time together that builds closeness. Spend time in mutual bodily pleasuring that is not designed to arouse but can provide enjoyment for both. Begin by learning to caress feet, face, and hands, including the whole body except the genitals, as described in *The Gift of Sex*.

Building intimacy can keep the two of you close while you struggle through the demands and failures of unsuccessful pregnancy attempts. Stress and tension have a way of wedging their way into a relationship and nudging people apart. The process is gradual. It is a result of not sharing the pain and of feeling badly about yourselves at a time when you need all the support you can get from each other. Learn to laugh and cry together. Maintain and develop all areas of intimacy.

Aesthetic, literary, musical, athletic, or craft and hobby interests should be continued. Pay attention to your spiritual life, too. This is vital! At a time of helplessness, God's all-knowing power and care are available to comfort and encourage you. Your times of corporate or personal worship, prayer, or Bible study can be a significant source of strength, especially as your helpless feelings find solace in your relationship with God.

These six steps are not magic. They are not going to make every sexual experience a honeymoon delight. There will still be a laborious quality to conception when fertility is a problem. But if the steps are applied in a steady, deliberate fashion, they can reduce the emotional and sexual distance that too often develops in couples experiencing infertility. They will help maintain at least a vestige of the former relationship that can be resumed once the struggle is over. This may even be a time to develop new and more fulfilling ways of connecting emotionally and sexually.

After the Trying Stops

Whether you are no longer trying because you have decided that pregnancy is impossible or because you have successfully conceived, a time of refocusing and relearning will be necessary for most couples. Paul and Gail spent five years working on this process. The difficulties they had in readjusting to self-directed sexual experiences that were aimed at pleasure and sexual fulfillment are not an extreme.

There are specific steps to take to ensure happier adjustment as you resume your ongoing sexual life. Let's look at this first from the perspective of the couple who have conceived as many children as they want.

1. Plan your contraception together (with your physician), being sure that both of you feel comfortable and confident with the method chosen. (Refer to chapter 2.)

2. Maintain some form of physical intimacy in the time between the birth of the child and the point when your doctor says you are physically ready to resume sexual intercourse. This could be just the normal day-to-day affection of hugging and kissing, giving each other body caresses and pleasuring, or some mutual stimulation, even to the point of orgasm.

3. Plan very carefully for your first sexual intercourse after childbirth. (Refer to chapter 5.) This needs to be a special event.

4. Plan and schedule physical times to be together that can grow into a sexual experience if both desire. There will be a natural resistance to scheduling, since that smacks of scheduling sex to conceive. Yet, if the two of you are going to come together in a way that brings fulfillment, active planning will be necessary. If you do not make touching a priority, you may end up in the same predicament as Paul and Gail, who found themselves never having sexual intimacy. By planning we mean allowing blocks of time in your schedule where lovemaking is possible. Plan an evening meal together or an hour away that has the possibility of growing into a sensual time. Life is going to be different with children in the home. As the two of you recognize that difference, talk about it, and make plans to bring your worlds together. You can make the necessary adjustments to find happiness in your sexual lives.

The next chapter addresses the sexual adjustment of those spouses who have to accept the fact that they will never bear children. Grieving the loss is painful. Most couples go through a clear-cut series of feelings after discovering their unresolvable infertility.

With infertility on the increase, all of us need a new sensitivity to the pain of those who struggle to get pregnant. They need our support. That will happen as being open about infertility problems becomes acceptable in our culture. Learning to share these problems with each other and with close friends and relatives is the start.

For Further Study

Aral, Sevgi O., Ph.D., and Willard Cates, Jr., M.D. "The Increasing Concern with Fertility. Why Now?" *Journal of the American Medical Association,* 250, no. 17 (November 1983): 2327–31.

Bernstein, Judith, R.N., and John H. Matton, M.D. "An Overview of Infertility." *Journal of Obstetrical and Gynecological Nursing* (September/October 1982): 309–14.

Elstein, Max. "Effects of Infertility on Psychosexual Function." *British Medical Journal,* 2 (August 1975): 296–99.

Hatcher, Robert A., M.D., et al. *Contraceptive Technology, 1990–1992*. 15th rev. ed. New York: Irvington Publishers, 1990. 475–502.

Larson, David E., M.D., editor. *Mayo Clinic Family Health Book*. New York: William Morrow and Co., 1990. 1131–37.

McIlhaney, Joe S., Jr., M.D. *1250 Health-Care Questions Women Ask*. Grand Rapids, Mich.: Baker Book House, 1988. 505–53.

Shapiro, Constance Hoenk. *Infertility and Pregnancy Loss*. San Francisco: Jossey-Bass Publishers, 1988.

4

Childlessness, Adoption, and Sex

Every little girl who plays with dolls grows up believing that someday she will have her own children. Playing house is practice for the real thing. This basic belief continues through adolescence to the point of marriage. A couple expects that children will be a part of their lives together. It usually isn't a question of *if* a couple can have children, but rather *when*. There are, of course, those few couples who decide not to do so. But most couples decide to wait through the years of their schooling until they can establish financial stability. Then they are ready to have the children who are seen as an inevitable part of their lives.

Infertility comes as a real shock for 10 to 15 percent of those couples (about one-sixth of the population), leaving them with a sense of powerlessness when they discover they may not be able to have children. Even though the infertility can usually be treated successfully, there still is a significant segment of the population that will remain childless.

Adoption is the first answer, yet 90 percent of single mothers are keeping their babies if they bring them to full-term. So the pool of couples looking for children is far greater than the pool of babies available. The wait will often be five or six years *if* the couple qualifies. Some are left to make their own personal connections for adoptions, or considering international adoptions—or resigning themselves to a life without children.

Frustration, anger, and anxiety are feelings most couples experience as they work with their physician in attempting to bring about pregnancy (see chapter 3). For those who decide to remain childless or are unable to adopt, the adjustment is major. It calls for internal strength and reliance on God as the couple is forced to readjust their view of themselves as individuals and as a couple, facing a future that will include only the two of them. They sense a feeling of loss as they realize they will have no one to live on after them.

If this is the situation confronting you, try to remember that many opportunities will come your way as a result of this change in your life—experiences not available to those who have children. We say this, even though we know that, when you are first going through the pain of adjustment, it does not help to have the benefits recited. However, you may be able to look at them later. Meanwhile, this time of readjustment, of accepting that your lives together will be without children, could seem very much like the period of adjustment right after marriage. Then you were working to become comfortable with one another. But you assumed that some day you would have a family. Lifestyle patterns and plans, both in terms of location and recreation, will need to be processed one more time. You will need much support, understanding, and encouragement when you finally face the reality that children are absolutely not going to be a part of your future.

Facing childlessness is indeed one of life's major predicaments. It is the erosion of hope—a steady, gradual loss of a life's dream. It is a life crisis. What is crisis? When we face an event that threatens life as we now know it, we usually experience the stress of crisis. Crises are those situations that go beyond the usual day-to-day problems and require special kinds of solutions. A crisis usually threatens something that has become an expected part of your life, such as a job, your health, a marriage, a home, or life itself.

Most crises are time-limited. That is, if a house burns down or a job is lost, the emotions are not dragged out over long periods of time. Infertility is more like a severe, long-term, perhaps fatal illness that moves us from crisis to crisis. Many times with infertility problems, the crisis is reexperienced every month as the woman again begins to menstruate. The failure to conceive is mourned each time. Hope continues to erode. Facing childlessness at the end of a fertility battle is much like facing death after a long-term illness. It is the final and most intense crisis of loss.

When a couple is in crisis, they have little to give each other, and often they feel very alone—especially when their infertility has not been shared in a supportive setting. Most of the advice they receive may encourage them to have a stiff upper lip, keep the faith, believe that it is God's will, pray harder, and be stronger. These are nonsupportive messages rather than expression of caring that listens to their pain and responds to their hopelessness. They need a group that stands with them through the struggle and is there to cry with them when the emptiness of childlessness becomes a reality.

Personal Consequences

Since childbearing is a natural stage in human development, the inability to produce children has a deep and cutting impact on our self-esteem. Something is wrong with us. It radically alters our self-image and view of our own sexuality. Even though most of us accept the sexual part of ourselves as having two purposes—one, the procreative purpose, and second, the purpose of pleasure—when we have difficulties with conception, pleasure is affected.

As we experience a decline in self-esteem, there is a direct impact on how we feel about our bodies and our body images. It is as if we have discovered a defect in our bodies and hence, we have lower worth. Our sense of wholeness suffers.

Social Consequences

Since the beginning of time, children have been the fruit of marriage. In the Old Testament, a stigma was attached to childlessness. While we think of our present culture as more open and sophisticated, this viewpoint is still part of our thinking, both within and outside the church. We complete our manhood by fathering a child, and motherhood is the most total expression of a woman's femininity.

In an article in the *American Journal of Obstetrics and Gynecology,* David Rosenfeld and Eileen Mitchell suggest that many of our views on normal adult mental health are specifically connected with parenthood. "Maturity, unselfishness, social isolation, and loneliness" are seen as directly related to our capacity to be parents. We may argue about the rightness of these expectations and promote individual wholeness without reproduction, yet most of us function with deeper feelings and beliefs that continue to connect marriage with childbearing. Children validate marriage.

Emotional Consequences

Barbara Eck Menning is the founder of Resolve, Inc., a national, nonprofit organization that offers help and support for couples experiencing infertility. She outlined a series of feelings typical of those facing infertility and then childlessness in *Infertility: A Guide for the Childless Couple.* She notes that most couples respond with surprise, denial, anger, isolation, guilt, and grief.

We respond this way because it is the all-American way to believe that we are in control of our destiny. We marry, wait awhile using birth control, and then expect that when we stop using birth control we will automatically become pregnant. No one is prepared for the surprise that comes when it is discovered that pregnancy is not possible. It leaves us in a state of shock.

Next comes denial: We refuse to believe that this can happen to us. While denial may be helpful for a short time as we adapt, it can have serious and detrimental effects if we allow it to persist. We may start rationalizing that we never really wanted kids anyway. Or we may keep believing that pregnancy is a possibility, even after the doctor has assured us it is not. The denial continues when we protect ourselves from feeling the pain of anger, isolation, guilt, and grief that needs to follow. We do not want to believe or accept the reality of our inability to have children.

When we finally do accept the loss, we are most likely to experience a major bout of anger. The angry response is there because of the loss of control over our bodies and our future. Sometimes the anger comes out at people who have children, those who have "too many" children, or those who choose not to have children when they could. Anyone who represents a choice we don't have and makes a different choice than we would make could be the cause of our anger. This angry response is very normal because we feel a mixed sense of fear, loss of control, and helplessness.

Isolation is a very common part of the experience of infertility and childlessness. The feelings of shame and low self-worth that are connected with infertility keep us from sharing our experience. We don't want people to feel sorry for us, nor do we want advice and home remedies, so we keep the problem a secret.

There are consequences to this isolation. Secrecy makes the couple bear the pain alone, rather than getting the support that would be available to them from their community. It also may keep them from each other. There may be feelings of blame. How they deal with the final pain of childlessness will depend on how they have handled the various infertility crises.

For example, if the man has kept all his feelings inside himself while the woman has spilled out her frustration and concern, they may have distanced themselves from each other. If they have kept communication open, kept the sexual experience alive, and shared the painful process, the isolation from the rest of the world may bring them together.

Nevertheless, most of us, with our Western thought patterns, look for cause and effect. Why did this happen? Whose fault is it? If we had done this or not done that, would we now be happy parents? We look for all manner of explanations to find some way to understand our childlessness. We feel guilty. We may blame past guilt-producing behaviors such as masturbation, premarital sex, abortion, extramarital affairs, or homosexual preoccupation. Sometimes even birth-control measures or sexual pleasure, itself, produces the guilt.

Many of us operate in a system that says that if we do good, God will reward us. The flip side is that if we do evil, God will punish us. In such a system, childlessness can be seen as a punishment for wrongdoing. Let us listen to Christ's answer to His disciples when He was asked why a man was blind. "Was it his sins or the sins of his parents?" his followers inquired. Christ's response was that it was neither, but rather that God would be glorified. We interpret his answer to mean that in the normal consequences of human life—sickness, illness, poverty—we cannot attempt to determine blame. It is humanly impossible for us ever to understand the total purposes of life and the universe.

Finally, when we have experienced the shock, denial, anger, isolation, and guilt of the reality that there will be no children, we are forced to deal with grief—a very normal and natural response to loss. In this instance, it is not a tangible loss, like a home or the death of a child, but rather it is the loss of a dream. It is a more ambiguous loss to deal with because there is no one moment of actual crisis.

When we lose a job, there is a point at which the boss says, "You're fired." When we get a divorce, there is that moment when the judge says, "You are divorced." When someone has a terminal illness and dies, there is the moment of death. When a child gets married and moves across the country, there is that point of saying good-bye and then watching him or her drive away. But with infertility there is no moment at which we can be declared absolutely infertile unless the reproductive organs are removed or totally unfunctional. Even then, the hope of adoption may linger. It is difficult to pinpoint the loss of a dream or the end of hope. Hence, it is difficult to pinpoint the moment at which one begins to grieve the loss of childbearing and accept the state of childlessness. Yet the pain of this grief needs to be worked through just as it does for more tangible losses.

Close friends of ours have been through this agony. With their permission we share their experience. One of them told us, "The hardest part is not knowing. It is very lonely! Living for ten years with an unfulfilled expectation is exceedingly wearing on the emotions and the relationship. After a while it is as if you live life waiting to miss your next period. If it is a day or two late, the warm, tender feelings begin to build—then comes the crushing disappointment." This couple never did get a diagnosis of what was wrong. The woman finally had to have a hysterectomy because of endometriosis. This was thought to have been the cause of the infertility.

Facing the fact that all possibilities of bearing a child had been removed was a cutting blow. Then when several adoption attempts also fell through, the reality had to be faced. They would never have children. That was deeply painful!

We asked how it was possible to live life with this ongoing disappointment. Their answer was, "Ultimately you have to get your peace from believing that God's will is being worked out in your life." This brings us to the last stage.

The final healing is the stage of acceptance, or "resolution," as Barbara Eck Menning calls it. In this stage you are past the steady pain; you can move on with the business of life. You will make decisions about how you are going to proceed with the reality of having no children.

At various times throughout your lives, the emptiness of not having children may bring deep sadness. These are grief pangs, the normal result of loss. They are reminders that hurt you, even when you have worked through the loss, readjusted to life, and found new fulfillment. Allowing yourselves to feel the pain, sharing it with someone, and asking God to heal and fill your lives with meaningful outlets—all these help you move through the stages of grief.

Some couples find that as they invest themselves in their careers and volunteer work, the rewards replace the loss. Taking care of other people's children for the weekend, teaching a Sunday school class, or coaching a Little League team are avenues of finding the joys and benefits of children. The two of you will need to discover the source of fulfillment that works best for you. A short-term therapy process with a qualified counselor can be most helpful. Talking together is essential.

Childlessness and Sex

Having accepted your childlessness, you need to sexually reengage in a caring, loving, slow process that can help the two of you move toward a life of sexual satisfaction and fulfillment. This will take planning, scheduling, and learning to focus on the pleasure of each other's bodies.

You could follow some of the steps outlined in *The Gift of Sex*. These begin with foot, hand, and facial caresses. Move on to total body pleasuring that doesn't include genitals. Next include genitals but without a great deal of stimulation, then with some arousal and stimulation, and finally moving on to intercourse. This process of rediscovering, of backing up and moving through every step of sexual intimacy, is essential in recovering sexual fulfillment. We would also encourage reading some good books on sex aloud to each other. Besides *The Gift of Sex* we would recommend Dagmar O'Connor's book, *How to Make Love to the Same Person for the Rest of Your Life—and Still Love It*. Both of these could help revive the sexual stirrings. We would also recommend attending a human sexuality class, weekend seminar, or retreat. Make your sexual life a clear priority.

Birth control continues to be an issue. The two of you need to decide whether you want to leave the rare possibility open that conception could occur, even at age forty or forty-five. Or do you want to permanently assure that conception is never going to happen so you can go ahead and plan your lives without any late-life surprises? Usually when the doctor has said that conception is an impossibility, it *is* an impossibility. But there are those situations when, miracle of miracles, suddenly the woman is pregnant. So you, as a couple, need to determine whether that surprise is something you can manage.

Adoption

Just as it's important not to marry on the rebound when a partner is lost by death or a fiancée is lost by rejection, the same thing is true with the rebound response of adoption when a couple faces infertility. Frequently those "second-choice" mates don't work out on a long-term basis. Similarly, when a couple has not emotionally worked through their inability to bear children, the adjustment to the adopted child may be difficult. He or she may never quite measure up to what they think their own children would have been. So it is vital that before you move on to the process of adopting you resolve the loss of not bearing your own children.

It is not only important that you internally accept adoption, but that you also accept it socially. Adoption may be seen as a sign or symbol of inadequacy, an announcement to the world of your infertility secret. Don't proceed with adoption until you are totally comfortable with it. Research has shown that how ready the parents are to give themselves to the newly adopted child is a much greater factor in how the child adjusts in the adoptive setting than the discovery later on that the child was adopted. How a child experiences love and acceptance from adoptive parents will be the most important issue for adjustment. This is why it is so crucial that a couple work through their loss of childbearing and their feelings about adoption.

Adoption or caring for foster children is a choice that is extremely fulfilling for some couples who are infertile. Adopted children become *their* children. They feel that same deep sense of joy, excitement, and completion as other couples do with the birth of a natural child. These children are accepted as very special gifts from God.

Adopting an infant is a long process with many screenings and hurdles to overcome. Specific information about when a baby will arrive may not be available. Even when the adopting couple knows the baby's due date the actual announcement usually seems sudden and startling. The adopting couple have not experienced the pregnancy that can help prepare not only the mother, but also the father and the immediate community for the arrival of the baby. No, waiting for an adoptive child is not the same as experiencing the pregnancy, themselves. They have not felt the sensation of the child kicking and moving in the womb; they have not heard the heartbeat or experienced other parts of the regular checkups by the doctor. So when the adoptive parents suddenly have the new baby in their arms, the infant can feel more like a stranger than might be true of a biological child.

Bonding has not yet occurred. Since it is so important that a special bonding happen between the parents and child, it might be wise to abstain from sexual involvement for a few weeks to let those special mother-child and father-child connections develop.

When a baby is born into a family, a sometimes-difficult healing and emotional adjustment has to occur as a result of the childbirth process. Usually there is a six-week recuperation and adjustment time. The mother is frequently breastfeeding. Adoptive parents experience obvious differences. Yet the process may be similar, since there is the adjustment to a new infant in the home.

The adoptive father may well experience the same kind of envy or jealousy of the child that would be true of a biological child. It is easy to experience a child as an intruder in the relationship, especially on the sexual life. The same time and fatigue adjustments are needed with adopted infants as with newborn babies that stay with their biological families.

Fortunately, the adoptive mother's body has not suffered the stress of labor and delivery, so she will have more energy available. Still, after the initial adjustment period, it would be important for her to follow many of the same steps recommended for sex after childbirth (see chapter 5). If there has been a long-term infertility struggle, the steps outlined for sex after infertility could help the couple readjust to their sexual life together (chapter 3).

Adopting Older Children

Most families go through four phases when they adopt an older child. These impact the sexual life. These four phases are: commitment, honeymoon, storm, and adaptation.

In the initial **commitment** phase, it is likely that your attention will be distracted from yourselves sexually with all your energy going into nurturing the new child. It would be unlikely that there would be much sexual activity at all during this first phase.

The **honeymoon** phase: Everyone in the family, as well as the new child, will be striving to be on their best behavior and to present themselves at their best. During this time, the sexual life would likely take a positive jump.

Then comes the **storm,** that period during which the adoptive relationships are tested. The child may feel rejected and the parents may feel inadequate. When parents are being tested in terms of their perseverance, discipline, power, and consistency, the sexual life will usually reflect that tension and either be purely functional or nonexistent.

As with any crisis, the family usually gets through the storm and **adapts**—but not always. The adoption either "takes," the storm lasts forever, or the child may actually be given back to the court. If the two spouses weather the adoption well, the adaptation takes place and the resulting good feelings allow for a full sexual life. However, if the storm has taken such a toll that it has been divisive between them as husband and wife, then some recommitment and reconnective work is going to be necessary—both in terms of communication and relationships as well as the sexual experience.

Adopting a child will inevitably be an event that brings stress, and stress always affects the sexual relationship. It does not need to be the end, though; it can be the time for a new beginning where the husband and wife discover each other sexually in ways that have not been enjoyed before. They can use this as an opportunity for growth in their communication and in their sexual life.

Adoption and Hope

Many of us know women who became pregnant a month after they adopted a child. This perpetuates the folklore that if the couple will just relax, children will be conceived and born. Statistics actually say something quite in contrast to this. The research has shown that after adoption, between 3 and 6 percent of the adoptive parents conceive—so this obviously is not a surefire method for dealing with infertility.

It is not fully understood why the few postadoptive pregnancies occur. It may be that in these instances, the reduction of stress did bring about the pregnancy. Some authorities suspect that it could be due to some subtle biochemical changes in the woman's body that happen as a result of parenting. Even though the numbers are few, this small percentage does hold out a measure of hope. We would encourage you to talk about that hope if either of you feels it. Recognize it as an unlikely possibility, yet take birth-control precautions if pregnancy after adoption would be negative.

Conclusion

For a few couples, the sexual relationship is unaffected by the struggle with infertility, the process of adjustment to adoption, or the grief of accepting childlessness. In fact, sex is the glue that holds their relationship together. For most, however, deterioration of sexual fulfillment is likely when this process is not counteracted with a conscious focus.

Whatever the outcome for the two of you, whatever the stress you go through in reaching that point, we trust that you will find peace with each other and with your situation. May

God's strength and blessing be with you. May you find the fullness of life God intended for you.

For Further Study

Menning, Barbara Eck. *Infertility: A Guide for the Childless Couple.* 2d. ed. New York: Prentice Hall, 1988.

O'Connor, Dagmar. *How to Make Love to the Same Person for the Rest of Your Life—and Still Love It.* New York: Bantam, 1986.

Rosenfeld, David L., M.D., and Eileen Mitchell, B.S. "Treating the Emotional Aspects of Infertility: Counseling Services in an Infertility Clinic." *American Journal of Obstetrics and Gynecology,* 135, no. 2 (1979): 135, 177–80.

Seibel, Machelle M., M.D., and Melvin L. Taymor, M.D. "Emotional Aspects of Infertility." *Fertility and Sterility,* 37, no. 2 (February 1982): 137–45.

Walker, Herbert E., "Sexual Problems and Infertility." *Psychosomatics,* 19, no. 8 (August 1978): 477–84.

Part 2

How
Children Impact
the Sexual Life

5

Sex During and After Pregnancy

Pregnancy and childbirth produce emotional and social changes as well as the obvious physical changes. All of these changes affect the couple. The process of having a baby can add enough stress to disrupt a relationship, or it can pull a couple together and deepen their relationship.

How is the sexual life affected? Recent studies have examined the patterns of sexual relations both during and after pregnancy. Sexual desire, frequency of sexual intercourse, various sexual activities, and the effect on orgasm have all been analyzed.

When one of the co-authors, Joyce, was studying nursing in the early 1960s, the cautious recommendations for sexual activity during and after pregnancy were unchallenged. Her maternity nursing textbook from the 1960s reads as follows:

> Sexual intercourse is usually permitted in moderation until the last six weeks of the pregnancy. However, many physicians advise against intercourse during the first three months of pregnancy or during the time of the regular menstrual periods because of the danger of abortion. If the patient has had previous abortions (miscarriages), coitus will probably be restricted until two weeks after the third missed menstrual period. Toward the end of pregnancy, marital relationships may cause premature labor or introduce infection. Relationships should not be resumed until after the six-week examination or until the doctor knows everything is normal.

What do we know today? Are these sexual restrictions necessary during pregnancy? Researching sexual behaviors and responses has answered many of the concerns about sex during and after pregnancy, but some are still awaiting clearer answers.

Sex During Pregnancy

Let's look first at how sexual activity is affected by pregnancy and then we can examine how pregnancy is affected by sexual intercourse and/or orgasm.

Pregnancy Affects Sex

Surveys indicate that as the pregnancy lengthens in time, sexual activity decreases, with a sharp decrease for many couples during the last three months. Why is this?

Socially and culturally there is an ironic attitude that pregnancy and sexuality don't go together. Historically, the pregnant woman has been regarded as an asexual being. One husband shared, "We haven't enjoyed each other sexually for a long time, not the way we used to before Meg got pregnant. I guess we lost the momentum. Once we found out she was pregnant, we pretty much stopped having sex. We weren't sure if it was OK. It just didn't seem right to be sexual with her."

His statement expresses how, even though it takes sexual intercourse to get pregnancy started, a pregnant woman may not be seen as sexual. She is seen as taking a hiatus from sexual desires and behaviors for the duration of the pregnancy, and even after the pregnancy. After all, she is now becoming a mother—and all of us know that mothers are not sexual!

During pregnancy, the woman is in transition between being herself and being the mother of a child. Most societies have rules or rituals that govern transition times from one social identity to another, similar to the rights of passage as one moves from childhood into puberty or from puberty into adulthood. Avoidance of sexual intercourse is a common ritual for a woman becoming a mother and even for a man becoming a father.

Some women don't *feel* as sexual during the early months of pregnancy. This decrease in desire is both emotionally and physically based.

Although hormonal changes are not thought to *cause* decreased sexual desire during early pregnancy, they do trigger the physical symptoms that may lead a woman not to feel sexual. Tenderness and enlargement of her breasts may elicit a pulling away from breast contact with her husband. Nausea and sleepiness may make her physically unavailable. The presence of medical complications will surely interrupt sexual activity. Closeness and reassurance of love continue to be very important for the woman who doesn't have the physical stamina for sexual intimacy. We encourage couples to increase the nonsexual physical closeness during pregnancy.

Emotional components also affect sexual desire. Difficulty in accepting body changes creates a guardedness in sharing freely in a sexual way. Pulling away from sex also may be a response to the feeling of connection with the new life inside. It is as if the woman's pregnant body belongs to the child, so it can't be enjoyed by her husband. Sometimes there is a sense of keeping the growing baby securely locked inside her as her exclusive property. The woman feels she must save herself for her baby. Just as it has been believed that a male athlete should not ejaculate before a competitive event (because sex would leave him physically spent), so some women feel they need to conserve their energy and vitality for the baby. Sometimes the desire to guard the pregnancy results from difficulty in conceiving.

Men also have emotional reactions to their wives' pregnancy that may cause them to avoid sex. Some men believe that sex with a pregnant woman is immoral, but most often the man's avoidance of sex during pregnancy relates to his fear of hurting the mother or baby. It is interesting that pregnant women sometimes say they think their husbands avoid them sexually because they are unattractive, but very few men react to pregnancy as a turnoff. This indicates a need to communicate. Whatever the feelings are during these early months of adjustment, the couple should talk about them. Harbored feelings can grow and separate the husband and wife. Shared feelings bring clarity and connection.

Other emotional reasons are blamed for avoiding sex. When either the husband or wife does not feel love for the other, but has only been sexually active to get pregnant, pregnancy will abruptly interrupt the sexual relationship. If the relationship has not been satisfying, pregnancy becomes a good excuse for avoiding the disappointing sexual experience.

On the other hand, sexual feelings in response to pregnancy can also be just the opposite. Some women report an increase in their sexual drive during these early months. These are the women who feel a sense of relief at not having to worry about trying to get pregnant or avoid pregnancy. Others who experience more desire during pregnancy connect it with an improved self-esteem. Pregnancy enhances their view of themselves sexually. Instead of seeing themselves as asexual, some women get a new sense of self-worth from carrying a baby.

Men can have this same positive response to their wives' pregnancy, as well. We have found this to be true for ourselves; Cliff always found Joyce's pregnant state very attractive. Many men are proud to be responsible for their wives' pregnancies. Increased sexual desire may be an expression of a new joy and connection between the husband and wife. For other couples, particularly those who have been pregnant before, sexual desire doesn't change at all with the onset of pregnancy.

Some studies of sexual desire during the second trimester of pregnancy (four to six months) report a gradual decline while others report that most women desire sex more frequently. Whatever is true for you is what you need to follow. Both husband and wife need to be free to listen to their feelings, share them with each other, and then make decisions about their sexual activity. In a normal, healthy pregnancy with both spouses desiring sex, the act can bring relaxation and increased intimacy.

Lack of sexual interest, reduced sexual activity, and even some decreased frequency of orgasm seem to be quite common during the last three months of pregnancy. Physical changes are mostly responsible. Pregnant women become weary with carrying the extra burden of weight. They feel awkward. Moving and turning is an effort. As one woman so vividly described it, "I walk like a duck, look like a cow, and feel like an elephant."

Because of the woman's large protruding abdomen, the position for intercourse will need to be changed. This is a great time to experiment and break out of old patterns. A side-by-side or sitting position may be preferred. Probably the most frequently recommended position has the man kneeling or standing beside the bed with the woman's legs being held by his arms. This gives freedom of movement for him without putting pressure on the baby. Sometimes a rear entry position is most comfortable. The woman can either be on her knees or lying on her side with her back to her husband and her knees bent toward her abdomen. One author recommended that the most important action to improve your sex life during the last trimester is to go out and buy more pillows—more than you think you will need.

How pregnancy affects a couple's sexual life varies greatly with their individuality, their relationship, and the circumstances, as well as the stage of pregnancy. Decreased sexual interest, activity, and responsiveness during pregnancy is usually connected with a lessening or absence of sexual stirrings and an increase in physical complaints and fears of harming the baby or mother. Keeping physical closeness and sexual activity alive will enhance the couple's relationship, the woman's feelings about herself, and her general well-being. We would encourage couples to plan weekly touching times into their lives. The activity of these times can vary with the feelings of the moment. Talking and touching are always important for handling life's changes.

Sex Affects Pregnancy

We have looked at the effects of pregnancy on a couple's sexual life. What about the effects of sex on pregnancy? When sex is avoided during pregnancy because of fear, that fear has to do with the concern that sex will have a detrimental effect on the baby or mother. Can intercourse cause harm during pregnancy? Are there times when certain sexual activities or responses need to be restricted?

The three primary concerns about having sexual intercourse and/or orgasm for the woman are that she will abort the fetus during the first trimester, that she will deliver the baby prematurely, or that she and the fetus could be infected. Let us look at each of these fears.

When a woman has an orgasm, her uterus contracts. Uterine contractions are what push the baby out of the uterus and vaginal passage during labor and delivery. So it is practical to wonder if allowing oneself to have an orgasm when pregnant might cause abortion or premature labor. Fortunately, we also know that the uterus undergoes contractions regularly during a pregnancy without triggering expulsion of the fetus. Much research has been conducted on this issue. It has been concluded from these studies that intercourse, orgasm, or both need *not* be restricted for the majority of pregnant women. Sexual activity appears to be safe throughout pregnancy for almost all women.

In normal pregnancy, it is not easy to set off labor before the body is ready. If intercourse or orgasm could terminate a pregnancy easily, unwanted babies would be avoided that way. But lovemaking alone cannot set off labor before the cervix is ripe (soft and opening). When the cervix *is* ripe, however, anything can set off labor, including sexual intercourse or orgasm.

There are situations in which sexual intercourse and/or orgasm are prohibited. Sexual stimulation to orgasm should be avoided by women who have suffered repeated miscarriages and have had difficulties in carrying a baby to term. When a woman has had difficulty keeping her pregnancy, for whatever reason, it is wise to avoid the uterine contractions of orgasm. Talk to your physician.

Similarly, this restriction of orgasm is also advised for women for whom premature labor is a threat. That would be true for women whose cervixes have dilated prematurely, who are bleeding, who have experienced previous threatened premature labor, or who are carrying a multiple pregnancy. Sometimes the physician will instruct the woman not to have intercourse because of one of these situations. Orgasm will not be mentioned, so the couple will continue other forms of sexual activity that bring the woman to orgasm.

This happened for us before Greg, our second child, was born. At that time, we were unaware of what happens in our bodies during a sexual response cycle. Joyce started dilating six weeks before she was due to deliver. Being faithful patients, we stopped having intercourse, as the doctor instructed, but we continued sexual closeness and caressing that led to orgasms for

Joyce. Fortunately, the other treatments we were following post-poned labor and delivery for three more weeks, and Greg was as healthy as a full-term newborn despite being born three weeks early. When intercourse is restricted, assume that stimulation of the woman to orgasm is also a danger, unless that difference is clarified.

There are times when vaginal abstinence, the avoidance of *intercourse,* is indicated. During the first three months of pregnancy, threatened or inevitable miscarriage (also called spontaneous abortion) is a clear reason for avoiding intercourse as well as orgasm. Once the sac or membranes have ruptured, vaginal abstinence is definitely a necessary restriction to avoid infection.

So intercourse and orgasm should be avoided in women with obstetric complications such as bleeding, ruptured membranes, premature dilation of the cervix, threatened spontaneous abortion, or premature labor. However, there is no reason to restrict such activity during a normal pregnancy. Most studies have shown that there is no connection between the onset of labor and intercourse, orgasm, and other sexual activity. In fact, it has been found that pregnant women who were orgasmic had a lower percentage of premature deliveries than did nonorgasmic women. So intercourse and orgasm, per se, are not related to premature births, but they may be injurious when prematurity is already threatening.

Infections are an unlikely complication of intercourse if the couple has a monogamous relationship. If either spouse has had other sexual partners, there is the risk of the mother acquiring a sexually transmitted disease. These can be a cause of death for the mother, the fetus, or the newborn. Since the baby is in the well-protected sac, it will not be infected unless the mother is infected with a blood-borne organism. Then it is passed through the placenta to the fetus.

One sexual activity that is highly dangerous during pregnancy is blowing air into the vagina. Oral sex, itself, is harmless, but deaths have resulted when air has been blown into the vagina. Death occurs within minutes if the air forced into the vagina happens to form a bubble. When the air is forced from the vagina into the uterus and into the bloodstream through the uterine lining, a bubble, or air embolism, forms. It may travel to the lungs, brain, or heart, causing sudden death. The same danger is present with vaginal douching during pregnancy.

It is important to be aware of these necessary restrictions. Nevertheless, since we have spent more time detailing the limitations than proclaiming the freedom to fully enjoy sex during pregnancy, you may feel that it is better to avoid sex just in case. That isn't true! If you are concerned about any of the special situations for yourself, check with your physician so you can relax and enjoy yourselves.

Unnecessary sexual inhibitions or restrictions during pregnancy can be a source of stress that is detrimental to a successful pregnancy. If there are no complications and the woman has no history of miscarriage or premature birth, the couple can safely enjoy sexual intercourse and orgasm from the onset of pregnancy until the beginning of labor (or the opening of the cervix).

Sex After Pregnancy

Whether the pregnancy ends with a miscarriage, still-birth, or a newborn baby, the weeks afterward are a time of crisis and adjustment for the couple. Sexual adjustment is one of the more critical emotional adjustments of this time period. In the case of a miscarriage, the loss of the pregnancy or the expected baby brings the pain and separation of grief, the doubt about oneself, and the feeling of sexual abnormality. When the pregnancy does end with the birth of a baby, the changes in social and family relationships are tremendous. Each subsequent birth changes the shape of the family, causing the relationships within both the nuclear and extended family to shift. Sometimes these shifts are felt abruptly; other times they are almost unnoticed.

Miscarriage

The emotional effects of a miscarriage have a more jarring impact on the sexual life of a couple than does the physical trauma, although physical recuperation is more serious than the couple expects. A miscarriage, or spontaneous abortion, is the unintended termination of a pregnancy prior to the twentieth week of the pregnancy. Spontaneous abortions are estimated to occur in 15 percent of all pregnancies.

There are various reasons why the woman loses a baby: hormonal abnormalities, high blood pressure, anemia, diabetes, or severe emotional problems in the mother are examples. Genetic defects, infection, and anatomical abnormalities in the fetus are other proven causes. It is important for the couple to be informed of the cause when it is known; so don't hesitate to ask! Many times, however (about 50 percent of the time), the cause is unknown.

Since the cause is often not known or not explained to couples, many women live with misconceptions. It is common for them to feel they caused the miscarriage. Some women fear they will no longer be able to bear children. Or they may feel less feminine for not fulfilling their reproductive role. Sexual activity may be assumed to be the cause; this will affect the sexual relationship.

It is important for the couple to acknowledge the importance of the lost pregnancy. Each spouse may experience the grief and loss differently. Sharing and accepting those differences can strengthen the marital relationship while feeling guilt or blaming the other adds to the stress. It is highly unlikely that either the husband or wife did anything to cause the miscarriage, despite any feelings that they did. Even when the pregnancy was unplanned, the experience remains emotionally upsetting. Feelings of sadness, anxiety, depression, and hostility are common. Often the woman is affected longer than the man. She may be weepy for several weeks and even experience loss of sexual interest, while he may have resolved the loss and be impatient to move on with life. If sexual intimacy is to be resumed with enjoyment, emotional needs and differences must be addressed. Take time to talk to each other and to other caring listeners.

Stillbirth

The grief of a stillbirth or the death of a newborn is amplified by the sense of having produced a "bad baby"—one who was defective or unable to live. All too often, there seems to be no place on the maternity ward for the mother without a baby. The staff doesn't know how to handle the loss; it is prepared to care for mothers with babies, not mothers without babies. As a result, the mother often is hastily sent home. Then she may feel that she has lost her baby, her status as a mother, *and* her role as a patient. Yet she is a person who needs extra care and attention.

A medical journal reported a case of a woman who, after delivering a stillborn baby, was put in a room alone, and no staff members even looked in on her for twelve hours. She wasn't checked physically or even offered anything to drink.

One of Joyce's friends from nurse's training had a baby who died in the hospital a few days after it was born. When the baby wasn't brought to her at its usual feeding time, Jan started calling the nurse. No one responded. After some time, she walked up to the nurses' station, but couldn't get anyone to talk to her. One of the nurses told her someone would be with her in a moment. Finally, a nurse's aide (who had no training) took her to a supply room, had her sit on a chair, told her that her baby had died—and walked out. Jan, feeling physically weak and totally dazed, had to find her way to a telephone to contact her husband. She had to manage this unexpected, devastating news without the support or care of the hospital staff.

These are extreme cases. Usually hospital personnel are better able to deal with the woman's loss than was true in these two situations. Yet it is not unusual for a woman who has lost her baby to feel like an outcast. Most of us are uncomfortable around her and don't know what to say, so we avoid her. We treat her like she has the plague at a time when she needs us beside her, sharing her pain.

Whether or not to see the dead baby, what to do about funeral rituals, and choosing or not choosing a name are all issues that the couple must decide. The amount of information and choice the couple is given (with support) will help ease this difficult situation.

Mothers whose babies live even a few moments are better able to handle the tragedy than those whose babies are born dead. Mothers who deliver stillborns are better able to mourn when they can see their dead baby and know what will become of it. Even if the baby is grossly defective, it is recommended that the parents be given the choice of seeing their child. Cleaning and wrapping the baby in a receiving blanket lessens the shock of the defects. Then the parents should unwrap and examine the baby at their own pace, if they desire. If you have experienced such a loss, you may have your own sense of what would have been best for you. The primary concern is that feelings of loss are taken seriously and that you as a couple are given the support you need.

If you are friends of a couple who has lost a baby, go to them. Give them a hug. Bring them a meal. Be with them. You don't have to say anything except that you are sorry, that you care, and that you want to be available in any way they need you.

Contrary to what is commonly believed, both parents will experience profound grief from the death of a baby they have never known or enjoyed. That grief may not be resolved for years. The grief begins with a sense of shock and disbelief and is followed by a time of confusion and pain. As the death becomes real, feelings of anger and guilt take over. The mother may mentally search through the pregnancy for evidence of something she did wrong or should have done better. Overwhelming sadness can naturally lead to depression, which may be accompanied by a sense of loneliness that can last several months.

During this time it is unlikely that the grieving couple will feel sexual. Yet closeness and physical affirmation are extremely important. Holding each other and crying helps lighten the despair. As the grief lessens, "the light begins to appear at the end of the tunnel." Heaviness is relieved and life's functions are reestablished. Sexual joy may need to be rediscovered. Taking time to "find" each other is time well spent. Bodily pleasure lessens pain.

Bringing Baby Home

Most of the time couples face both the joy and the stress of bringing home that wonderful new creation—the precious little person who will change their lives so dramatically. Sexual adjustment can go smoothly or be difficult. The six to eight weeks following labor and delivery are known as the postpartum period. It is during this time that the woman's genital organs return to their previous condition. The uterus shrinks back to almost its pre-pregnancy state, shape, and position. It takes only two to three weeks for the cervix (the opening of the uterus) to close and the vagina to return to normal. The breasts prepare to nurse the infant.

When is it possible to resume sexual intercourse? In the past, enforced abstinence was the rule during the six weeks following birth. However, at this time, all of the literature indicates that there is no need to wait that long. No evidence has been found to indicate that having sexual intercourse earlier than six weeks has an adverse effect on the healing. This is particularly true when there has not been an episiotomy (incision to enlarge the vaginal opening) or when the episiotomy has been carefully repaired with little tissue damage.

Some couples prefer to resume comfortable intercourse in the second or third postpartum week. The only reason not to return to sexual intercourse would be pain, vaginal irritation or infection, or the physician's instructions. Any stitches should have healed within ten days. Some women report having had intercourse five days after delivery without any complications. Provided the woman hasn't developed an infection and both partners are freshly washed and following good hygienic practices, it is up to them to determine when to resume intercourse.

We encourage couples to make the first lovemaking time after childbirth a special event. Plan very carefully; this would be best as a scheduled, rather than a spontaneous, time. Make a decision that you are both ready for sex and then prepare for it. Plan a time when the baby has just been fed and is least likely to awaken. You may want to have someone close to you take the infant for an hour or two.

Many women think of this time in the same way they thought of their first intercourse. It is like being a virgin again. Use the same precautions to avoid pain. That is, take plenty of time to caress and enjoy the pleasure of each other's body. Proceed to entry slowly, with the woman in control of guiding the penis into the vagina. Use a lubricant. Albolene (a facial cleanser) is one we like. Allercreme (non-lanolin), which is excellent to pleasure the total body, also works well as a lubricant. Both of these products are petroleum-based and should not be used with a diaphragm or rubber condom (see chapter 3). It would be helpful for the man to have ejaculated within twenty-four hours before this time together so that he will not ejaculate too quickly. This can be taken care of through self-stimulation or through manual caressing by the wife, if that is enjoyable for them.

Plan for some special romance as part of the setting of your enjoyment together. Joyce had experienced so much sexual pain after Julene was born that after the birth of Greg, our next child, we went to see a romantic movie together before our reinitiation. It worked well! Joyce had extensive stitching from a breech (feet-first) delivery with Julene. Greg was an easier birth, so that helped also. To the best of your ability, see to it that the first sexual intercourse after childbirth occurs under ideal conditions in terms of setting, fatigue, preparation of your bodies, and time of day.

Take the necessary birth-control precautions, even if the mother is breastfeeding. Though many women do not ovulate (and, as a result, cannot become pregnant) during the first few months of breastfeeding, some do. Some women ovulate before they have their first menstrual period. You may want to refer to chapter 2 in deciding what birth-control method would be best for both of you during this important time of reconnecting sexually.

How Sex Is Affected

Tiredness and fatigue are natural deterrents to sex. The woman's body has experienced a major blow. First of all, she has been carrying around this twelve- to fifty-pound basketball of extra weight for nine months. She is recuperating from the physical trauma and emotional intensity of the birth process. Her body has not returned to its pre-pregnancy shape. Her breasts are sore and seem to belong to the baby. They are no longer there for her or her husband's sexual pleasure. Also, she has a totally dependent infant to care for.

If this is the first child, both spouses may be using up any extra energy with anxiety about being good parents. They may be getting up every few hours during the night. Household tasks have to be handled, meals prepared, the house cleaned, and other children tended to. Fatigue is an almost inevitable part of those first months after a newborn comes home. This combination of exhaustion and anxiety may mean that the woman never becomes aroused. If she ever does have enough energy to feel interested and get things started sexually, about the time she relaxes enough to enjoy herself, she's likely to fall asleep or hear the baby stir. Thus, many women report diminished sexual desire after the birth of a first child. Even though sex is still as enjoyable for many, the frequency of sexual activity is less during that first postpartum year than it was before pregnancy.

In addition to the tiredness, there is a change in focus after the first child arrives. Instead of the primary focus being between the husband and wife, now the two of them are focused on the child. Sometimes the husband feels that the only connection is between the mother and infant, leaving no place for him. Couples need to work together to get the father and infant bonded. If the father is home during the baby's fussy times, he can take his shirt off and carry the baby on his shoulder. (Infants attach as they smell our bodies and feel our skin.) This will also give the new mom a break. Fathers should be active in sharing the responsibility for the baby.

The new mother may feel not only tired, but also depressed. Depression causes sexual apathy. Postnatal depression may be the reason for infrequent sexual intercourse up to three months after delivery. The weepy, postpartum blues often begin within a few days of the child's birth. In addition to being overwhelmed by the new responsibilities of motherhood and being exhausted, some women are affected by sudden hormonal changes—and in different ways. Even though the lack of interest in sex is temporary, women worry about it and feel guilty, while husbands feel frustrated and unsure of how to bring relief.

For women who do feel sexual desire after childbirth, the fear of pain from the episiotomy (the cut that allows the baby to be born without tearing the perineum) may cause the parents to wait to be sexually active. Intercourse after childbirth can sometimes be distinctly uncomfortable. Forty percent of women report soreness or pain during intercourse after childbirth. Pain needs to be taken seriously and remedied with the physician's help. When something that is normally pleasurable causes pain, it is likely that couples will pull away from the activity. Pain causes more havoc in sexual relationships than most people realize. It must be relieved!

Breastfeeding also can stir up feelings both in the woman and in the man. Initially, there may be anxiety for the woman about whether the whole process will work. She may worry about being able to produce enough milk. Once they are working, the breasts seem to belong to the baby. A woman may feel an incredible sense of heaviness from the infant's total dependence on her body for survival.

Joyce breastfed all three of our children. She began teaching at the local university when Julene was just six weeks old, yet Julene refused to take a bottle, even if it contained Joyce's breast milk. So Joyce would often drive home from work with that sense of urgency for Julene—the sense that the infant could not survive without her. There were many intense prayers for safety on those trips home! The joy of arriving and being there for her baby was all-encompassing. When Joyce walked in the door, Cliff was often thrilled, too, because his Ph.D. studies may have been sidetracked by walking Julene for the past hour while waiting for Mom to come home with the "goodies."

Some women who breastfeed find they are less sexually interested, while others get turned on when breastfeeding increases their desire for their husbands.

The sexual feelings that stir in women in response to the baby sucking their nipples may come as a real surprise, even shock and embarrassment. These feelings are a pure, natural, physical response to that part of the body being stimulated. The feelings in no way impart the message that the mother is using the child as a sexual object. The increased sensitivity of the breasts may be very intense. Yet they may get so used to the baby's sucking that the mother is not able to switch gears to her husband's touch or lips and tongue. Besides, when her breasts fill up, they may ache and leak.

We offer two helpful suggestions: First, breastfeed immediately before a sex playtime so the breast will feel more comfortable and available. Second, take time to discover the type of breast and nipple play that feels arousing but different than the baby's sucking. It is important that the man not take these adjustments as a rejection of him, but rather as a time of rediscovery.

The man may have his own sexual inhibitions after bringing a baby home. He may have difficulty responding to the mother of his baby. In his eyes she may have become almost sacred, not a sexual person to be enjoyed for his pleasure; this is the madonna syndrome. He may feel more like worshiping her than making love to her! Her being the "food factory" may enhance this nonsexual image to her husband. These barriers to sexuality need to be discussed.

Enhancing Sex after Bringing Baby Home

The ongoing sexual relationship of the couple with a new baby requires nurturing. Life's responsibilities will need to be balanced so there is time for each spouse to get rest and have time for the other.

Write out a plan for each day, listing the essential activities; decide what can be skipped. Get as much help as you can afford. Allow friends to help by bringing a meal, taking an older child while the baby sleeps, or coming for a night or a few hours each day. Plan for the new mother to rest every time the baby sleeps. Divide responsibilities between the two of you, so that the stress is equally distributed. How many responsibilities each of you assumes depends so much on the rest of your lifestyle. If the husband works 6 A.M. to 8 P.M., he is not going to be able to take on much more. If there are three children at home under the age of four, and there is no outside help, the mother will be able to handle only the minimal essentials.

Once the duties have been sorted out, decide what kind of time you each would enjoy with the other. Take turns being responsible for the times of your choice. For example, if the wife wants a time of relaxation for talking and low-key touching, she may schedule a babysitter to come in for an hour or two right after the baby has been fed. She may prepare the master bedroom for candlelight, slice some cheese and apples, leave a message with her husband that he is to be hers from 8:00 to 9:30 that evening, and then invite him to the bedroom with a clear message of her desires for that time.

If the husband would like to get away from the responsibilities of home, he might invite his wife to a short, light dinner out for an hour and a half. Getting away will be difficult during the first year after the child is born. If time away is important for your relationship, you will have to be deliberate in making it happen. Once breastfeeding has been well-established, pumping milk for the baby to be fed by bottle is a possibility. Start this in the first month or so to get the baby used to both breast and bottle. Conducting a trial run before the real event is important. As we mentioned before, Julene would never suck from a bottle, even if it was Joyce's milk.

An important element of sexual enhancement is the woman's physical condition. Pelvic exercises (also called Kegel exercises) for the woman will increase her sexual awareness. She can speed the healing of the episiotomy and the return of her genitals to good tone by faithfully exercising her PC (pubococcygeus) muscle. This is the muscle that forms a figure 8 around the openings of the urinary tract and vagina in the front, and the anus in the back. It controls the opening and closing of these orifices. Tightening these muscles can stop the passage of urine or feces. Tightening and relaxing them during lovemaking can enhance sensation. These muscles contain many nerve endings that record pleasurable stimuli. Their activity and liveliness are vital for every woman's sexual satisfaction. A man also enjoys the firmness of his wife's muscles when she contracts them rhythmically during sexual intercourse. They play an important part in mutual pleasure.

To increase the PC muscle's tone and vitality, start exercising it one hundred to two hundred times daily. Slowly tighten the muscles that you use to stop urination until you cannot tighten anymore; hold it tight to the count of four, then gently let go. Practice this while urinating. Stop the flow of urine several times while you are emptying your bladder. You can do the same thing with the anal muscle.

When you're focusing specifically on the vagina, think of starting to tighten the vagina by bringing your labia (lips) closer together. Imagine that your vagina is an elevator and you are starting at the ground floor. Bring the muscles up from floor to floor, tightening and holding at each floor. Do not hold your breath while you tighten. Go to the fifth floor, then go down one floor at a time. These more thorough exercises can be done twenty-five times a day.

Exercise some pelvic muscle every time you change a diaper, while you wash the dishes, cook dinner, breastfeed, read stories to your older children, and so on. The exercise will make a difference both in feeling and in keeping your internal organs in place!

Keeping the sexual relationship alive will take a conscious effort. Recognize that special times for the two of you are a priority.

Conclusion

Sex during and after pregnancy need not change. Except for the pain Joyce experienced after Julene's birth, our sex life was not that different from before conception. We never thought that much about it. Our lifestyle, Joyce's quick labors, and a mutually satisfying sex life for five years before bearing children may have contributed to the lack of change. With Cliff as a full-time student and Joyce as the full-time financial provider, roles had to be shared. We did not fit the traditional husband-wife, father-mother stereotypes. Mutuality became a must!

Each couple is different, each pregnancy is different, and every birth is different. Finding what is mutually satisfying for you as a couple is vital. Do not be forced into a pattern of behavior just because the books or experts say that is how it should be. Learn the principles, then apply them to your lives. Enjoy a happy family life together.

Learn to laugh and cry together when stress is more than you can handle.

For Further Study

Cane, William. *The Art of Kissing.* New York: St. Martin's Press, 1991.

Close, Sylvia. *Sex During Pregnancy and After Childbirth.* San Bernardino, Calif.: Borgo Press, 1986.

Jessner, L. "Pregnancy as a Stress in Marriage." In *Marital and Sexual Counseling in Medical Practice,* edited by D. F. Abse, E. M. Nash, and L. M. R. Louden. Hagerstown, Md.: Harper and Row, 1974.

6

Mommy, What Are You and Daddy Doing in There?

It's Saturday morning. Your seven-year-old son had a friend over for the night and they love to watch Saturday morning cartoons. Even though you are not sure about all the learning that is taking place from those cartoons, you brush it aside with the thought that somehow this one time isn't going to make any difference. The television does function as a good baby-sitter.

You go to the bathroom and brush your teeth. Then you wake up your spouse in anticipation of a relaxed, enjoyable sexual time together. You're refreshed and feeling that specialness of making love right when you wake up. The bodies are warm and relaxed, and the minds are sleepy.

You get into the sexual experience and are just beginning to get aroused. You're laughing and giggling together. All of a sudden there's that knock on the door. "Why did you lock the door? What are you guys doing in there? Can I come in? Tommy just spilled his milk all over the carpet."

Suddenly, the morning that started with such great promise has been jolted by reality. The fact is that you live in a home where you aren't completely in control of your time, nor can you choose exactly when you're going to make love.

Children are an interruption and an intrusion in a couple's sexual relationship. Yet the stability and solidarity of a home is enhanced by the mutually satisfying, ongoing sexual life of the parents. Thus the marriage must take priority. There will still be many times when the needs of the family are attended to first. But the long-range priority has to be the marriage. The solidarity of the marriage is very much like a good foundation for a building. If the foundation is set on solid ground, with good reinforcement steel in the concrete, then the building will withstand all the buffeting of the above-ground activity. The same is true for a marriage. One of the best gifts we can give to our children is the gift of a marital relationship that is solidly based on love—and a fulfilling sex life. This is a major source of security for a child.

Building a Solid Marriage

A solid marriage has a number of ingredients. We would recommend the following:

Keep open. Open communication between husband and wife, and then within the family, is basic. As you maintain openness with one another, the children will model that style. When we talk about openness, we are not commending inappropriate exposure of private feelings and behaviors that would be confusing and emotionally upsetting to children, but rather we encourage an openness about feelings, reactions, impressions, expectations, and dreams that help members of a family share together.

Keep the decks clear. Don't let anger, resentments, and frustration build between you. This can be accomplished by following the Marriage Encounter format of writing to each other. Another way is to provide a time to share specific events on a regular basis. Or perhaps this sharing happens spontaneously in the course of your lives together. By always keeping the feeling channels open and clear, you will be a positive example for your children.

Keep together. This is not a united front against the kids, Mom and Dad on one side and the kids on the other, but rather a joint front with and for the kids. This also does not mean that the two of you can't disagree in front of the children. But it does mean that in the middle of your disagreement you send a message of respect, care, and concern for each other. You do *not* undermine the other parent as a way of furthering your own purposes or gaining some advantages with the kids.

Keep committed. Every marriage is very much like driving along a mountain road. The ground underneath may be as solid as granite, but you are always only a few feet from going over the precipice. To function at a high level a relationship needs a diligent focus to keep it soundly on the road. Getting close to the edge may lead to havoc and destruction. Those edges usually involve overcommitment in other areas such as work, church, volunteering, or community action. Extensive involvement in other relationships, with either the opposite or the same sex, also test those edges. Overcommitment to the children, so that the marriage is always in second place, can be a danger, too. If you are going to show your children that your marriage is a priority, it must be evident in your actions.

Keep balanced. While each of us has different needs, we all require variety. We need private times, social times, times for exercise, work, reflection, even time for paying the bills. When we become overfocused in one area, we take away from the balance that allows us to be whole individuals, able to share the intimacy of a marriage and give ourselves to a family. Check out that balance with each other on a regular basis to help keep yourselves on track.

Keep scheduled. Due to the busy lives most of us lead, it is usually necessary to do some planning for our times together. Otherwise, the demands of the immediate family, the extended family, and the community—church, school, sports events, and other social involvements—usurp all available time. The time left over, if there is any, is given to the marriage.

Couples who are determined to maintain a solid marriage must make time together a priority. Think about it. How often have you been invited out to dinner, looked at the calendar, and discovered that you had set aside that time to spend time alone with your spouse? Did you then say, "No, we're not doing anything that night; we'd be delighted to go"? This sends the message that you, as a couple, are a low priority rather than one that must be taken seriously.

Keep "turned on." A young couple in a class we were teaching asked, "Could you speak on keeping your sexual love relationship exciting for both partners throughout the marriage years? What are some obstacles that might occur after the honeymoon is over? What are ways to continually be *pleasing* to each other?"

This couple is already taking steps to keep their love relationship alive by thinking about it and asking questions. They accurately imply that it takes a conscious effort to keep the sexual relationship exciting. The reason it takes a conscious effort is that the intense passion and craving for each other that is present before marriage changes once the partners can have each other day after day, week after week, for the rest of their lives. In fact, now sex is not only readily available, it has become an expected part of the relationship, sometimes a demand.

Even though marriage is the most secure and trusting relationship in which sexual joys can grow, there is also much about married life and the family that we associate with being asexual. We didn't see our parents as sexual, so when we become parents, ourselves, we may turn off our own sexuality. Here are some guidelines that can help you keep turned on in your marriage:

1. Make certain your sexual experiences are satisfying for both of you. The experiences need to be free of demand and anxiety and full of care, warmth, pleasure, and fun.

2. Both of you must be able to allow intimacy, to be willing to lose yourselves with each other, and be open with your sexuality.

3. Take care of your bodies. Staying in good physical condition will help keep you in tune sexually. This includes eating the kind of food that is best for your body, getting the right amount of rest, doing physical exercise that stimulates your cardiovascular system, and practicing good grooming.

4. Keep in touch with your own sexual feelings and physical responses. You may need to discover those for the first time. Until each of you knows your body, it may be difficult to share yourself with another person.

For the woman, it is important to learn to do the pubococcygeus (PC) muscle exercises (also called Kegel exercises). Let yourself be aware of your sexual thoughts; affirm your body's sexual feelings as you experience them. Let yourself be aware of all your sexual dimensions physically, emotionally, and mentally.

If sexual feelings are triggered in response to others of the opposite sex, manage and control those feelings by channeling them into your marriage. Bring the spark home to bed!

5. Make your sexual relationship a priority. Scheduling quality time to be together physically is most difficult for many couples. From what most of us experienced before marriage, what we've read, and what we've seen in movies and on television, we believe that a truly romantic sexual experience will automatically and spontaneously burst forth from within us. We believe we will make mad, passionate love throughout our marriage, and if we don't, something is wrong with us.

The fact is that most of the time this is not how it works. After a few months we find that the newness becomes repetitive. Other claims upon our time are barging in on us. We find ourselves having to make more of an effort to be sexual.

This should not be surprising. Something we've been looking forward to for years, that was forbidden before marriage, is now completely open and available to us. As availability is gained, intrigue is lost. That initial sparkle has to be kindled through other means. For many couples, it is important to schedule blocks of time to be physical together.

These are times that are designed for physical pleasure and may or may not lead to sexual intercourse. There can be talking, touching, caressing, and loving without demand for response. If that should lead to sexual interest and arousal for both, then proceed with a total sexual experience. Some resist the idea of scheduling "sex." Many feel that scheduling takes away the aura of romance. Often those couples who fear "losing the mystery" are the ones who are experiencing conflict. We are all for spontaneity when your sexual life brings you total happiness without scheduling. But if you are in conflict about what you want, or if you are unhappy with what happens between you, or find that sex is a quickie at the tired end of the day after the eleven o'clock news, then you may be a couple who could ignite the flame by quality, scheduled times.

6. Learn to give and receive bodily pleasure without demand for sexual response. Before marriage there is usually hugging, kissing, and caressing, "making out," or petting with an intense turn-on. After legitimizing our sexual activity by being married, we tend to cut out all these preliminaries because now we can do the "real thing," sexual intercourse. What we fail to recognize is that all of the touching, caressing, and pleasuring is part of the sexual experience. When we neglect that part, we diminish the joy, pleasure, and satisfaction.

So it is crucial that we learn to touch one another totally, bodily, without demand for arousal or release. Arousal is likely to grow out of this touch when we are relaxed, but it doesn't always—and that's OK. Chapter 13 in *The Gift of Sex* explains the process of learning to receive pleasure through touch. The whole body is a receptor of pleasure. Allowing the tingling sensations of skin-to-skin contact can help us keep the sexual spark alive as the years go by. Many women, especially, report that they would rather touch and cuddle than have intercourse.

7. Take responsibility for your own sexual pleasure. Go after what feels good to you. Don't demand that your spouse produce a positive response in you. Many of us have the idea that we are in the sexual experience for the other person and will get the most out of it when we are focused on bringing the other one happiness. But our finding is that we actually give the most when we take responsibility for our own sexual feelings and enjoy our spouse's body for our pleasure. Of course, this means eliminating anything that violates, hurts, or offends the other person. We must each let the other spouse know if something feels negative.

It is a vital thing, especially for the woman, to learn that being in a sexual experience for her own pleasure will ultimately bring the most pleasure to the man. The reason we emphasize this for the woman is that many men already tend to function that way, but women don't. If you ask your husband, he will affirm to you that he enjoys the sexual experience immensely when you get the most out of it—not just when he gets his own satisfaction. So it is vital that you go into the sexual experience taking responsibility for your needs and verbalizing them, so your spouse can relax and enjoy you. You should not see this as selfish, but rather as the way you can give the most in the sexual experience.

8. Plan special treats. Like every other part of life, sex can become boring and humdrum. You can add sexual excitement by bringing treats to the experience. These tell your spouse that you have thought ahead. Such actions send a little extra message that you care.

No major productions are necessary. It may be a rose on the bedside stand or lighting the candles while she is in taking her shower. Or it may be preparing a love nest in front of the fireplace that's ready when he gets home late from work, or buying a sexy nightgown, or having a bowl of fresh fruit in the bedroom that you're going to feed each other. The special treats can be as elaborate as surprising the wife with a special weekend in a city or resort nearby, or as simple as a message to him under the dinner plate that says, "I'm going to attack your body tonight."

9. Be free to experiment! Plan experimentation in your sexual experience. This is especially important if the two of you find that experimenting does not come naturally. For some couples, creativity and experimentation are as natural as getting up in the morning and brushing their teeth. But for others, it is much more difficult.

Whenever we do something exactly the same way repetitively it is likely to get boring. If you started eating your favorite meal every day for the next six months, or if you got together with a social group and planned exactly the same event over and over again, or if you went to church on Sunday morning and sang exactly the same songs and heard the same sermon, you would become bored. Our sexual lives are no different.

There is no way to discover the five or ten or twenty steps to perfect sexual happiness and then follow them for the rest of our life. We can practice principles, but the actual behavior must

vary. Each sexual experience is a new event waiting to be discovered. As we are willing to stretch ourselves and experiment,
to play, tease, and explore, we will discover that we have an
endless capacity for new experiences and feelings. Continually
uncovering the unknown keeps sex alive.

10. Include specific times for teaching. These are times
when you focus on teaching each other what brings you pleasure,
showing how you like to be genitally stimulated, how you like
to kiss, how you like your body touched. This is like a periodic
review, not only in words but also in action. These can be fun
times which may even turn into sexual arousal, but that isn't the
goal.

**11. Schedule sex-talk times when you are not fatigued
and not in the middle of a sexual experience.** Keeping
yourselves turned on over the years of marriage will mean
learning to talk about sex. From time to time you need to touch
base by talking about how you are feeling in the sexual experience. What is it that you would like to change? What would you
like more of, and how would you like to experiment? Some
couples go through their whole married life never talking about
sex and report that they are happy. But most of us need to talk
about our sexual feelings and experiences regularly.

12. Seek help when necessary. You may find that problems are persisting. There may be a lack of sexual desire, difficulties with arousal for the woman, impotence for the man,
orgasmic problems for the woman, premature ejaculation for the
man, or persistent pain during intercourse. Get help early in
dealing with the problems. Start self-help methods. Read, attend
classes, or consult your physician.

If self-help doesn't make a difference, get a referral to a
sexual therapist. Ask your doctor or minister for a recommendation. Give us a call. You will find our number in the front pages
of this book.

As we were writing this, we got a call from the wife of a
sixty-year-old man. She said her husband has been struggling
with impotence, difficulty in achieving and maintaining an erection, for fifteen years. He doesn't believe he can be helped. Our

strong encouragement to her was to get help. Sexual problems can be reversed. Early treatment diminishes the distress and the length and cost of treatment.

Being Parents and Lovers

When we have focused ourselves on keeping all dimensions of the marriage relationship solid we will be able to be parental *and* sexual. Children need not usurp our roles as lovers.

We believe it is great for our children to know that we delight in loving each other. If we teach them to wait until marriage to have sex and then we behave as if sex doesn't exist in our marriage, what are they waiting for?

We can communicate to our children the importance of our times alone. There is nothing wrong with the children knowing that we have sexual times and that we have fun. One couple struggled because their only lovemaking time was after all six kids were in bed. They finally decided to designate one night a week as their evening to focus on each other. Whatever room they were in that evening—whether it was the television room, the bedroom, or the guest room—was not to be disturbed. The older children were responsible for keeping the younger children out. It soon became an established part of this family's life that Thursday night was Mom and Dad's time. The children eventually felt a sense of pride at cooperating with these evenings.

This approach ultimately builds a deep-down security. These children are hearing of families that are falling apart—and here their parents are so enjoying each other that they have special times just for each other.

Research has shown that when parents share positive, open attitudes about sexuality in the family setting, those attitudes are passed on to the children. This does not mean that we expose children to our sexual play, nor does it mean that we give a debriefing the next morning at breakfast! It does mean that we openly communicate that sex is still an enjoyable part of our marriage and we expect it to be for the rest of our lives.

As we mentioned earlier, most of us grew up not viewing our parents as sexual, so we struggle to allow ourselves to be lovers once we are parents. We have separated the sexual part of ourselves from the parenting part. The idea of being a mother and being intensely sexual is as dissonant as a striptease at the Sunday school class.

As parents, we have to start by giving ourselves permission to be lovers. In 1 Corinthians 7:5 the Apostle Paul tells us not to forsake coming together sexually, except for brief seasons of prayer, and then to come back together again to avoid being tempted. Paul's assumption is that the sexual life will go on for the purpose of enjoyment. Children are not a reason for limiting our sexual relationship. The Song of Solomon, which is purely an erotic, sexual, love poem, gives us an example of the breadth and intensity of love play that is expected of a couple. All of that is available to us, even when we are parents!

Yes, children bring changes. Since sexual intercourse is a private act, we can no longer freely romp around the house. Children demand our time and energy, so we have less available for each other. This is the reason for a significant decrease in sexual activity for most couples during the first year after a baby is born. (See chapter 5.) Fatigue, pain, and change in body image all may lower the wife's desire and, thus, decrease the frequency of sexual activity.

Once the child reaches toddlerhood and is mobile, there is a new concern. We have to be cautious about being interrupted while we are engaging in sex. When we are on guard, fearing an intruder, we will not freely enjoy each other sexually. This is the time to get a lock on the bedroom or love-room door. A first priority when moving into a new home is to get that lock put on your bedroom door—and use it. Many couples enjoy a special kind of security when the door is locked during lovemaking time. They know that nobody is going to walk in on them. This can be important, even if a lovemaking time occurs in the middle of the night (particularly when the children are younger). There is something about a locked door that enhances freedom.

Should it occur that at some point your child walks in on you while you are making love, it is completely appropriate to ask him or her to leave. You may need to explain, especially to younger children, that "What Daddy and Mommy were doing was a loving thing, not a hurtful thing." To a young child the vigorous thrusting and the noises of release could seem painful.

The concern with noise becomes more pronounced as children get older. Where the walls are thin or children's bedrooms are right next to the parents' bedroom, precautions need to be taken—both for the child and for you as a couple. One thing you can always do is put a musical barrier such as a speaker or a radio between your room and the child's. Your sounds will be behind it so that the music serves as a buffer for your noises and helps you relax.

One mother reported about her curious ten-year-old who used to come knocking on the door. When the parents didn't respond, she called them on the telephone (they had two lines). "What's going on in there?" she asked. "It sounds like either Dad is sick or there's a dog vomiting." Such questions provide a great opportunity to give a little sex education, since these are not images that we want connected with the sexual experience. We must keep in mind that the sexual noises are a different set of noises than our children will ever hear us make. It does take some explanation if the children are inadvertently exposed to them. Privacy, both in terms of a closed door and the noise, is as important for the couple as it is for the children.

As the children grow older, they begin to understand adult sexual behavior. For some parents this is a serious dilemma. The awareness that their children know what's going on makes them feel self-conscious about being sexual. So they are only together after all the children are asleep or away. Then they feel they must be very quiet. This inhibiting attitude is based on the belief that it would be dramatically and negatively shocking to the child to be aware of adult sexuality. This issue needs to be addressed. Healthy attitudes can be communicated to the children. This is the surest way for them to grow up with good sexual feelings about themselves and about marriage.

As children reach adolescence, parents may feel even more limited. The dilemma we discovered with having adolescents in our house is that they are often studying or coming home from social events later than when we want to go to bed. We find ourselves needing to gear our special times together around their time schedules. Sometimes it can seem as though there is no time when we have our home to ourselves.

Conclusion

In every stage of the children's growth there are adjustments for the sexual life of the mother and father. But there also can be much joy and fulfillment when time and privacy are provided for the two of you. The more you can appropriately share yourselves, the more open your children will be able to be with you.

In this chapter we have emphasized the great importance to the whole family of keeping the marriage a priority. And within the marriage, keeping the sexual life is a priority, too.

Whatever your dilemmas and whatever the joys, if the two of you stay connected and share this with your children, you'll give them something that will become a basic part of who they are. It will stand them in good stead as they move into being lovers *and* parents, themselves.

For Further Study

Cane, William. *The Art of Kissing*. New York: St. Martin's Press, 1991.

Leman, Kevin. *Sex Begins in the Kitchen*. Ventura, Calif.: Regal Books, 1983.

McGinnis, Alan Loy. *The Romance Factor*. San Francisco: Harper and Row, 1990.

O'Connor, Dagmar. *How to Make Love to the Same Person for the Rest of Your Life—and Still Love It*. New York: Doubleday, 1986.

———. *How to Put the Love Back into Making Love*. New York: Doubleday, 1989.

Penner, Clifford L., and Joyce J. Penner. *The Gift of Sex*. Waco, Tex.: Word, 1981.

Part 3

Teaching Children
About Sex

7

Modeling and Communicating Healthy Sexual Attitudes

We are frequently asked, "At what age do you recommend that parents begin the process of sex education for their children?"

Our answer, "at birth," often shocks parents. But we think about our sexuality as a vital dimension of who we are throughout life. Our sexuality is so much more than sexual intercourse. We are male or female from the moment of birth until the final event of death.

This is true both physically and emotionally. All the sexual anatomy is present at birth, and it is working! A little boy has his first erection within minutes of birth and a little girl lubricates vaginally within the first twenty-four hours. These are the first physical sexual responses, even in adulthood.

Parents relate differently to infant girls than they do to infant boys. So emotionally, we begin at their birth to influence the sexuality of our children. Think of yourself. Remember or imagine yourself talking to a newborn baby boy, then to a baby girl. How might you communicate differently?

Recently friends of ours had their first baby. We received a call from the husband shortly after the delivery. His announcement was, "We've got a 'tiger.'" There was no doubt in our minds that they had a baby boy. There is a difference in how parents respond to babies of each sex. Little girls are referred to as "sweet," delicate, and pretty. Little boys are referred to as "tough" and "big guy." Moms love to fuss with bows in girls' hair.

This difference in treatment is important to help our children establish accurate gender identity. During the first two years of life adults give the baby many cues about its gender. The way parents dress the baby, the tone of voice they use, and the toys they choose for him or her are all important in developing the sexual identity of the child. All parents teach their children about sex whether they know it or not. The question is, "How can parents guard against transmitting negative messages?"

Children learn about sex throughout their lives. The home is the primary place where this learning takes place. This is true whether or not parents *decide* to teach them. They will learn about what it means to be male or female. They will get a sense of what roles are associated with each sex, how the same and opposite sex interacts, and what value we place on being male or female. Sexual feelings and attitudes will be picked up from parents. Vitality may become associated with one sex or the other. And eventually, attitudes about specific sexual behavior, all the way from touching to intercourse, will be learned. Our children will learn by our modeling, relating, and communicating about sexuality.

Modeling

When both parents are in the home, the children learn by the interaction they witness between Mom and Dad—the affection, the communication, and the exercise of power. If Mom pulls away when Dad reaches out to pinch or touch, they probably learn that sex is something the man pursues and the woman resists. Or the opposite message may be transmitted when the roles are reversed. It is important that children see their parents express affection. It's wonderful for them to know their parents love each other and enjoy touching, kissing, and hugging. It is even good for them to become aware that parents have special times together when they are alone, and that those times are sexual. Being sexual with each other as parents models to children that sex in marriage is fun!

The communication habits we model to our children also influence their development into men and women. Do we give each other verbal praise? How do we communicate needs? How do we share our needs? How do we respond to each other's communication of needs? Do we take time to share our worlds with each other? Are we regarded and listened to by each other? How do we handle disagreement? All of these are part of sexual interaction as men and women. What do our children learn about the husband-wife relationship by observing us?

John and Nancy, a couple we saw in sexual therapy, attributed their sexual tension to the modeling of John's parents. His parents fit the stereotypical husband-wife communication pattern. His father would come home from work, grumble a greeting, grab the newspaper, sit in his recliner, and read. His mother would be preparing dinner, chattering a mile a minute about nothing. His father would grunt every now and then, but there was no obvious connection between them.

Now John found he was unable to connect with his wife. Nancy was eager to hug and kiss when they got home from work. She was interested in sharing reports of their days with each other and expressing their love. John was, too, but he felt awkward, so he often avoided her and hid behind the newspaper. Seeing himself emulate his father and wanting a more intimate relationship with Nancy, John decided that after work they would have a time just for the two of them. Sexual activity flowed more easily once they had time to bring their worlds together.

What about the exercise of power in the relationship? For a family communication exercise, we had each person in our family, including our three children, answer a questionnaire about power distribution in the family. It was most helpful to get the children's view of us. They saw Cliff having control in some areas and Joyce in others. Some of their answers surprised us. We saw ourselves differently than they experienced us.

What kind of feedback do you get from your children? Who do they see as having the final word? Who makes the final decision about money, food, gifts, entertainment, church, devotions, and so on? When mutuality flows between Mom and Dad in most areas, children learn a sense of mutual sexual respect and responsibility.

What about the single parent? About 45 percent of the children in the United States spend some or all of their most formative years with only one parent. How can the male-female interaction be modeled to children when there is only one parent in the home? The children will learn by observing the parent in opposite-sex interactions. They might be present when Mom or Dad is leaving for a date or talking on the telephone to a male or female special friend. The special friend may be included in family events.

When there has been a divorce and the parents are still in contact with each other the children will learn from that interaction. There may be hurt and anger. These feelings need to be worked through, so that the children can learn positive respect. What needs to be modeled is that, even when there is stress, the parents communicate respect and care for each other. It's important never to put down or belittle the children's other parent.

There is nothing wrong with our children observing our anger. But it is important that we are clear about the feelings behind the anger—the hurt, fear, frustration, helplessness—and use those emotions constructively. Dr. Neil Warren's book, *Make Anger Your Ally,* is most helpful in teaching effective ways to deal with emotions that are felt as anger. We recommend it highly.

Children from a single-parent situation can also be provided with other couples as models. This can happen in extended family events, social situations, and church or Christian communities. This may take some effort and planning. You, as a single parent, may want to select a couple whom you admire. Then reach out to care for some of their needs in exchange for their spending time with you and your children. Swap services!

If you were in a healthy marriage the first eight years of the children's lives, most of the modeling will have been accomplished by that age. They will have learned a sense of mutual respect, affection, and positive male-female interaction. If the marriage was tense and shaky, the children may need to work through their insecurities and sexual identities in a therapeutic situation. Both you and your ex-spouse can take an active role in providing some healthy models for them. That model may also be a stepmother or stepfather.

Relating

Not only do children learn male-female interaction from the parental or other couples' model, they also learn by the way the parents interact with *them*. From the same-sex parent, they learn what it means to be male or female. If a mother feels good about her body, the daughter will too—even though she may go through the awkward, uncomfortable stages of puberty. If a father enjoys being a man with all that involves for him, his son will, too.

Children learn to relate to the opposite sex by the relationship they have with the opposite-sex parent. When a father shows his love and high regard for his daughter, she will grow up with positive expectations in relation to men. And we can say exactly the same thing for a mother and son. How a son is expected to treat his mother is probably how he will treat his wife.

Both parents and children may experience sexual feelings in relating to each other. These feelings are very normal. How they are handled is vitally important. It is natural for a mother to experience sexual arousal when breastfeeding her infant. Those feelings are a physical response to the sucking and are not harmful in any way. Likewise, children or parents might notice turned-on feelings at other times in the child's development. It is important to recognize that these feelings are normal. As parents, we must be responsible that those feelings never lead to sexual actions with our children. That is molestation and will hurt them. On the other hand, do not let the feelings keep you from being warm and affectionate at all ages. Remember the principle that we are to give love and affection to our children, but they are never to be the *objects* of our sexual gratification.

Communicating

We would like to share some guidelines we often offer Christian parents for developing healthy sexual attitudes in their children.

We, as parents, are the key to our children's sexual education! Our children's attitudes about sexuality are usually learned from us. We must begin by looking at ourselves. What are our attitudes about sex? What did we learn about sex in our homes? Did we get mixed signals? If the only time sexual language was used was to tell dirty jokes, then we learned that sex is something that is not valued highly. Was sex to be avoided, expected, matter-of-fact, anticipated? Was it something healthy and wholesome, or a bother? Was it the woman's burden and the man's delight? What specific sexual instructions did you receive? Maybe sex was nonexistent.

Picture the kind of messages you got from your home. What did you learn about your sexuality? What about masturbation or the male-female relationship? Then think of how you might be communicating these same attitudes. It is natural to communicate the same attitudes that were communicated to us. When those attitudes were positive, we have it easy. But when we don't want to live out the attitudes we learned, we have to make a conscious effort to be different.

Even we, as sex therapists, do not automatically respond in the manner we desire. We find we have had to learn not to fight or judgmentally react to our children's specific bodily discoveries or other more blatant sexual situations. Our spontaneous response is guarded rather than open. In contrast, it is natural for us to be generally warm and affirming. There is a real positiveness about being male and female, because our parental homes instilled that warm regard.

Joyce remembers proudly the first bra-buying experience with her mom. Starting her period was a positive sign of becoming a woman. Clear preparation had been made for this event. Similarly, beginning to shave, use a deodorant, and encountering other indications of becoming a man were experienced by Cliff as affirming events. Our parents delighted in our growing up. Thus, it is inevitable that we exude a similar delight as we interact with our children as they become men and women.

What can parents do to overcome their negative inhibitions so they don't pass them on to their children?

Sexual attitudes *can* be changed! Human beings are not limited by their backgrounds. Parents can increase their positive feelings about sexuality by educating themselves, affirming their bodies, and experiencing fulfilling sexual relationships in their marriages. Since parents tend to communicate to their children what they believe about sex, they must look at themselves to realize what they are communicating to their children!

How satisfying are your sexual experiences? Do you feel sexually inhibited? We chose to first write *The Gift of Sex,* a guide for enhancing the sexual relationship in marriage, to emphasize our belief that the parents' sexual relationship must be positive if they are going to communicate positive attitudes about sex to their children. So your individual sexuality and your sexual relationship in marriage must be addressed. For the married couple, we recommend reading *The Gift of Sex* out loud to each other. We would also recommend *The Gift of Sex* for the single parent (who has a Christian perspective). In addition, two secular books may be helpful: Julia Heiman and Joseph LoPiccolo's *Becoming Orgasmic for Women* and Barry McCarthy's *Male Sexual Awareness: Increasing Sexual Satisfaction.*

Once you and your spouse have taken a good look at how your backgrounds and your sexual relationships are affecting your communication about sex to your children, ask yourselves, "What do we want to communicate?"

Parents should discuss sexual facts with their children. When parents can openly discuss physical processes with respect and dignity, children will develop pride in their bodies. When children sense that their parents view sex as healthy, they tend to adopt healthy attitudes, themselves. Communication about sexuality is an important part of growing up. The following principles are basic to what we believe needs to be communicated to children.

1. Sex is good and of God. Our sexuality, bodily pleasure and sexual intercourse in marriage are part of God's perfect design and plan. They are good!

2. Sexual curiosity is natural. Children should never be punished or embarrassed for showing their curiosity. It is natural to ask questions about sex and to discover their own bodies, as well as observe others' bodies and have questions about them.

3. Sexual responsiveness is natural (when social and emotional barriers have not inhibited that). Our sexual responses, whether aroused through self-stimulation, fantasy, mutual stimulation, or sexual intercourse, are a part of the functioning of each person's body. It is not a skill to be learned. It is an involuntary response that comes from within. It begins at birth and continues throughout life in healthy people.

4. Sexual responsibility belongs to each person. Sexual feelings need to be differentiated from sexual actions or behavior.

Sexual feelings arise from our natural, involuntary sexual responses. What we decide to do with those feelings is our responsibility. Our sexual actions or decisions are in our control. Men are as responsible as women, and women as responsible as men for their sexual actions.

5. Mutual respect and biblical standards are the guide for all sexual relationships. Spouses must respect each other's rights and needs. Children must be taught and expected to respect their parents' sexuality and their sexual relationship. Parents must respect their children's developing sexuality. When there is respect, no one will be violated! Abuse will not be present.

When we believe and practice these principles, our children will receive a healthy view of sexuality.

Sexual Identity

What can parents do to ensure that their children will grow up with a clear sense of being a man or a woman?

Since the "free speech" movement of the sixties and the "individual rights" movement of the last three decades, all of us have become aware that sexual identity is a vital issue in our society. Parental concern regarding the sexual identity of their children must be understood against the backdrop of the seemingly ever-increasing incidence of homosexuality. It is not our intention to give a definitive treatise on the subject of sexual identity, but rather, a general framework regarding this vital issue.

Just as there is a wide range of heterosexual behavior, there is also a wide range of homosexual behavior. In contrast to what is often taught, a homosexual orientation is no more a choice than is a heterosexual orientation. We can choose our behaviors, that is, whether we act homosexually or heterosexually, but usually the feelings of attraction to the same sex and lack of attraction to the opposite sex are not chosen. This is particularly true for men. Research has shed some light on why this is the case.

A research article in the *Journal of Sex Education and Therapy* by Dr. Frederick L. Whitman of Arizona State University reports on the "Childhood Predictors of Adult Homosexuality."

The research reports that, in studying the lives of homosexuals (especially men), there were clear indicators of the tendencies already present between the third and sixth years. The indications were that those who grew up to be homosexual frequently preferred the toys, clothes, and activities of the opposite sex during their preschool years. Lest we alarm parents, let us hurriedly add that it is completely normal for all children to occasionally exhibit interest in and engage in behavior typical of the opposite sex. But in this case, we are talking about a *clear preference* of the boy for dolls rather than trucks, for playing house rather than climbing trees, for skirts rather than jeans, and for the company of girls rather than boys. It should also be made clear that even in those instances where there was early cross-gender behavior, it did not necessarily mean that these children grew up to be homosexual. Rather, this tended to be in the background of those who did have a homosexual preference.

With the Bible's condemnation of homosexuality, society's deep hesitancy and discomfort with it, and the painful, never-satisfied quality so often present in the homosexual's life, it is important that we parents do all we can to help our children make a positive connection with who they are as male and female.

How can we understand this dilemma? While no one knows for sure, we would like to present our theory about "critical periods" in the developmental process. This is theory, though, not fact! It grows out of our clinical experience, not research.

Since there is no convincing evidence to suggest a biological basis for homosexuality, we have to assume it is learned during *three critical periods:* (1) birth to age two, (2) age three to six, and (3) early adolescence, ages eleven to fourteen.

1. In the first two years of life, the messages about being a boy or a girl are sent very indirectly but often clearly. Even those boys who might naturally be quite effeminate, not fitting the image of the masculine male, can grow up feeling strongly positive about themselves as boys or men if they are treated as such. That is, to develop strong feelings about himself as a man, a little boy must get positive messages about his masculinity, even during the first two years of life. His parents must delight in the fact that they have a boy. They must dress him so that the people in the world respond to him as a boy. For example, in our culture today it is not appropriate to dress baby boys in dresses as was done several generations ago or may still be customary in other cultures. All this begins the shaping process.

2. During the preschool years (three to six), the importance of a same-sex model is crucial. A boy needs to have a man around with whom he can identify, and a girl needs a woman. It seems obvious that one reason why there are more male homosexuals than female is that boys have more opportunity to model women than girls have to model men. With the increasing divorce rate, we should continue to expect an increase in the occurrence of the homosexual preference.

Both boys and girls need reinforcement and affirmation for sexually appropriate behavior and identification. We are not talking about forcing all boys to play baseball or all girls to always stay pretty and clean. Some very masculine boys will enjoy music, art, and other, more delicate dimensions of life. Many very heterosexual women enjoy and are accomplished at what are normally considered male interests and activities. What is most important is that the identification occur with the same sex gender. Sometimes the identification is evidenced in the choices of the child's activities. This is why it is so important, during this critical period, to provide ongoing reinforcement to the boy or girl for being male or female.

If the parents have a low view of themselves as male or female or are verbally derogatory of the opposite sex, either can have a severely negative impact on a child. In the past, the research often described a pattern of a domineering mother and a cold, passive, uninvolved father. More recent research has suggested that the father became cold and uninvolved once he sensed his son was going to be a "sissy." Whichever was the cause or the effect, the lack of a strong, involved male model during the preschool age is detrimental to the development of male identity. Of the three critical periods, we would see this preschool stage as the most important.

3. The third vital age is the time during early adolescence. This is when the child is moving away from parents toward attachment to peers. This usually begins with attachment to peers of the same sex. In fact, in developmental terms, these years are sometimes referred to as the "homosexual stage." This is the time when boys are usually first learning to ejaculate and will sometimes compare experiences, watch each other, or even participate with one another in sexual encounters. In later years some then worry that they are "latently" homosexual. But just because a boy has engaged in homosexual play as a thirteen-year-old does not make him a homosexual. While less common, this kind of mutual play and discovery does occur among girls as well.

Also during these years a boy may be approached by an older homosexual male. If he already has weak male identification from the earlier critical periods in his life, he may respond to the invitation. Then the tendency toward the same sex gets sealed or confirmed. If it is not acted on, however, a positive connection with the opposite sex can still be made, even when there is an inclination toward the same sex. At the same time, some men don't act on their inclinations until their thirties, forties, or fifties, often after they are married and have a family. The strong homosexual preference has been present but not acted on for all those years.

During the junior-high years, it is so important that the connection and attraction shift from the same sex to the opposite sex. Since this is the beginning of direct sexual behavior (even if it is the bumbling discovery of the kiss-and-run variety), it is vital that boys and girls experience affirmation in these early heterosexual activities. This forms the basis for all later heterosexual involvement.

In summary, our critical-period theory is this: In their first two years, children learn about their sexual identity by how they are handled and talked to. During the preschool years, direct learning takes place from role models as well as gender-related activities. Finally, in the time of early adolescence, behavior confirms or interrupts the tendency that is already established.

Once homosexuality is confirmed, either by feelings or by activity, it is difficult to reverse. While the behavior can be controlled, the same-sex preference is stubborn. This is true even after extensive psychotherapy or spiritual conversion. Some approaches to dealing with the homosexual are now claiming greater success—especially in the charismatic wing of the church.

Masters and Johnson are also claiming long-term success with those who want to change.

Because of the difficulty of changing sexual orientation later in life, we need to do all we can to prevent the development of homosexual tendencies. This prevention begins with a healthy acceptance of oneself as a man or woman. The outgrowth of that will be the vigorous endorsement of our children's maleness or femaleness. If you walk around with buried hostility toward the opposite sex, it will be communicated. Endorse who the child is and the natural ways of expressing that personhood—always in the context of the child's maleness or femaleness.

Spend time modeling what it means to be a man or a woman. Your child will learn from you. We have little evidence to suggest that, left just to instinct, the child will develop normally. Mothers are the example to their daughters of what it looks like, sounds like, and feels like to be a woman. In work or play, spend time together so your child can learn both from your direct teaching and by osmosis.

It is rare to discover one's sexual preference by accident. But traumatic molestation experiences of a homosexual nature usually leave a child confused about sexual identity. The false guilt aroused by the molestation can be overwhelming. We must do all we can to teach our children the reality that they are in charge of their own bodies, and neither a stranger nor relative should touch or violate them in any way which leaves them uncomfortable.

One last word on this subject of homosexuality. People with a sexual preference for those of the same sex are human beings in need of our love, care, and respect. They may be doctors, lawyers, truck drivers, waitresses, or gardeners. They have feelings, they get lonely, and they experience pain just like any other person. They need our compassion and understanding as they struggle to make choices about their impulses and behavior.

For Further Study

Barbach, Lonnie. *For Yourself: The Fulfillment of Female Sexuality*. New York: Anchor Books, 1979.

Heiman, Julia, and Joseph LoPiccolo. *Becoming Orgasmic.* New York: Prentice Hall, 1988.

Ketterman, Grace H., M.D. *How to Teach Your Children About Sex.* Old Tappan, N.J.: Fleming H. Revell Co., 1981. 7–76, 167–83.

*Kolodny, Robert C., et al. "Development and Sexuality." In *Textbook of Human Sexuality for Nurses.* Boston: Little, Brown and Co., 1979.

McCarthy, Barry. *Male Sexual Awareness.* New York: Carroll and Graf, 1988.

Warren, Neil C. *Make Anger Your Ally.* Brentwood, Tenn.: Wolgemuth and Hyatt, 1990.

Whitman, Frederick L. "Childhood Predictors of Adult Homosexuality." *Journal of Sex Education and Therapy,* 6, no. 2 (Fall/Winter 1980).

*This book is no longer in print but is still available in many medical libraries.

8

Affirming Sexuality in the Infant and Toddler

Children are born as sexual beings. They learn about themselves as sexual persons throughout life. Sex education does not begin with the parent-child "birds and bees" talk.

From our understanding of human growth and development, from hearing hundreds of case histories, and from reading over a hundred sexual autobiographies, we are convinced that there are common developmental stages for learning about ourselves sexually. In other words, children will learn when they are ready, not when we are ready to teach them.

Touch: The Basis for Intimacy

During infancy (from birth to age two), children learn about sex from their primary caretaker, usually their mother. However, the father may be an equal source of sexual affirmation for the child; he may even play a dominant role. There may be a primary childcare substitute. The person or persons with whom they bond will be their lifeline to learning physical intimacy.

Ideally, this bonding begins immediately with the mother at birth, and shortly thereafter with father. Skin-to-skin contact will help these babies grow happily and securely. It is this warmth and closeness to the bodies of those who love them that gives the tiny, helpless infants the emotional security to be able, as adults, to give their bodies to the spouses they marry.

It is sad that our Western culture went through a twenty-year time span—from the 1940s to the 1960s—in which hospital personnel's control prevented this immediate bonding of mother and newborn. When both of us were born in 1941, home delivery was common practice, with the mother's arms becoming the first bed for that new little creature. When our younger brothers and sisters were born, though, our mothers were rushed off to the hospital where they were frustrated by the hospital routine that took control of all contact between parent and child.

This mode was predominant until about the time our oldest child, Julene, was born. Because we were graduate students receiving free medical care from a wonderful but elderly physician who felt uncomfortable with the modern trends, Julene was born with the hospital-in-control system. Joyce's labor and Julene's birth were an easy, three-hour process without medication.

Joyce describes the horror that soon began:

> At midnight, about an hour after the baby's birth, I was wheeled into my room (darkened because my roommate was sleeping), Cliff was told he had to go home, and Julene was taken to the nursery. I was wide awake and so eager to see and touch my new baby, to have her close to me, and to talk with Cliff about our experience.
>
> Even though I requested many times during the next twenty hours to be able to have my baby, she was not brought to me until 8 P.M. the next day. I never found out why this happened. Many fears overwhelmed me and many tears were shed waiting to be certain she was totally mine. I was never so happy as the day we were able to take her home from the hospital.
>
> Of our three children, she was the baby who sucked for hours when she breastfed. I believe that was her way of making up for the separation pain that occurred between us because of "hospital policy."

What we learned, and what we would recommend to you, is to have the confidence to take charge of situations like the delivery and postbirth process. Inquire beforehand about the hospital's policy. Find ways to get your needs met. Remember, what happens during those first hours is an important part of becoming a family. Fortunately, today the widespread trend in hospitals is to encourage involvement of both parents throughout labor, delivery, and after delivery. In most cases, both parents now have the opportunity to bond immediately with the baby.

Infants begin to know about themselves as sexual persons by how they are touched and held, the tone of the parent's voice, and the comfort or discomfort they experience. Bodily pleasure is felt from the beginning. Babies who receive calm, warm stroking and close holding with unconditional love will feel good about their body sensations and thus be affirmed.

If the mother or primary caretaker has difficulty with intimacy or difficulty giving freely of herself, the child will feel anxious, distant, and unsure, and will tend to have difficulty forming intimate relationships later in life. Sometimes the mother keeps the child at a distance because the mother fears her own sexual warmth in relation to the child. Those feelings of warmth and closeness between parent and child are natural and good. *Never* is the infant's body to be used sexually for the adult's pleasure! But warmth, closeness, touching, and stroking in a general, loving, affirming way is necessary for positive personal and sexual development.

As sexual therapists, we are convinced that our toughest cases are those where bonding never happened between the mother and infant. One most attractive couple came to us within the first year of their marriage with the wife complaining about her husband's lack of interest in sex. Even though he really wanted help, he resisted every attempt at working on the dilemma in the same way he resisted his wife's sexual advances. It was as though he could not help himself.

After their first child was born, they talked with us about the husband's interaction with his own mother when he was a baby. His mother had wanted the baby to meet her needs, but was never able to give herself warmly to the infant. It became obvious to us that the husband was suffering from a deep-seated difficulty; he was unable to give and receive bodily pleasure. Thus there was an almost complete inability to form a physically intimate attachment to his wife. His mother had probably never really been able to *give* him warmth and closeness. She only knew how to enjoy a baby for *her* pleasure.

If you see yourself as a person who is needy or unable to give that radiant warmth and unconditional love to your infant, get help! Find a mothering, giving person who can give to you and model the kind of mothering you want to give to your children, but may not have received from your own mother. Joyce has recently taken on that role with a young couple in our community. It has been most rewarding to see them gain the confidence to give relentlessly to their little family. Parenting requires servant leadership that can seem like endless giving of oneself. Christ is the ideal model of that kind of giving.

As children grow from infancy to toddlerhood (two to four years old), they move from total dependence on their caregiver to self-discovery as they learn to master various dimensions of their world. This process includes learning the control of elimination, genital discovery, and the naming of body parts. This is a most critical time for forming attitudes about sexuality.

Learning Control of Elimination

Since elimination and sexual functioning are connected with the same parts of the body, what we teach children about elimination will affect their view of their sexuality. If we are rather matter-of-fact, using praise and rewards for learning toileting, children will gain a healthy respect for their sexuality. If we are punitive and rigid, they may have difficulty freely sharing in genital discovery in marriage. If we are totally permissive, the children may not learn how to make decisions and feel in control of their sexuality, just as they may have felt out of control as it related to elimination.

It is important that we teach good hand-washing practices after toileting. But we should not send the message that the genitals are "dirty" or "yucky," or that what they produce is repulsive. Young children will naturally feel proud of their excretions. That pride can be enhanced and carried into their adult sexual functioning. This is not too young an age to let them know that bowel movements have germs, but urine, vaginas, and penises do not. In fact, our genitals are a very special part of us. Children will hear enough "shady" messages in their lifetimes, so the more positive messages we can give them the better. The belief or teaching that sex is dirty often has its origin in what children are taught about their own genitals. If they get only the "unclean" message, they connect that to sexuality.

Genital Discovery

Genital self-discovery may begin during diapering, but it certainly will be a part of this two- to four-year-old stage. We remember when our son was two-and-a-half. We heard him giggling in the bathtub, only to find that he had discovered his penis. It is natural for both older infants and toddlers to reach down and touch their genitals, to play with them, and rub them in a soothing manner, almost like sucking their thumbs. They naturally poke their fingers in their noses, in their ears, and in their belly buttons, but somehow when they poke their genitals, we tend to react uncomfortably. We may say "No," and move the hand away or give it a little slap, sending messages similar to when they go near a hot stove. The sexual part of us is very intense. It grabs us totally. These emotions complicate the way we deal with our children's self-discovery, which is a very natural, healthy part of their development. By sending negative messages in this early, impressionable stage of life, we may teach our children that our genitals are "untouchable"—that they are *certainly* different than the rest of our bodies.

Where do you draw the line for a toddler who is discovering his or her body without making the child feel bad about being curious? The messages we want to transmit to toddlers are these: Your genitals are special. They feel good to touch. They are private. We don't touch them in public. If these attitudes are taught with the same matter-of-fact style that we teach children not to put objects in their ears or their noses, then touching genitals will not become an emotionally loaded activity.

Along with our messages of acceptance of the genitals, we must make certain that we are providing our children with enough touch. Regular stimulation of the genitals by toddler-age children may be a signal to the parents to increase the amount of holding and hugging. In fact, that response is a good distraction when your toddler's self-stimulation makes you uncomfortable. A parent might interrupt a child by saying, "Nancy, I haven't had time to hold you on my lap and read to you. Choose your favorite book so we can read for a while."

Children will discover that their genitals feel good. When they are receiving enough general body affirmation from their parents (and are not given guilt-producing responses), the genital touching will not be an ongoing, controlling part of their lives. Instead, it will be a natural response to how their bodies were made.

Naming the Genitals

Naming body parts properly is important as the two- to four-year-old learns to talk. We spend time teaching our children to say, "nose," "eyes," and "ears." We're so proud when they can identify "elbow" and "wrist." Then we get to the genitals and we revert to "wa-wa" and "do-do." Call a penis a penis and a vagina a vagina, even if it shocks the grandparents. Knowing and naming genitals is an important gift we need to give to our children. Giving children correct anatomical names for genitals will help them develop the attitude that genitals are as valid and acceptable a part of their bodies as are their toes, fingers, and nose.

Conclusion

If touching the genitals is accepted as normal, control of elimination is guided with praise and a sense of accomplishment, and genitals are named with pride, by the time children are four years old they will have been given the gift of their genitals as their friend—a valid part of God's perfect creation. In contrast, when their hands are taken away and given a slap, the four-year-olds will think of their genitals as *untouchable*. Similarly, when there is discomfort in naming genitals they become *unmentionable*. Thus, toddlers' development may bring an integrated acceptance of their genitals—or a disassociation with them, making it difficult to share their genitals freely as adults in the sexual relationships of their marriages.

What if your children are all older than four and you've blown it? One parent confessed: "I have already mishandled my child's sex education. How can I undo the mistakes I have already made?"

Children are incredibly resilient. It is never too late to go to them and say, "Hey, we made some mistakes. We'd like to make some changes in what we taught you." We've had parents in their fifties have a talk like this with their young adult children, and it made an important difference! Take courage and go for it!

For Further Study

Ketterman, Grace H., M.D., *How to Teach Your Child About Sex.* Old Tappan, N.J.: Fleming H. Revell Co., 1981. 79–97.

*Kolodny, Robert C., William H. Masters, and Virginia E. Johnson. "Childhood Sexuality." In *Textbook of Sexual Medicine.* Boston: Brown, Little and Co., 1979.

Prot, Viviane, and Philippe Delorme, M.D. *A Story of Birth.* Ossining, N.Y.: Young Discovery Library, 1986.

*This book is no longer in print but is still available in many medical libraries.

9

The Curious Years:
Preschool to Puberty

By the time children reach preschool age, their view of their genitals and their ability to give and receive touch has been well established. So what happens from preschool to puberty? Curiosity takes control.

Question Asking

Curiosity about sexuality begins around four or five years of age. We refer to this as the question-asking age. Parents are concerned about how to respond to these early questions—and rightly so! Many adults report that they never asked their parents another question about sex after age five because they got the message that sex isn't something you talk about with Mom and Dad. What happened?

Children's sexual questions often catch us off guard and trigger strong adult emotions. Sex is such a loaded topic for us that it is difficult to take the innocent questions from our young children for what they are. We tend to impose our adult feelings on what is being asked.

So what do you say when your preschooler asks, "Where do babies come from?" or, "How does the baby get out of (or into) Mommy's tummy?"

The five R system—reinforce, reflect, review, respond, and repeat—is most helpful in dealing effectively with emotionally loaded questions, especially sexual ones. It serves two functions: stalls for time, giving us a chance to collect ourselves, and it affirms the appropriateness of the child's curiosity. We both win!

1. Reinforce. Commend children of any age for coming to you with such an important question. Emphasize that it is a family question and you're glad he or she came to you rather than a friend who might not have correct information. This positive, outward response to the child's openness with you is particularly important when the question asked or experience shared elicits an inward, alarmed response in you. Reinforcing the child helps him or her feel good about sharing without being burdened with your reaction. If you respond this way, your child will probably come to you again, because children want your verbal reward. This is a good way to foster an open relationship with your children.

2. Reflect. After reinforcing the question, we encourage reflection, getting a clear picture of what the child is really asking. Find out what is behind the question. For example, when we respond to the question, "Where do babies come from?" we are drawing from vast information. Therefore we tend to think that the child's question is more complicated than is usually the case. As we reflect the child's question, it becomes clear what specific bit of information he or she is really seeking. This way we avoid giving a twenty-minute lecture on sex education when one short sentence may have been the most accurate response. It is important to ask the child, "What do you mean when you ask, Where do babies come from? Do you mean, Where do they grow?"

3. Review. Once we're fairly clear about what our children are really asking, we need to review what they already know. What is the context of the question? It is important to get into their world and find out where they are. They may have misunderstood previously shared information. They may have gotten misinformation from peers or television. If they share what they have heard and understand, we can respond to that before we load on our views. It gives us a chance to correct and teach without adding confusion. This becomes even more important as children get older and gain more of their information from outside the home.

4. Respond. The time does come when we need to answer the question. We can stall only so long! If you know the answer and feel comfortable in giving it, then do so. If you are unsure, go to another resource. Be sure you get the child an answer somehow. It is best to give simple, factual, short answers, but be as specific and explicit as the question warrants. For example, if we have determined that the child is wondering where the baby grows, then an appropriate response would be, "The baby grows in a special, thick, soft pocket in the mother's abdomen. This special place is called the uterus." It gets more difficult when they want to know how the baby gets started there. A factual response is, "A seed from the daddy joins with an egg from the mommy."

The next question usually is, "How does Daddy get the seed in there?" Now, we really get uncomfortable! But again, once we're pretty clear that we've heard the question accurately and we've reviewed what they already know or have heard, then the answer can be simple and honest. A natural answer is, "The daddy's penis puts the seed into the mother's vagina." As children get older they will ask for more of the emotional components. "When do moms and dads do this? Isn't it yucky? Did you do that?" Eventually they'll need to get the picture that sexual intercourse is a pleasurable expression of love between a husband and wife and not just for producing babies—that you still "do it."

Parents might doubt that the child is ready for the facts. Our response is that when children ask, they are ready for the answers to their questions. If they have been set up by someone older to ask the question, you will have discovered that by the time you have reinforced, reflected, and reviewed. When you determine that the question is not theirs, find out what *they* would like to know and start the process again.

5. Repeat. Once we've responded, there's a temptation to wipe our brow with a, "Whew, that's taken care of!" But it isn't. We will need to repeat ourselves, explaining the basic facts of reproduction, intercourse, and sexual pleasure a dozen times or so. From preschool to puberty (four to ten years old), children's ability to picture the sexual process changes greatly. At each level of understanding, the questions will mature, and the information will need to be repeated, but with greater depth.

What if your children don't ask questions about sex? You may feel as if you're continually looking for an opportunity to teach them about sexuality, but it doesn't occur naturally. First, look and see if you are subtly stifling communication. Or realize that some children tend to be shy and easily embarrassed. Whatever the cause, become active in providing opportunities for sex education. Associate with pregnant women. Talk about the pregnancy with the children: "Did you know Aunt Beth is going to have a baby? She looks fatter, but that's not fat, it's the baby growing inside her." Take the children to visit farms, zoos, or pet stores when the animals are having babies. Watch sex-education series together on television. Plan a time to talk afterward. Have the children write down thoughts or questions while they're watching. Do the same with sex-education programs at school. Talk to them afterward concerning your beliefs about what was taught. Read books on sexuality aloud with them, making sure the books are age appropriate. Create every opportunity to open the topic of sexuality.

Self-Discovery (Masturbation)

Just as the curiosity of this age leads to question-asking, it also stimulates children's interest in their own bodies. When our daughter was four years old, Joyce walked into Julene's room after her bath. She found Julene sitting on the floor with her legs spread apart and her head down as she tried to examine her genitals. When she heard Joyce enter the room, she remained in the same position and casually asked, "Mom, what is that hole in my bottom?"

Joyce's first tendency was to respond with shock, but Julene's ease with the situation made her stop and think. She remembered that just the day before Julene had spent a long time in front of the bathroom mirror looking down her throat, trying to examine and watch her uvula at the back of her throat. There was no difference in Julene's intent in discovering another part of her body. She did not think that looking at her throat was fine, but looking at her genitals was "sinful."

Repressing her own tendency to react with alarm and discomfort, Joyce took advantage of the curiosity for a teaching experience. She got a hand mirror so that Julene could better see her own genitals. She sat down with Julene and pointed to the various openings, the lips, and the clitoris, and indicated their technical names. Julene's curiosity seemed satisfied. She responded rather matter-of-factly, got dressed, and ran off to play.

Kristine, our younger daughter, went through a similar curiosity teaching experience with Joyce. Greg, our son, never pursued information about the anatomy of his genitals. This is less likely to happen with boys, because their genitals are accessible and easily observable. There are no hidden parts to discover.

Boys and girls of this age will continue to touch their genitals. The good sensations will be discovered. That is the way God made them. This genital pleasure does not cause guilt unless we send negative messages about the activity. If the child is getting enough other physical affection, and if sexual feelings in the child have not been prematurely aroused by exposure or abuse, genital stimulation will not become a habit or preoccupation. The genital touching is likely to increase for children at this age, especially when they are tired, sick, lonely, or sad. It is self-comforting, very much like sucking a thumb or holding a blanket.

In responding to children regarding genital exploration or stimulation, it is vital that we, as parents, do not make too big a deal of it. It is usually not that important to the child. The basic principles to follow are: Think of the genitals as a part of the body, rather than a unique separate entity. Recognize that adult erotic emotions are not a part of children's genital touching. Remember that physical affirmation needs to continue throughout life—our children need our hugs. Teach children socially appropriate behavior in relation to the genitals just as you do in any other area of life (keep them covered, don't play with them in public, use the toilet to urinate and defecate, and so on). And finally, think of inappropriate or excessive sexual exploration and stimulation as a *symptom* of a problem, not the problem itself.

Exploratory Play

Let's say you discover your young son and your friend's little daughter playing "doctor." How will you deal with the incident so they will not feel they are "bad"?

Similar to the self-discovery of the four- to ten-year-old, exploratory play is a natural manifestation of the sexual curiosity of this age. Not only are children interested in how they are put together, they're also interested to see their cousin or neighbor. "Playing doctor" is almost inevitable between the ages of five and seven. It is reported to us over and over again. When it occurs between children of the same age who have not been abused or exposed to adult sexual behaviors, and if it is handled as a normal part of growing up, it causes no harm. When it is met with a traumatic reaction from parents, it leaves children with incredible confusion about their sexuality.

Age-appropriate exploratory play is innocent curiosity. It needs to be responded to as just that. Use it as an opportunity to teach. Get out the anatomy book. Explain safety precautions. Just as objects shouldn't be put in ears and nose, it is important that we don't stick things in vaginas. We can talk about the purpose of the genitals—for excretion, for reproduction, and for sexual pleasure. This is a good time for parents to share their values and teach their children about the specialness of sexual pleasure in marriage.

Set some limits. Recognize the naturalness of their curiosity and the good feelings of the genitals, but that underpants need to be left on and the doors need to be open. Teach them about making decisions about sharing their bodies. Let them know that their bodies are their personal property. They are special and they must choose carefully when and with whom they will share themselves. Basically, the helpful response includes a balance of acceptance of what is happening with some teaching and limit-setting. But keep it low-key and matter-of-fact. Provide controls and safety without trauma.

Nudity in the Home

Before age four or five, children usually don't notice whether parents or older brothers and sisters have clothes on or not. But at this age of sexual curiosity, children begin to differentiate their bodies from those of others, and develop a sense of modesty. They are aware of male-female differences. Feelings that are difficult to handle can be aroused in young children by nude adult bodies. Therefore, it is recommended that while nudity should not be studiously avoided, it also should not be flaunted. Take more precautions about being exposed to the children for extended periods of time, without communicating discomfort with nudity. If children walk into the bedroom and the parent is undressed, there is no need to quickly go for cover. However, cooking dinner in the nude is not recommended, either!

From the stories adults tell us about their childhood experiences, we find that both extreme modesty and totally free exposure have led to difficulty in sharing bodies openly in marriage. When nudity was not comfortable at all, the children learned a self-consciousness and negativity about the body that carried over into marriage. Sometimes there was an opposite reaction, especially for boys, that led to an extreme, obsessively curious, "peeping Tom" type of behavior. When nudity was experimented with as a lifestyle, the children tended to feel violated and exploited. As adults, they became very protective, easily feeling violated and exploited by their spouses.

One woman could enjoy touching her husband's body totally but would panic if he tried to touch her, reported that her father required that they have dinner in the nude. Another woman with a similar reaction to her husband shared that her father always wanted to be in the bathroom while she was bathing. We have heard many other such stories.

Nudity in the home needs to be a comfortable openness of accepting our bodies with respect for privacy and without demand, exploitation, violation, or teasing. Never should the children's bodies be exposed to us or ours to them for our emotional or sexual pleasure. That is sexual child abuse!

Parents often ask, At what age is it best to discontinue bathing with opposite-sex siblings? There is no age that is right for all children. Your observation of the children's behavior is a key to decide when separate baths would be recommended. It would be necessary sometime between the four- to eight-year-old age span. When it changes from being a functional, fun event to a specifically sexual event in terms of attention or play, it's time to change to separate bathing. It is best if that change can be announced as a positive sign of growth, rather than treated as a withdrawal of a privilege. For example, the older one can now use the shower or bath at another, private time, as Mom and Dad do. There are many possible invitations to a new system of bathing enjoyment. Again, the principle is to see bodies and sexuality as natural, without exposure to erotic stimulation that is not age-appropriate. Children need to feel safe while they learn both bodily acceptance and socially appropriate modesty.

Stranger Danger

The teaching that occurs in the home regarding exploratory play and nudity can help prevent child molestation. Additional, specific teaching to prevent child molestation needs to be regularly reviewed with preschool and school-age children.

Children should be told that there are some very sick people in this world. No, they don't have the flu. Their sickness is that they get a thrill out of hurting children. Those people must be avoided—*Stay away from them!* But these people look like us, so how are our children going to know one when they meet one? Two things can help them. One has to do with strangers. (But not all of these sick people are strangers; sometimes they are friends, neighbors, or even relatives.) So first, to avoid being hurt by a stranger, have your children follow these rules:

1. Always go to school or other places on the route planned with a parent—a route that is in plain view of others, never through alleys or out-of-the-way places.

2. Never use a public restroom by yourself. Have someone you know go with you—or don't go. (In this case, it's important, then, that parents don't punish the child if he or she has an accident resulting in wet pants.)

3. If someone stops his or her car and tries to get your attention for any reason, turn and run the other way. If the person asks for directions or says he or she is sick or hurt, still run, but ask an adult to go back and help them.

4. Never accept anything from a stranger.

Here are some other suggested answers to share with your children; these responses are intended to help them avoid being hurt by someone who is *not a stranger.*

1. If anyone talks to you in a way you know is not right or tries to touch you or wants you to touch him or her in a way that feels uncomfortable, say, "No!" If you can, leave that person. If you can't leave, keep saying *"No!"* until your parents come.

2. Remember, you can be in control. Your body is yours and you don't have to share it with anyone, even if the other person is bigger than you, says nice things to you, or tries to scare you.

3. It is not your fault when a person behaves this way to you.

4. It is important that you tell us, so that we can protect you and get help for the sick person. We will listen to you and believe you, even if it may seem unbelievable.

This is basically the kind of talk children need to have about once a year from age four through ten and maybe even older.

Conclusion

Preschool to puberty often has been thought of as the nonsexual age, but that is not true. This is a critically formative age from a sexual perspective as attitudes and a sexual view of the self are developed. It also is the children's age that is most important to us as parents. They are most influenced by us during these years. We should take advantage of it. This is our special time to implant positive Christian values in our children!

For Further Study

Andry, Andrew C., and Steve Schepp. *How Babies Are Made.* Boston: Little, Brown, and Co., 1984.

Christenson, Larry. *The Wonderful Way That Babies Are Made.* Minneapolis: Bethany House, 1982.

Cole, Joanna. *Asking About Sex and Growing Up.* New York: Beech Tree Books, 1988.

Edens, David. *The Changing Me.* Nashville: Broadman Press, 1973.

Hummel, Ruth. *Where Do Babies Come From?* (Originally published in 1982 as *I Wonder Why?*) St. Louis: Concordia Publishing House, 1988.

Ketterman, Grace H., M.D. *How to Teach Your Child About Sex.* Old Tappan, N.J.: Fleming H. Revell Co., 1981. 99–117.

Mayle, Peter. *Where Did I Come From?* New York: Carol Publishing Group, 1973.

Nixon, Joan Lowery. *Before You Were Born.* Huntington, Ind.: Our Sunday Visitor, 1980.

Sheffield, Margaret. *Where Do Babies Come From?* New York: Alfred Knopf, 1978.

Wabbes, Marie. *How I Was Born.* New York: Tambourine Books, 1990.

10

The Squirrelly Years: Junior High

Preadolescence (ten to thirteen years old) is a great age, yet it is a tough one.

The great part is that preadolescents are full of energy. Hormones, chemicals that cause body growth and change, are being released into the bloodstream. These hormones also affect feelings and provide the energy for the sexual drive. This energy can be used to get things done in life. Thus, junior-highers are loaded with the potential to develop all of who they are. Physical activity is vital for the ten- to thirteen-year-old. Investing long hours in academics and developing talents will make use of that energy in a productive and self-fulfilling manner. When that energy is constructively directed, preadolescents will be happier with themselves and will get more affirmation from family and friends. Their self-confidence will be stronger.

The tough part of preadolescence is the awkwardness of being neither child nor adolescent. In fact, when we speak to junior-high groups, we usually refer to them as students. Calling them children would be a putdown; referring to them as adolescents doesn't quite fit. Yet referring to them as preadolescents is somewhat cumbersome.

With all the changes going on around them, preadolescents' self-worth is in a constant state of flux. Their rapid body growth tends to cause clumsiness. They seem to knock things over at the table, drop things, and generally feel out of control of their bodies. In addition, their emotions are changing; their feelings fluctuate. They sometimes seem as if they are on a roller-coaster ride—up one minute and down the next. A critical comment or a disappointment devastates them, while success or a positive look from us elevates them. There doesn't seem to be an inner sense of self; instead, value is contingent on external input. It is difficult for us as parents to keep up. We're still concerned about the last low when they're on their next high. Unpredictable behavior is part of this syndrome also. Responsibilities that were handled competently at age eight or nine are suddenly neglected. At times, the internal confusion of all the change seems to keep them unsure of themselves, self-conscious, and mentally preoccupied.

Time of Transition

Moving from dependence to independence contributes to the awkwardness. The transition from childhood (with parents responsible and in control) to adulthood (in charge of one's own life and decisions) begins during preadolescence. Peers become the transitional authorities. Because of their need to feel separate from parents while still feeling unsure of themselves, preadolescents have a strong tendency to conform—to do and be like the other kids their age. The more self-confidence junior-highers feel, the less peer pressure will control their lives. Peers do become more and more the source of sexual information (and many times misinformation).

The primary question that haunts the preadolescent is, "Am I normal?" Many feel they are the only ones thinking and feeling the way they do. It is important for them to know that everyone at this age has times of isolation and loneliness—of feeling different. Physical changes are inconsistent from one child to another. Some children start developing at nine, others not until fifteen. Those who develop early feel self-conscious because they're ahead of their peers, and those who start late worry that they will never become adults.

Sexuality

Sexually, the juices of these young saplings are beginning to flow. Erotic feelings stir, leaving them restless and "squirrelly." They don't know why they're feeling the way they do. An explanation is often helpful. This can be followed by reminders like, "It might be helpful to go jogging to wear off some of that energy."

Group Experimentation

The actual sexual behavior that is age-appropriate is what we call the kiss-and-run games. It is primarily group experimentation. A group of guys and a group of girls meet behind the ice cream parlor. One guy in the group likes one girl from the other group. So, sort of like a pep squad, the groups are giving the guy and girl courage to kiss each other. They run and kiss and return to their group to giggle or act cool. This type of experimentation with male-female sexual interaction is very necessary to developing self-confidence in later serious relationships. That is why it is important that we don't set absolute rules like "No kissing until you're eighteen." The kissing that will be done at eighteen is *certainly* not the kissing the ten- to thirteen-year-olds will be doing if they are behaving age-appropriately.

Obviously, according to the statistics, some thirteen-year-olds are having sexual intercourse. They are engaging in sexual behavior that is adult in nature, not just junior-high experimentation. These prematurely exposed children usually are extremely confused about what they are experiencing.

"Going Steady"

The ten- to thirteen-year-olds who are functioning at their age level *will* have boyfriends and girlfriends. However, these relationships are much different than adolescent or young-adult relationships. They are usually negotiated through others. Jennifer asks Tim if he likes Jody. Then Jennifer tells Jody that Tim wants to "go steady." Jody gives her response to Jennifer and Jennifer tells Tim. Now, before we react, it's important to find out what "going steady" means. When Julene, then in third grade, announced she was "going steady," Joyce's first image was of our personal experience of "going steady"—a step toward engagement. But when Cliff calmly asked, "What does it mean to be going steady?" Julene replied, "It means we don't talk to each other any more because we wouldn't want anyone to know." When Kristine, our fourth grader, announced she was "going steady," and we asked what it meant, she shrugged her shoulders and said, "I don't know!" As junior-highers, "going steady" for all three of our children was a verbal arrangement, usually negotiated by a third person, without any direct contact with the other person. It did not include typical dating behavior, and simply meant they couldn't "go steady" with anyone else.

Social Awkwardness

It is OK to be awkward and experiment as a junior-higher. It is less OK as a high-schooler, and usually quite uncomfortable for a college-aged young adult. That is why severe restrictions of age-appropriate boy-girl interaction in junior-high school is not recommended. Adult-supervised group activities are best at this age. These times allow for opposite-sex interaction within safe boundaries.

This time is painful for the shy or socially unaccepted child. Many times the child will not have the opportunity for boy-girl interactions, or will not feel comfortable if they occur. If adolescents' sociability doesn't progress by high school, they will continue to lack confidence in relating to the opposite sex. They don't have a chance to experiment while it is still innocent play.

Shy or socially unaccepted children need to be encouraged to get involved in as many social settings as possible. Junior-high activities at church and school are great. Have mixed groups in your home and give the youngsters a job such as serving refreshments or snacks so they have a structured way to interact with the group. Let them know it's OK to feel awkward. Everyone feels awkward at this age, even though some may hide their discomfort better than others.

Dirty Jokes

In addition to boy-girl experimentation, "dirty" jokes are another element common to preadolescent sexuality. What has been shocking to us is to discover that our ten- to thirteen-year-olds, raised in suburban Los Angeles, heard the same sexual jokes that we heard thirty years earlier in our small, rural Mennonite communities. This tells us that these stories are developmental. They are a part of the process of growing up—of trying to make sense out of the whole concept of sexual intercourse, even though it sounds rather strange.

This doesn't mean we encourage our children to tell sexual jokes. What it does mean is that we recognize it as a reality of what is probably happening. In fact, a great way to open up communication between parent and preadolescent is to ask, "What are the jokes being told at school these days?" or, "What are the sexual slang words used at school these days?" Then it is helpful to explain the accurate, clinical meaning of the words being used and jokes being told. The kids are often shocked to hear what these words really mean. It is an opportunity for education and a way of limiting that kind of language. It teaches internal, rather than external, control without forbidding use of the particular word. Often, the youngsters no longer feel comfortable using the word when they know what it means. Nor do they need to use it because their curiosity has been satisfied—and curiosity is the primary reason for this kind of communication.

Masturbation

Masturbation becomes an emotionally loaded issue during puberty. Touching one's genitals changes from a soothing, self-affirming act to erotic self-stimulation, probably leading to orgasm. This may not happen until adolescence, but for many boys it will begin around age twelve. Girls tend to discover their erotic responsiveness later in life. And some boys and girls never do masturbate. About 95 percent of boys do, and about 50–80 percent of girls do.

It is now known that there are no physically harmful effects from masturbation and there is no psychological damage, except when self-stimulation is associated with guilt and sin. Although masturbation has been and still is condemned by some church groups, the facts are that the condemnation tends not to limit the behavior, but only makes it more secretive and guilt-ridden. This can sometimes lead to obsessive, uncontrolled masturbatory activity, which can be very destructive to the self-image of the young person who feels so ashamed of the horrible thing he or she is doing.

Since the Bible has no direct teaching about masturbation, our encouragement is to teach developing children about their bodies and how they function. In the process, it is natural to let them know that God designed the clitoris in the female and the penis in the male as sexually pleasurable to touch. They need to know that the primary place to experience sexual pleasure is within marriage, but that their hormones will be giving them feelings that are sexual now. They will need to decide how to handle those feelings between now and when they are ready for marriage, which will not be for a long time. In the meantime, they will probably discover that the genitals are pleasurable to touch and this is natural and normal.

For a sensitive discussion of this issue, listen to Dr. James Dobson's tapes on "Preparing for Adolescence." Masturbation during adolescence is certainly a tough issue. Just this week we received a letter from an older adolescent who attempted suicide because of her guilt about masturbation. After several years of trying to stop masturbating and feeling condemned by what she was hearing from Christian leaders, she was in despair. She believed that God had put a drive in her and then rejected her because she couldn't help responding to it. We need to be careful not to make proclamations about issues that are not addressed in God's Word.

The Parents' Role

What specifically do preadolescents need from us as parents? They need our *stability*. When their emotions are up and down, they need us to be understanding and caring—but not ride the roller coaster with them. They need our steady perspective.

Our *acceptance and praise* can make such a difference. We may have a tendency to want to correct, to shape them up. But the more we correct and criticize, the worse our children will feel about themselves—and the more negative their behavior will become. We can have definite expectations and stick to those. But then we need to let our children know how much we love and enjoy them. Or if we're not enjoying them right now, we need to take extra and special time alone with them.

Find small attributes that you can genuinely praise. Look for the positive. Assume they still need you, even if they behave as if they don't. Make special dates with them. Keep up the affection—back rubs, wrestling, and hugs are all comfortable ways of being physically affirming as our children's bodies are changing to adult bodies. Be warmly strong!

Our children need *limits*. It is best if our limits are clear and consistent, but allow growing freedom. Preadolescents will be making more and more of their own decisions as they move into adolescence and young adulthood. It is important that they learn to make decisions while we are involved. When our seventh grader asks if he can meet a girl at the pizza parlor down the street, the tendency may be to give an immediate answer. It helps him more if we guide him through the process of deciding. What does he think? How does he feel about it? How does this fit in with what he has sensed are our values? What are the plans? Help him examine whether it is a natural, harmless event or something that might lead to more pressure than is comfortable at his age. *Assisted decision making* within boundaries is what we recommend at this age.

The limits parents do set should be based on the *values* they teach—and how important it is to keep teaching and living those cherished values! Don't harp on everything. Reserve your messages for the important things. You may want to write down what is absolutely most important to you for your kids. Then look at how those values are being instilled. Is your life consistent with the values you have listed? In other words, do your children observe you living what you believe or want for them?

Specific sexual instruction is most important for children from ten to thirteen. These are the years of greatest openness to being taught about sexuality. Preadolescents need to be prepared for bodily and emotional changes. Both girls and boys need to know their body parts and their names. They need to know that boys grow hair under their arms, on their legs, chest, face, and around the penis and testicles. They need to know the penis and testicles grow larger and the voice becomes deeper. Erections, ejaculations, and wet dreams need to be explained as normal functions. For the girl, hair grows under the arms and around the vulva and vagina, breasts enlarge and develop, and the vagina may discharge a white, sticky substance. Menstruation, ovulation, and the process of fertilization all need to be clearly understood (refer to chapter 12 on sex education for more detail).

Above all, open communication with mutual regard for one another will be the most helpful in guiding our children out of childhood into adolescence.

For Further Study

Betancourt, Jeannie. *Am I Normal?* New York: Avon/Flare, 1983.

———. *Dear Diary.* New York: Avon/Flare, 1983. (Note: *Am I Normal?* was written for adolescent boys and is still available; *Dear Diary,* the companion book for adolescent girls, is out of print, but is still available in many libraries.)

Gardner-Loulan, Jo Ann, Bonnie Lopez, and Marcia Quackenbush. *Period.* San Francisco: Volcano Press, 1990.

Gordon, Sol, Ph.D., and Judith Gordon, M.S.W. *Raising a Child Conservatively in a Sexually Permissive World.* New York: Simon & Schuster, 1989. (This is a clearly secular approach to this topic.)

Hock, Dean, and Nancy Hock. *The Sex Education Dictionary.* Pocatello, Idaho: Landmark Publishing, 1990.

Ketterman, Grace H., M.D., *How to Teach Your Child About Sex.* Old Tappan, N.J.: Fleming H. Revell Co., 1981. 119–66.

*Kolodny, Robert C., William H. Masters, and Virginia E. Johnson. "Puberty and Adolescent Sexuality." In *Textbook of Sexual*

Medicine. Boston: Little, Brown, and Co., 1979.

Mayle, Peter. *What's Happening to Me?* New York: Carol Publishing Group, 1979.

*This book is no longer in print but is still available in many medical libraries.

11

The Decision-Making Years: Senior High

Adolescence and sexuality—as parents we would like to believe there isn't such a thing! It would be most convenient for us if we could strip all thirteen- to eighteen-year-olds of their sexuality—sort of put it on hold for five years. Then we could send them off to college and hope for the best.

Adolescents' sexuality scares us, and rightly so. All of that dynamic drive for intimacy, closeness, and connection with the opposite sex is racing within them. Yet they're still struggling with who they are, pulling away from their parents, and so influenced by their peers that we're not confident of their inner strength, even though they believe they are invincible. Besides, most of us are somewhat aware of the statistics. The number of sexually active teenagers continues to increase, in spite of the current emphasis on abstinence to prevent disease and pregnancy. This is shown by the following estimates from *Facts in Brief: Teenage Sexual and Reproductive Behavior in the United States,* published by the Alan Guttmacher Institute:

- 50 percent of unmarried women and 60 percent of unmarried men age 15–19 have had sexual intercourse (97 percent of women and 99 percent of men age fifteen to nineteen are unmarried).

- Teenagers are having sex for the first time at younger ages. Most of the increase in female sexual activity in the 1980s was among white teenagers and those in higher-income families.

- By the time they are eighteen, boys have had sex with an average of five girls. Eighty-seven percent of them report they worry about AIDS and venereal diseases.

- In-depth studies of a few specific sex-education programs have shown that some approaches contribute to a greater delay in teenagers becoming sexually active, at least in the short term.

- Each year more than one million teenagers—one out of ten of all women aged fifteen to nineteen and one out of five of the women who are sexually active—become pregnant.

- About half of all teenage pregnancies end in births; four out of every ten teenage pregnancies (excluding miscarriages) end in abortion. Fewer than 10 percent of teenagers who give birth place their babies up for adoption.

In addition to these alarming statistics about sexual activity, pregnancy, and birth, is the frightening fact reported by the Centers for Disease Control in the October 1991 issue of *Contemporary Sexuality* that one in seven of America's teenagers contracts a sexually transmitted disease (STD).

As professionals who work in this field, we found it interesting that these statistics include an indication that sex-education programs have been shown to help delay teenagers' initiation into sexual activity. We also have been pleased to find a government publication that contradicts recent, generalized accusations that secular sex-education programs in public schools promote, rather than discourage, teenagers' sexual activity. The publication, produced by the Centers for Disease Control, is "Guidelines for Effective School Health Education to Prevent the Spread of Aids," in the *Morbidity and Mortality Weekly Report,* (19 January 1988). While its primary focus is prevention of AIDS, its guidelines also should be encouraging to parents concerned about any teenage sexual activity. An excerpt of those guidelines is reprinted here:

The principal purpose of education about AIDS is to prevent HIV infection. The content of AIDS education should be developed with the active involvement of parents and should address the broad range of behavior exhibited by young people. Educational programs should assure that young people acquire the knowledge and skills they will need to adopt and maintain types of behavior that virtually eliminated their risk of becoming infected.

School systems should make programs available that will enable and encourage young people who **have not** engaged in sexual intercourse and who **have not** used illicit drugs to continue to—

- Abstain from sexual intercourse until they are ready to establish a mutually monogamous relationship within the context of marriage;

- Refrain from using or injecting illicit drugs.

For young people who **have** engaged in sexual intercourse or who **have** injected illicit drugs, school programs should enable and encourage them to—

- Stop engaging in sexual intercourse until they are ready to establish a mutually monogamous relationship within the context of marriage;

- To stop using or injecting illicit drugs

Despite all efforts, some young people may remain unwilling to adopt behavior that would virtually eliminate their risk of becoming infected. Therefore, school systems, in consultation with parents and health officials, should provide AIDS education programs that address preventive types of behavior that should be practiced by persons with an increased risk of acquiring HIV infection. These include:

- Avoiding sexual intercourse with anyone who is known to be infected, who is at risk of being infected, or whose HIV infection status is not known;

- Using a latex condom with spermicide if they engage in sexual intercourse;

- Seeking treatment if addicted to illicit drugs;

- Not sharing needles or other injection equipment;

- Seeking HIV counseling and testing if HIV infection is suspected.

State and local education and health agencies should work together to assess the prevalence of these types of risk behavior, and their determinants, over time.

Despite such recommendations, sexual activity continues to increase among teenagers—with the resulting, alarming statistics. Why? The emotional fluctuation, uncertainty about "who I am," and the incredible internal need to be accepted by peers all continue from preadolescence into adolescence. But at this time when ego strength is still shaky, adolescents' internal drives and sexual impulses are on fire! So at a time when they need to "play" at learning adult behavior as they played house at age five, their bodies and peers are pushing them to do more than just play at being couples. They are physically ready for the real thing!

Sexuality on Fire

Sexual hormones are the basis for these bodily urges. These hormones begin spurting about three years before any of the actual physical changes of puberty are evident. Now, during the high-school years, they are being secreted in full force. It is the hormones that trigger the *sexual drive.*

Fortunately, our *sexual drives* give us energy for much more than just bodily pleasure and sexual intercourse. The sexual drive is the energy for life. Activity, productivity, developing talents and skills, all burn up sexual-drive energy. Emotional intensity also expresses sexual-drive energy. The increased need for touch and physical closeness is a manifestation of sexual-drive energy. Nevertheless, this drive *does* stimulate the desire for sexual arousal and release.

All of this outgrowth of sexual drive is new to adolescents. They do not know what to do with it. They tend not to recognize the potency of their drive, so they get themselves into situations where the passion of the moment controls. They engage in sexual behavior inconsistent with their values or emotional readiness. Alternative expressions are often not utilized fully.

Masturbation may not be acceptable because it has either been condemned as wrong or is seen as the "chicken's way out." The challenge might be presented as, "If you're a real guy, you'll

have a woman!" In contrast, young women may have discon-
nected from their genitals in growing up, and may not even think
of self-stimulation as a way of releasing some of the intensity
they feel in their bodies.

Because of feelings of low self-worth, adolescents may not
be burning up their drives by working diligently on academics,
talents, or skills. Physical touching in the home is likely to decrease, at the very time when the need for touching is increased.
Parents of thirteen- to eighteen-year-olds would do best to increase the amount of contact time. That is difficult, just by virtue
of the fact that adolescents spend less time at home. Require
them to spend a certain amount of time at home and be available
for talking and being with you (not on the telephone). Then stick
to this requirement, even if they argue against it. Know that they
need this time, even though they're not likely to make it happen,
themselves. *You* will need to make it happen.

Be available when they are there. Tousle their hair as you
pass by when they're studying. Rub their shoulders. Give them a
peck on the cheek, a pat on the back, or a hug. Offer a back rub
at bedtime. That's how Joyce has kept up the physical affirmation
with our children throughout their teenage years. Virginia Satir, a
leading expert on marriage and the family, says we all need four
hugs a day to survive, eight hugs to maintain, and twelve hugs to
grow. Start a hug chart! It can be a fun way to get past the awkwardness of hugging your adult-bodied children.

Dealing with Sexuality

What are the ways adolescents deal with their sexuality?
Some respond with *denial*. They shut down their sexual feelings
totally. As soon as they sense any physical urges or thoughts,
they become uncomfortable. They may become socially and
relationally isolated. The feelings are so scary, their way of handling them is to withdraw. If they don't date, this lack of experience leaves them feeling naive, anxious, and uncomfortable with
the opposite sex.

There are two risks for these socially and sexually withdrawn
adolescents. First, when they do choose a guy or gal, they tend
to hang on and stick with a relationship that is not necessarily

right for them. The other hazard is that these adolescents are most prone to sexual accidents. Their sexual feelings take them by surprise because they've been denied so long. In addition, they crave affirmation from the opposite sex since they have not been a part of the dating population. So they are especially vulnerable!

One constructive way that adolescents can handle their sexual drive is with *replacement*. We've mentioned this already. Adolescents need to keep aware of their needs and drives, feel good about those tingling sensations, but decide to use them in ways other than sexual play. They may be active in mixed social groups, but not in one-on-one relationships. They may become active in giving to others. Our daughter Julene was a leader for a group of junior-highers at a local church when she was in high school. Both she and Greg worked as counselors at a Christian summer camp and as peer counselors for the junior high school. Other alternatives might be to work for a charitable organization.

Developing themselves physically also is a vital way for adolescents to use this energy. Greg swam or worked out with the water polo and swim teams when he was in high school. Now he goes mountain biking. Julene danced and played the harp and now power walks. Kristin is a diligent piano and violin student, in addition to her jogging and dancing. They all study hard. It's OK for adolescents to keep busy. In marriage, we want to save that energy for each other, but adolescence is the time to really go after all there is in life, to burn up that sexual-drive energy.

Self-stimulation (Masturbation) is a choice that most adolescents find comforting. It helps them be in a boy-girl relationship and to be responsible. By providing themselves with sexual release, they are better able to focus on developing the other dimensions of relating and are not so driven by sexual needs. Yet this can be a source of conflict and pain for many Christian adolescents. Dr. Dobson's tape series, "Preparing for Adolescence," has been helpful to many in understanding the facts of self-stimulation and making decisions regarding it.

Others decide to get much of their needs met by being active in a relationship with the opposite sex, but having clear *limits for sexual involvement*. When deciding to handle their sexuality in this way, adolescents need knowledge about their bodies and how they function sexually. They need to know that when you "get together," you are stimulating sexual arousal that is designed to lead to sexual release. So sexual play, even though it is limited, may leave feelings of frustration. Yet this is probably the most common choice made by responsible, sexually aware adolescents who are dating. And it is a very natural step in their growth and development. Their bodies and emotions are ready and desirous of physical closeness. But to be physical with limits requires a strong individual in a relationship that has *mutually accepted boundaries.* Adolescents need to avoid relationships in which one is pushing for more and the other is always having to draw the line.

Finally, some adolescents do handle their sexual drive by *mutual stimulation to sexual orgasm and/or sexual intercourse.* A few may make the decision and proceed responsibly, but most fall into this activity in the passion of the moment. The force leading them may be their own drives, the feeling that they have to nurture the relationship, or not knowing how to say no. Many adolescent girls report feeling pushed into having sex. Yet their adolescent male partners would not see themselves as having pushed sex on their girlfriends.

The Sexually Active Adolescent

When adolescents become involved in total sexual play, particularly sexual intercourse, what happens? They feel inept, afraid, guilty, and inappropriate. Their experience is like being lost in a flood of their own emotion rather than feeling close and warm with their partner. They are mainly focused on themselves. Because of their own discomfort and feelings of vulnerability, they tend to pull away and avoid each other afterward, when both need reassurance from the other. But neither is secure enough to reach out and give. So both end up feeling rejected and uncared for.

We would encourage you to use scenes from television shows and other media as conversation starters to teach these principles in your home. The old movie *Little Darlings* did a great job of depicting these realistic reactions to sexual intercourse during teenage years. We recommend that you see it if it's available from a video-rental store. Then if you feel comfortable with it, watch it with your teenagers and discuss it. This procedure can be used as a tool for opening communication.

Sexual intercourse is so much more than just releasing our physical drives and bringing two bodies together genitally. It is the union of two people totally. Two become one. We lose all of who we are with another person. That takes incredible security. Yet adolescents are still struggling with *who they are.* Their ego identity is unsure. So, at a time when they are supposed to be finding themselves, they are losing themselves to another person. It's most confusing!

When adolescents become sexually active, they bypass many steps of relating. They move quickly into physical intimacy without learning how to get along together. They develop sexual relationship patterns that are not fulfilling for them later in their marriages. They don't know who to talk to about their feelings, how to let others know their likes and dislikes, how to share mutual interests, and how to resolve differences. In fact, many times young girls come into pregnancy detection centers, crying. When they're asked how it happened, their response is that having sex was "easier than talking."

One authority wrote: "When you learn to fly, you don't get straight into any airplane and take off solo. When you learn to use your sexual powers, you don't start by trying to have sexual intercourse with somebody." Even the most liberal authorities on sexuality don't recommend sexual intercourse for teenagers. They see it as detrimental to psychological growth and development. The only reason they teach birth control is to encourage having responsible sex, if adolescents are going to have it anyway. But the big push today is teaching adolescents that they have the power (and the right!) to say no. It is important for all adolescents to recognize that their bodies are theirs to share only when they are good and ready to, and when they believe it is right.

Since 85 percent of the teenagers who have sexual inter-course say it is unpremeditated the first time, they are not pro-tected. Sexual infections are a high risk that can lead to pain, a maimed sexual self-image, sterility, and even death. Teenage pregnancy also is a high risk. There are no easy solutions to teenage pregnancy. A sixteen-year-old girl who finds herself pregnant is jarred out of the innocent bliss of adolescence. If sexual intercourse causes the adolescent to bypass important relational stages of growth and development, you can imagine how pregnancy interrupts. It is always sad and painful. As parents, our most important response is to stand alongside our child. Our rejection will help no one. Grieve the loss of her adolescence with her. Use the decision-making process we describe later to help her decide how she is going to handle the pregnancy. Make certain she has accurate information regarding moral, religious, physical, and emotional issues. Be there for her!

Positive Parenting

How can parents teach their children that a sexual relationship outside of marriage is wrong, yet that God planned for sex to be a great joy within marriage? How can parents be positive, and avoid the negative "thou shalt not" messages about having sex before marriage?

That is a most difficult balance to present. The goal is to teach values that have limitations, yet promote a positive view of sex. It is best when the limitations are presented as part of the facts, rather than the overall slogan. For example, "This is what the Bible teaches about sex. The reason God gave us that rule was not to make us unhappy, but to take care of us. Sexual union is a deep, special act. It unites us with another person emotionally, spiritually, and physically. We are really married to a person once we have sex with him or her." Then present the facts of what happens in our bodies during a sexual experience (see chapter 7 of *The Gift of Sex*). One way to do this is to say, "It is a complex and beautiful response. We want to be very careful about sharing something so intense and special. But sex is to be enjoyed. Marriage is the place for it—and that is God's plan."

Maximizing the Positives

How can parents and adolescents maximize the positives of dealing with sexuality during this age?

1. Be aware. Recognize the dilemmas and pressure adolescents face. There is an increasing gap between physical maturity and readiness for marriage. Education and financial demands are delaying marriage for most. That means the period from when their bodies are ready to function sexually until marriage is longer than ever before. At the same time, the media flaunt sexual stimuli everywhere. The general behavior and attitude of society pushes children to be sexual before their time.

2. Be educated. Both parents and adolescents need to read accurate sexual information. Knowledge breeds responsibility, not sexual promiscuity. Premature sexual behavior is the result of the general influence of society, along with incomplete knowledge and lack of internal strength to resist external and internal pressures.

As parents and adolescents, we are responsible for educating ourselves about how our bodies function sexually and for understanding the sexual drive and how it can be channeled. We are responsible for having a deep understanding of God's purpose and will for us as sexual persons. We are responsible for avoiding unintended sexual activity and for preventing venereal diseases. We need to be educated about these diseases' signs and symptoms, as well as about how they are transmitted. We are responsible for the prevention of teenage pregnancy.

3. Be a decision maker. We believe strongly that the most important place to start in effectively managing adolescents' sexuality is with decision making. Adolescents are moving toward making many of their own decisions about what is right for them. They will need to start thinking about the kind of persons they want to be and how they want to be known or regarded. As they begin to wonder what life will be like for them when they're on their own, they will begin to question values. They will start to think about questions such as, Why does one decide to have sex? When is it right to become sexually active? Why wait for marriage?

It is helpful, while adolescents are asking these questions, for parents to *discuss* these issues with their children, rather than simply try to dictate what values they should accept.

Parents could begin by sharing their own values and explaining why they believe what they believe. Yet, at the same time, they should show that they understand the teenager's struggle with these issues, especially if the family's values differ from the adolescent's peers. Understanding parents also should be prepared for questions such as, "Why do you believe this?" and "Why shouldn't people have sexual intercourse before marriage?" An adolescent might ask, "If teenagers are behaving responsibly, having sex but using protection, why is it wrong?"

For many parents, the answers to these questions might include the following points:

- Christians follow biblical directives prohibiting premarital sex, so that they don't have guilt with their sexuality.

- Abstaining from premarital sex prevents us from making comparisons later between the spouse and past sexual partners. Usually, more trust and less jealousy exists in married couples who come to the marriage without having had sexual relations with other partners. There's also less fear that the spouse will have sex with someone else outside the marriage.

- Saving sexual intercourse for the marriage relationship reduces the chances of becoming vulnerable, and then being rejected.

- Emotionally, sexual intercourse during adolescence can be destructive. To "give yourself away" so totally to another person when you are still attempting to "find yourself" often leaves a person feeling very empty inside.

- Finally, of course, abstinence means freedom from the fear of sexually transmitted diseases.

In helping youngsters make decisions about sexuality, begin by differentiating sexual feelings from sexual behavior. Sexual feelings include the *urge* to be touched, to be close, to be "turned on." Those feelings are part of who we are. They are good! Our sexual behavior—our actions—is what we decide to do with those feelings. That is where decision making is so necessary. These decisions need to be based on what we value and believe. As Christians, we are to use the Bible as our guide and strength for defining these beliefs.

Adolescents make choices, and they are the ones who have to live with the consequences of their decisions. Ultimately, the decision about the extent of their sexual activity is theirs to make. To help with their decision making, we suggest that they apply the following seven steps of a problem-solving process.

Define the problem. As an adolescent, how am I going to handle my sexuality? (Or ask yourself some specific version of that question.)

Identify your alternatives. Refer to the "Dealing with Sexuality" section for ways adolescents can handle sexual feelings and to the "Decision Making in Regard to Sexual Behavior" form at the end of this chapter for a full range of sexual behaviors.)

Identify the consequences for each alternative. The following two steps will help you determine these consequences. The questions you need to ask are, If I choose this alternative, what is likely to happen? How am I going to feel? How does it fit with what I believe to be right?

Gather data about the possible alternatives. Take time to know yourself. Write down your feelings. Clarify the physical, emotional, and spiritual consequences of the possible choices.

State your values. What is important to you in life? Brainstorm, listing everything that comes to your mind; then prioritize your list. Where does God fit in? What about your family, friends, and Christian community? How do the various alternatives fit with what you value?

Make the decision. First, try it out in your mind. Then plan your activities and relationships around that decision. Don't get yourself into situations that make it virtually impossible for you to stick with your decision. Make your plan work. For example, date others with similar values and choices.

Evaluate the consequences of the decision. Is it working the way you thought it would? What changes need to be made?

Parents, use this problem-solving process with your adolescents, and teach them to use it for themselves. As much as possible, be an active consultant with them. See yourself as their ally—someone who is standing alongside them! Allow them to struggle with all sides of the issue. That is difficult to do. Having our children consider possibilities that we don't believe are right makes us incredibly uneasy. But what we have to keep in mind is that we are not going to be with them when these decisions about sexual behavior are put into action. We don't go with them on their dates. We're not with them at school when they're making contacts. Unless they have thought through their options (and their consequences), they are not likely to be strong enough to stick with what they believe to be right for them.

We have to trust that what we have instilled in them since infancy is part of who they are. Ultimately, they do want to please us and God, and they want to do what is best for themselves. When they rebel against that and seem self-destructive, it is usually because they are not getting enough love, affirmation, and acceptance from us—not enough quality time. We can demand that! Or maybe they feel too smothered and controlled by us; maybe the move from dependence to independence has not been allowed. In this case, the adolescents have not sensed parental confidence in their decision making.

One exception to these recommendations of encouraging decision making for teenagers is the use of drugs or alcohol. Whatever the substance, when a person of any age is controlled by a chemical, he or she is incapable of competent decision making. Sometimes sugar can even influence certain people like a drug! Then you are not relating to this person, you are relating to the chemical. When this happens, you *do* have to take charge. Get help immediately!

With the one exception of the chemically controlled adolescent, active decision making by the adolescent produces behaviors most consistent with the values he or she has been taught. This is most true when parents have been reasonable, rather than rigid and controlling. They have considered the child as a person, talked with him or her, and listened to his or her situation. They have expressed their own concerns, being clear about the important issues: alcohol, drugs, sexual intercourse—or whatever their important issues happen to be.

It works well to communicate something like this: "We want you to take charge of your life more and more. You know what we believe is important in life. A meaningful, ongoing relationship with God is number one. Developing your full potential is number two. Family times are number three. We'd like to be open in working with you on making decisions that are right for you. We'd like you to be thinking about the kind of person you want to be, about your goals in life, and how your choices fit with that.

"We hope we can be the kind of listeners who will allow you to work through your thoughts with us. When we're uncomfortable with the choices you're making, we'd like to express that, but then listen to the reasoning behind your choice. Our feelings may be unfounded, but sometimes they may be right and necessary to at least consider. We'd like to practice a system of mutual respect. Above all, we'd like you to know that we are on your side. Even though we might get anxious when you start moving out more on your own, we want to trust you. We love you more than you can ever imagine."

In summary, we can help teenagers be wise decision makers by: enhancing ego development (self-confidence) and reinforcing self-worth, allowing independence to grow, expressing trust in them, giving daily touching affection, allowing mistakes, and keeping communication open.

4. Communicate openly. Obviously, being involved in an active decision-making process requires open communication. How open we can be with our teenagers depends upon several factors:

- Our attitudes about sex
- Our knowledge of the sexual facts—biblically, physiologically, and emotionally (*The Gift of Sex* is a great resource for parents.)
- Our willingness to talk openly about ourselves:

  What did we struggle with as teenagers?

  What mistakes did we make?

  How do we wish our experiences had been different?

  What did we feel good about?

- Our being willing and able to listen without passing judgment. This does not mean that we always agree; but we should reflect to them what they are sharing and feeling. We become a mirror to help them see themselves accurately. We are there to care, understand, and accept.

Often teenagers say they have difficulty discussing sex with their parents. Some parents feel uncomfortable discussing sex with their children. Are there acceptable alternatives or teaching tools for those who cannot seem to communicate verbally about sexual matters?

When verbal communication is uncomfortable, we recommend reading something like this chapter out loud together, listening to tapes like Dr. Dobson's, attending sex-education programs, watching and discussing sex-education specials on television together, and so on. The outside input gives you content, words, and a framework for talking.

5. Keep involved. Don't leave teenagers alone at home. Be present at their parties. This isn't necessary because you distrust them, it is necessary because they need your support. Peer pressure can be so strong. Your presence is a message that you care. Go to their activities, even if you have to take off work for them. Invite their friends into your home—and love them, too.

Plan special times alone with each child. We have developed special events with our children. With our teenagers, it was (or is) a breakfast or lunch out or a shopping day. Cliff took Greg for a snow-skiing-talk-about-sex weekend each winter. Joyce took Julene on a desert-spa weekend that focused on sex, Christianity, or decision making. Kristine automatically has one-to-one time with us because she is the only child at home. Because of that, we have to be careful not to miss special focus times with her.

Special family times are vital, too. We have attempted to keep Sunday dinner and evening for the family. When we allow life to infringe on that time, we notice the difference.

6. Negotiate contracts. With issues like dating, curfews, and household and family responsibilities, it is best to negotiate a plan. Both the parent and teenager should write out a plan for what they think is acceptable. Then negotiate the differences. Both should decide on the consequences that result when the contract is broken. Deal with issues factually, rather than emotionally. This will be a great preparation for your teenagers as they form life relationships.

7. Be the parent. This might seem contradictory to what we've suggested so far, but it isn't. Even though we're allies and consultants and on our kids' side, we *are* the parents. We're not to behave like fellow adolescents. We need to be strong and tender. We need to be firm with limits when those are necessary. But we must reserve those limits for important times and issues that are within our control. Many times, however, parents have more power than they accept. We all need affirmation from our parents—and need breeds power. Use it wisely!

Conclusion

We want to encourage you by being very honest with you. If we could follow all of our guidelines at all times, we would be thrilled! Obviously, this is an ideal approach. And all of us are human. We bring our own backgrounds and limitations to our relationships. Fortunately, children are amazingly resilient and God's grace is bountiful.

A few years ago, Dutch Professor Dr. med. C. van Emde Boas published "Ten Commandments for Parents Providing Sex Education" in the *Journal of Sex Education and Therapy*. We quote these "commandments" with our additions and comments in parentheses.

Ten Commandments for Parents
Providing Sex Education

1. Thou shalt not separate sex education from any other education, but realize that sex education starts in the cradle.

2. Thou shalt realize that skin and hands are our most important sex organs.

3. Thou shalt neither curb spontaneous sex expressions of the child (when it is age and biblically appropriate and not harmful), nor ever stimulate it artificially.

4. Thou shalt answer every question of the child according to truth, wherever possible immediately but always according to the emotional and spiritual level of the child; never answer more than was asked for.

5. Thou shalt realize that a living example carries more weight than words.

6. Thou shalt realize that sex information at school can never be anything but an addition to sex education in the family.

7. Thou shalt realize that overstressing of the biological aspects of sexuality must lead to underestimating of the emotional and relational aspects.

8. Thou shalt teach that sexual exploitation of another human being is equally as reprehensible as any other form of exploitation.

9. Thou shalt teach your children that the stem "co" in coitus means "together": being together, belonging together, becoming one, and thus presupposes an intimate relationship (scripturally and in marriage).

10. The Pill: rather a year too early than one night too late. (We would say: a clear decision about sexual behavior a year too early rather than one night too late.)

Decision Making in Regard to Sexual Behavior

Level of Sexual Activity

Complete this form to define for yourself the level of sexual expression that fits with who you are and what your values are.

Individual Activity

Masturbation: I do ___ I don't ___ It's okay ___ Shouldn't do ___ Causes me guilt ___

Sexual fantasies:
      Are a part of my masturbating activity ___
      Pass through my mind occasionally ___
      Preoccupy my mind frequently ___
      Seem natural and normal ___
      Aren't something I've been aware of ___
      Are sinful ___

Relationship Activity

The following activities express the whole range of possible sexual involvement. *With the knowledge that God designed sexual intercourse for marriage,* determine the limits of your sexual activity. Decide which activities are right for you now and which you would save for marriage.

None ____
Handholding and hugging ____
Polite kissing ____
Total mouth kissing ____
Intense, passionate hugging ____
Full-body rubbing, with clothes on ____
Breast stimulation over clothes ____
Genital stimulation over clothes ____
Breast stimulation under clothes ____
Genital stimulation under clothes ____
Full-body pleasuring, no clothes ____
Oral-genital stimulation ____
Total sexual experience, except entry ____
Total sexual experience, including intercourse ____
Ejaculation/orgasm by:

    Manual stimulation ____
    Oral stimulation ____
    Actual intercourse ____

Birth control or no birth control ____

If yes, what kind and what degree of safety? _____
I would like to get control of my sexual activity by

_____

I would like to gain more comfort with my sexuality by

_____

My goal for myself: _____

(Having decided to what degree you would see yourself being sexually active, how are you going to be responsible for that? What other types of intimacy might you develop? How might you use your sexual-drive energy to be productive in other ways? What types of situations and activities encourage your goals and what gets in the way?)

For Further Study

Burns, Jim. *Handling Your Hormones.* Eugene, Oreg.: Harvest House Publishers, 1986. (We recommend both this text and its companion volume, *Handling Your Hormones, Growth Guide.*)

Colgrove, Melba, Harold Bloomfield, and Peter Williams. *How to Survive the Loss of a Love*. New York: Bantam Books, 1984.

Comfort, Alex, and Jane Comfort. *The Facts of Love: Living, Loving, and Growing Up*. New York: Ballantine, 1986. (Parents need to add their values to the information in this book.)

"Games Teenagers Play." *Newsweek,* 1 September 1980, 48–53.

Grossman, Linda M., Ph.D., and Deborah Kowal, M.A. *Kids, Drugs, and Sex: Preventing Trouble*. Brandon, Vt.: Clinical Psychology Publishing Co., 1988.

"Guidelines for Effective School Health Education to Prevent the Spread of AIDS." *Morbidity and Mortality Weekly Report,* 37, no. S-2 (19 January 1988). Available from the U.S. Department of Health and Human Services, Public Health Service, Centers for Disease Control, Atlanta, Ga. 30333.

Alan Guttmacher Institute, 111 Fifth Avenue, New York, N.Y. 10003.

McDowell, Josh, and Dick Day. *Why Wait?* San Bernardino, Calif.: Here's Life Publishers, 1987.

Shearer, Lloyd. "Teenage Sexuality." *Parade Magazine,* 16 January 1983, 15.

Shedd, Charlie. *Letters to Karen*. Nashville: Abingdon, 1977.

———. *Letters to Phillip*. New York: Jove, 1985.

Short, Ray E. *Sex, Love, or Infatuation: How Can I Really Know?* Minneapolis: Augsburg-Fortress, 1990.

Wilder, E. James. *Just Between Father and Son*. Downers Grove, Ill.: InterVarsity Press, 1990.

Wood, Barry. *Questions Teenagers Ask about Dating and Sex*. Old Tappan, N.J.: Fleming H. Revell Co., 1981.

van Emde Boas, C., Dr. med. "Ten Commandments for Parents Providing Sex Education." *Journal of Sex Education and Therapy,* 6, no. 1 (Summer 1980).

12

Sex Education
with Values

Why sex education? Those who severely oppose sex education say, "The major goal of nearly all sex education curricula
being taught in the schools is to teach teenagers (sometimes
children) how to enjoy fornication without having a baby and
without feeling guilty" (*The Phyllis Schafly Report,* February 1981).
Yet even extreme liberals are saying,

> We don't think it's a good idea for teenagers to have inter-
> course. Sex for teenagers is a health hazard. . . . Teenagers are
> too young, too vulnerable, too available for exploitation. They
> don't know that the first experiences of sex are usually grim. . . .
> We cannot teach sex education without values. Sex education
> without values is valueless. . . . We believe in morality, in values,
> and in the family. We need to reemphasize that the family and
> parents *are* the sex educators of their children whether they do it
> well or badly.
>
> "Sexuality Education in the 1980s—No More Re-
> treats," editorial, *The Journal of Sex Education and
> Therapy,* Fall-Winter 1982

Controversy

Why the controversy? One dilemma is that sex-education
programs vary as much as the individuals responsible for them.

Thus, generalized conclusions about all of them are often based on one inadequate, irresponsible program. Another issue is fear without facts. What tends to happen is that a very small, loud minority will raise opposition to a sex-education program without thoroughly evaluating that program. Conclusions are drawn because certain educators or groups are known as humanistic. So the assumption is made that their program promotes anti-Christian values. Many times that isn't true, but no one has bothered to check what *is* being taught. In addition, the average parent may fear that educating young people will cause them to experiment sexually or to turn against the values of their family.

Should children be taught about sex? Doesn't educating them just give them ideas? In so doing, don't we destroy their innocence? What if the sex educator *does* communicate values that contradict ours?

We would like to address some of these concerns. As we've mentioned in previous chapters, children will be curious about sex and they will experiment. This happens without any formalized sexual program, even in primitive societies. It is part of the developmental process. And children will learn about sex, whether or not we expose them to a planned sex-education program. So refusing to provide sex education is not the answer to keeping them innocent.

Views in opposition to our Christian principles may be presented in a secular sex-education program. But we see that as a negative that can be turned into a positive. In fact, opposing thoughts can provide an excellent opportunity to implant our beliefs effectively. Throughout their lives, young people will be confronted with values in opposition to those of their parents. Most times when our young people are exposed to contradictory values, we are not present to teach what we believe and why. So the outside information is added to what they've heard from us, leaving them confused and unsure of what to believe. Our presence and ability to clarify at the moment (or shortly thereafter) can have a positive effect similar to parents countering the effect of television on their children. That is, research has shown that when parents watch television with their children and react to what is being shown, the children do not absorb what is seen as true reality. They learn to discriminate. Expressing our views in contradiction to other views teaches children to critically examine the outside information. It teaches them to think for themselves and to realize that not everything they hear is the truth. So the important element to control the effect of opposing views is our presence or awareness of what has been presented and our willingness to interact with the young person about that input. In fact, we include both secular and Christian books in our resource list because we find it helpful for parents to read both views with their children and then discuss the differences while clarifying their beliefs.

We would like to mention an additional attitude. It comes in response to the fear that our children are going to become sexually active if they attend sex-education programs. The atmosphere in our homes will have a greater impact on how our children behave sexually than will any sex-education program. We parents have a lifelong interaction with our children. We have the opportunity to instill enough positive input that the limited external teaching will not undo all our efforts (their own drives and peer pressure may, but not sex education, per se).

Many times parents don't recognize the impact they have on their children's lives. Because some parents don't accept their position of power and influence, they fail to utilize it effectively. Parents react in two ways to their feeling of powerlessness in relation to their children. Either they assume a powerless, helpless role, leaving the children without any clear direction, or they tend to dominate and dictate, eliciting rebellion in their children. Accepting our position of power and influence with our children enhances mutual respect for one another in the family. It promotes a sense of wanting to make the very best use of these limited years with our children. It causes us to use every opportunity to listen to them, spend time with them, teach them, and share with them our thinking and feeling.

Formal Sex Education

Obviously, we are *for* responsible sex education. As sincere, evangelical Christians, how can we take such a stand?

We believe negative Christianity that takes a stand *against* issues rather than promoting the positive has too often been the dominant voice of our evangelical churches. We are active in teaching positive, responsible, biblically based sexuality to married couples, singles, and parents of children of all ages. We believe there is so much we can be *for,* that it is a shame to spend our energy only attacking and condemning. We'd like to see Christians everywhere become involved in the sex-education programs of their communities. Think what a positive influence we could have! Even if all we do is present the biological facts with a clear call for responsible decision making, we could encourage a positive trend.

What are the *benefits* of a formal sex-education program outside the home?

First, the facts presented in a formal program can be more complete and graphic than what we, as parents, can share with our children in our homes. For example, there is no way that we can communicate all the detail of how the reproductive system works, as do some of the films. Nor can we as vividly portray the varying growth patterns that are so typical during puberty. Many of the teaching films do an excellent job of capturing the attention of young people while describing both the physical and emotional dimensions of growing up.

Second, attending sex-education programs with our preadolescents or having our adolescents share the content of their programs with us can be an excellent way to open discussion between parent and child.

Third, some parents need to utilize sex-education programs outside the home because they are unable to share the necessary information at home. Either their discomfort with their own sexuality prevents them from communicating openly or they lack knowledge about the topic.

Fourth, some parents have not developed a rapport with their children that allows the children to feel comfortable discussing sexuality with them.

Fifth, it is very helpful for children of all ages to hear the questions their peers are asking in a group setting and to hear what the sex educators are saying to everyone their age about certain issues. It helps them realize that what they are thinking and feeling is normal. Sometimes a one-to-one discussion can make children feel that they are the only ones their age who need this talk—or, at least, that this is how their parents view them.

Sixth, if adolescents are going to decide *not* to be sexually active, they are going to have to be informed. They are going to need to know about their bodies and how they work, to be aware of sexual feelings and drives and how to handle them. They are going to need to know how to separate feelings from behavior so that they can say, "No."

Seventh, in her "Research Notes," Bowling Green State University researcher Elizabeth Rice Allgeier reported on long-term comparison studies between adolescents who have had sex education and those who have not. Her report indicated no difference between the two groups in the level of sexual activity— or that "those who did *not* receive sex education had a higher rate of sexual activity than those who did receive such education." All studies report pregnancy and abortion rates to be significantly lower for those who have received sex education. Even though our ultimate goal would be to reduce adolescent sexual intercourse for both moral and sexual-infection reasons, we also are very concerned about eliminating out-of-wedlock pregnancy and abortions.

It is not surprising to us that effective sex education would reduce, rather than increase, sexual activity. When we understand that most thirteen- to fifteen-year-olds are experiencing full hormone production and, thus, high sexual drives, we realize that they have to have tools to help them harness that energy. As one author wrote, they already have the keys to the car (their sexual drive). The tendency will be to go out and use those keys and have accidents (unintended sexual intercourse, pregnancy, and/ or sexually transmitted diseases) unless we give them systematic driver's training (sex education).

Who Should Do the Teaching?

Where should formal sex-education programs be offered? The church is our first place of choice. We would love to see the church assume responsibility for sex education so that sexuality and spirituality develop together. When sexuality becomes linked with spirituality, it will be enjoyed in marriage. Unfortunately, most children receive their sexual information through television, movies, and friends. In those situations it is often linked with sin and guilt. Thus, sex becomes connected with something fun and exciting outside of marriage and outside of the church. When sin and sex go hand in hand, adults have difficulty enjoying sex without feeling guilty. The adrenaline rush of the guilt adds intense passion to sinful sex. We would love to have children grow up in the church with positive input regarding their sexuality—that it is a God-given force within them, that it has dynamite power they can use positively or negatively, and that having information will help them make wise decisions regarding their sexuality.

Community organizations and schools are also important places for responsible sexual education to take place. Christian schools presenting a sex-education program can have the same effect as the church teaching about sex. We have participated in such programs for Christian schools in our area. When sex education is offered in a secular setting, we recommend having clergy persons of all religious groups there to interact with their people about the content of the presentations. This is best handled by adjourning to small meeting rooms after the larger group presentation.

The only way to influence sex-education programs is to be involved. As Christian parents we must take an active role in ensuring positive sex education for our children. Rather than trying to protect them because of our fear, let's turn that energy into giving them facts that lead to value-based decisions.

The persons presenting the sex-education material or interacting with the audience must be comfortable with and well informed about the topic of sex. There has to be an ease in handling any question that might come from the audience. There will be some students in every crowd who attempt to shock or stir up the presenters. It is important to be unshockable and nonjudgmental. In other words, our advice to the presenters is, Keep cool! Being secure with regard to our own sexuality has been invaluable to us when we give these presentations. We have learned the importance of having thought through our own values so that we communicate them when appropriate without imposing our beliefs on others. It helps for us to have a strong sense of ourselves, yet respect each other's feelings and views.

When parents and students are attending together, we recommend that questions be written and that students be allowed open discussion from the floor—but *not parents.* The reason for this is to prevent the insensitive parent from embarrassing his or her child. We have experienced some most unfortunate situations when that limitation was not set. One mother openly and condemningly discussed the masturbatory habits of her daughter—with the girl and her peers present. The chance of one child being hurt that severely is not worth allowing open discussion for parents from the floor. Always have pencils and cards or paper available for them to write their responses, questions, or concerns. Encourage each student to write something so that no one will feel embarrassed asking a written question.

The Content

What should be taught and at what age level? Ideally, sex education is a circular process for all ages. Because many adults have not been educated regarding their own sexuality and sexual relationships, we believe adult education needs to occur first. That is why we wrote *The Gift of Sex* before we wrote this book. How parents experience the sexual dimension of their own lives will have a significant effect on what they communicate to their children. A friend of ours once observed, "You know, it's interesting that most of us as adults spend a major share of our lives in a marriage relationship and as parents, yet our educational process did almost nothing to prepare us for those responsibilities."

We move from teaching couples how to handle their own sexuality to teaching parents about teaching children. Before their children are in about the fourth grade (ages nine or ten), our primary focus is on teaching parents how to handle sexuality with their children. Parents need to know what and how children learn at various levels of sexual development. Chapter 8 (infant and toddler sexuality) and 9 (preschool-to-puberty sexuality) of this book will be most helpful with this age group. We will summarize that information in the Sex-Education Model that appears later in this chapter.

Starting at age nine or ten, formal education is recommended as a supplement to the ongoing process of informal teaching that occurs in the home. Education for ten- to thirteen-year-olds is best directed toward the children, but with the parents present and sitting with their children.

At adolescence, peers become the key to influencing positive decisions regarding sexuality. At this age, most children "turn off" to sex education from an adult authority, particularly in a large group setting—i.e., church or school. There is a self-consciousness about the topic, as well as an overconfident attitude of already "knowing it all." It's as if the content is too close to what they are trying to sort out for themselves. It's too close to be comfortable, so there is a low receptivity to formal sex education during the high-school years. Peer power is dominant; teenagers are listening to each other. Therefore, we recommend that a select group of desirable, emotionally and spiritually mature adolescents be trained and supervised by qualified counselors. These peer counselors need to be visibly available to their peers through some formal or informal plan.

Having started sex education with teaching married couples of all ages, we then complete the circle of sex education by teaching adult singles (refer to chapter 13 for details on singles and sexuality) and couples preparing for marriage.

Sex education for the single adult is not much different than that for the adolescent. The same issue is alive: Sexual drives are flaming while sex within marriage is not available. The gap between physical readiness for sexual involvement and the actual possibility of marriage is widening. Puberty is occurring at a younger age while our economic and educational system is delaying marriage until later in life. Responsible decision making based on knowledge and self-awareness is the only solution.

Premarital classes for couples can be an incredible boost to starting a happy sexual life in marriage. Much of the content will be the same as what adult married couples receive. There are some specific instructions to help couples with that first sexual intercourse. We were fortunate that before we were married Joyce received premarital instruction from her gynecologist as well as a premarital class that was part of her school-of-nursing program. She shared this content with Cliff as she received it. The content, as well as the sharing, was a great way to start a sexual relationship in marriage.

This process of sex education targets all age groups. It begins with married couples and ends with those who are about to be married. We find the groups most receptive to education are the fifth- and sixth-graders and the married couples. They are eager and ready to learn, and they ask excellent questions. The *least* receptive are the high-school students and the premarital couples. For both of these groups, there is an element of newness as it relates to sexuality in their lives; thus, they feel self-conscious and somewhat certain they don't need the information.

What follows is an outline of the content in this sex-education process as we have utilized it. The process could be put into use by a community, a school, a church, or by an individual professional. The entire program could be adopted to reach all ages within a certain community. Or any part of the program could be utilized for a particular age group. The teaching tools suggested will become outdated with time, and should be replaced with similar, newer tools as they become available.

Sex-Education Model

I. Educate married couples to enhance their sexual relationship, by teaching:
  A. Positive sexual attitudes—concept of mutuality
  B. Biblical endorsement of sexual pleasure in marriage
  C. Bodily openness and familiarity between the couple
  D. Physical facts of how the male and female bodies function during a sexual response
  E. The emotional and relational dimensions of a sexual encounter
  F. Solutions for common sexual problems
  G. Open communication about sex in marriage
  H. Freedom without demand in the sexual relationship
  I. Guidelines for resolving sexual conflicts
  J. Special issues for married couples (See chapters 1–6 and 14–20.)

K. See *The Gift of Sex* for details about enhancing married couples' sexual relationship.

II. Educate parents to model and teach healthy sexual attitudes to children 0–10 years old. (See chapter 7 for specific details of this content.)
   A. For infants 0–2 years—teach expectant and new parents how to affirm through touch and bonding. (See chapter 8.)
   B. For toddlers 2–4 years—teach parents how to instill a positive acceptance of genitals by the way they respond to the touching, naming, and controlling of the genitals that occurs at this age. (See chapter 8.)
   C. For preschoolers 4–5 years—teach parents how to communicate acceptance of, and boundaries for, the sexual curiosity of children in this age group. (See chapter 9.)
   D. For the 3–6-year-olds—teach parents how to affirm gender identity and development. (See chapter 9.)
   E. For school-age children 6–10 years—teach parents how to help their children develop a respect for their bodies and a regard for their sexuality in relation to others through the appropriate reaction to exploratory play, the handling of nudity in the home, and the prevention of molestation. (See chapter 9.) Parents should also help their children gain an understanding of AIDS. The U.S. Department of Health and Human Services suggests:

> Education about AIDS for students in early elementary grades principally should be designed to allay excessive fears of the epidemic and of becoming infected.
> AIDS is a disease that is causing some adults to get very sick, but it does not commonly affect children.
> AIDS is very hard to get. You cannot get it just by being near or touching someone who has it.
> Scientists all over the world are working hard to find a way to stop people from getting AIDS and to cure those who have it.
>
> "Guidelines for Effective School Health Education to Prevent the Spread of AIDS," *Morbidity and Mortality Weekly Report,* 29 January 1988

F. For details of the physical developmental process, refer to the Puberty Timetable in Table I at the end of this model.

III. Educate preadolescents with parents present.
   A. 9–10-year-old girls (fourth- and fifth-graders) and their mothers. This session focuses on menstruation. As they arrive, greet them with a snack and juice, a three-by-five card and a pencil, and a pretest. (The film "Julie's Story" has one; this film is available from Kimberly-Clark Corporation, Neenah, Wis. 54956.)

   Have mothers and daughters sit together and work on the pretest while they wait. (It gets them to talk with each other.) Begin the program by having the girls give the answers to the pretest as the presenter asks for them. Talk to the group about menstruation, then show the film. After the film, ask each girl to write a question on the three-by-five card. While collecting the cards, ask the mothers to share with their daughters something they learned from the film. Then answer the questions with clear, warm, factual responses. You might show diagrams of the uterus, demonstrate samples of sanitary pads and tampons, and describe, on a large calendar, how to calculate the menstrual cycle. List definitions of menstruation, uterus, vagina, ovary, etc. on a large poster board and have the group read them out loud together.

   Dismiss by giving each mother an assignment to tell her daughter how and when she learned about menstruation, and give the daughters an assignment to ask questions. Have sanitary supplies available at a table on the way out of the auditorium.
   B. 10–12-year-olds (fifth- and sixth-graders) with one or both parents. This session focuses on the biological and emotional changes of puberty, elementary biological facts of sexual reproduction, facts about masturbation, and values of responsible utilization of sexual energy.

   As the participants arrive, instruct the students to sit with their parent(s) and give them a three-by-five card and pencil. Introduce the film. We use either "Then One Year" (available from Churchill Media, 12210 Nebraska Avenue,

Los Angeles, Calif. 90025, telephone 213-207-6600) or "Sexplanation" (from Wisdom Video, P.O. Box 35014, Minneapolis, Minn. 55435). After the film, ask each student to write a question on the three-by-five card. While you collect the cards, have each parent share with the student something he or she learned from the film. Respond to the questions factually and sensitively. If inappropriate slang terminology has been used in a question, reword it in correct terms. For example, you might say, "Someone asked a question about sexual intercourse but used the slang word for that. Let's talk about sexual intercourse." Then go on to talk about the physical, emotional, and spiritual union that occurs during sexual intercourse.

If the teaching is occurring in a Christian setting, either close with or begin with a ten-minute talk on the positive biblical view of sexuality and sexual intercourse in marriage. In addition, work into the answers to the questions the positiveness of becoming men and women, of our sexual energy, and yet the problems that occur when sex is misused: unwanted pregnancy, emotional hurts, and sexual infections. Emphasize that this is the reason it is so necessary for students to have accurate information about their bodies and their sexuality. Teach them about preventing, stopping, or reporting sexual abuse (any uncomfortable touch, look, or exposure). And teach them about AIDS:

Education about AIDS for students in late elementary/ middle school grades should be designed with consideration for the following information.

Viruses are living organisms too small to be seen by the unaided eye.

Viruses can be transmitted from an infected person to an uninfected person through various means.

Some viruses cause disease among people.

Persons who are infected with some viruses that cause disease may not have any signs or symptoms of disease.

AIDS (an abbreviation for **a**cquired **i**mmun**o**deficiency **s**yndrome) is caused by a virus that weakens the ability of infected individuals to fight off disease.

People who have AIDS often develop a rare type of severe pneumonia, a cancer called Kaposi's sarcoma, and certain other diseases that healthy people normally do not get.

About 1 to 1.5 million of the total population of approximately 240 million Americans currently are infected with the AIDS virus and consequently are capable of infecting others.

People who are infected with the AIDS virus live in every state in the United States and in most other countries of the world. Infected people live in cities as well as in suburbs, small towns, and rural areas. Although most infected people are adults, teenagers can also become infected. Females as well as males are infected. People of every race are infected, including whites, blacks, Hispanics, Native Americans, and Asian/Pacific Islanders.

The AIDS virus can be transmitted by sexual contact with an infected person; by using needles and other injection equipment that an infected person has used; and from an infected mother to her infant before or during birth.

A small number of doctors, nurses, and other medical personnel have been infected when they were directly exposed to infected blood.

It sometimes takes several years after becoming infected with the AIDS virus before symptoms of the disease appear. Thus, people who are infected with the virus can infect other people—even though the people who transmit the infection do not feel or look sick.

Most infected people who develop symptoms of AIDS only live about 2 years after their symptoms are diagnosed.

The AIDS virus cannot be caught by touching someone who is infected, by being in the same room with an infected person, or by donating blood.

"Guidelines for Effective School Health Education to Prevent the Spread of AIDS," *Morbidity and Mortality Weekly Report*, 29 January 1988

Have clergy persons clarify moral issues. Encourage parents and children to discuss these and other issues after the program. Recommend that parent and child have a discussion about the content of the program immediately following the session. Assign a specific question or topic for them to discuss.

C. 12–13-year-olds (seventh-graders) and one or both parents—This session focuses on biological, emotional, and responsibility changes of becoming an adolescent, biological details of sex and reproduction, a description of sexual intercourse as a special expression between a husband and wife that is for pleasure as well as reproduction, facts about conflicting views on masturbation, introduce decision making—the concept of active choices.

As the participants arrive, instruct students to sit with their parent(s), and give each student a three-by-five card and a pencil. Introduce the film. We use "Human Growth IV by Churchill Media, 12210 Nebraska Avenue, Los Angeles, Calif. 90025 (telephone 213-207-6600). After the film, collect their questions. Assign a topic for parents and students to discuss while questions are being sorted. Have a question-answer time and a time with clergy, conducted the same as for fifth- and sixth-graders, described previously. Small-group discussions the next day would be great.

IV. Educate adolescents (13–18-year-olds), informing parents of what is being taught. Have previews of films or videos for parents.

A. 13–14-year-olds (eighth grade)—Show a film to eighth-grade assembly or group depicting the peer pressures that students will be facing as they move into ninth grade with consequences of various choices shown. One such film is "Running My Way" by Children's Home Society of California (2727 West Sixth Street, Los Angeles, Calif. 90057, telephone 213-482-5443); it is excellent—if you can overlook the outdated styles. A decision-making form to lead discussion after viewing this film is in Table II at the end of this chapter. A newer, equally great video is "Choosing to Wait: Sex and Teenagers" (Sunburst Communications, Pleasantville, N.Y. 10570). Have the students write questions, then collect the questions and answer them. The presentation should include information on decision making, sexual infections, and pregnancy prevention (these topics may be handled in small groups, where possible).

B. Teach classrooms of high-school adolescents, separating gals and guys to promote freer discussion.

C. Teach mixed groups of peer counselors.

D. Content that needs to be taught:

1. Sexual anatomy and physiology: what happens to the body during sexual arousal and release. (See *The Gift of Sex.*)

2. Sexual feelings and drives as separate from sexual actions which require decisions. (See chapter 11.)

3. Various choices for responding to touching, relationship, and sexual needs; include statistics of adolescents and consequences of those choices. (See chapter 11.)

4. Values clarification *Choices* and *Challenges,* books by Mindy Bingham, Judy Edmondson, and Sandy Stryker, or *Sex Respect* by C. K. Mast may be used for this purpose. If the course is taught within the church, the Bible is the best resource. Josh McDowell's book *Why Wait?* is helpful also.

5. Facts about sexually transmitted diseases. (See chapter 19.) In addition, teach these facts about AIDS:

> Education about AIDS for students in junior high/senior high school grades should be developed and presented, taking into consideration the following information.
>
> The virus that causes AIDS, and other health problems, is called **h**uman **i**mmunodeficiency **v**irus, or HIV.
>
> The risk of becoming infected with HIV can be virtually eliminated by not engaging in sexual activities and by not using illegal intravenous drugs.
>
> Sexual transmission of HIV is not a threat to those uninfected individuals who engage in mutually monogamous sexual relations.
>
> HIV may be transmitted in any of the following ways: a) by sexual contact with an infected person (penis/vagina, penis/rectum, mouth/vagina, mouth/penis, mouth/rectum); b) by using needles or other injection equipment that an infected person has used; c) from an infected mother to her infant before or during birth.

A small number of doctors, nurses, and other medical personnel have been infected when they were directly exposed to infected blood.

The following are at increased risk of having the virus that causes AIDS and consequently of being infectious: a) persons with clinical or laboratory evidence of infection; b) males who have had sexual intercourse with other males; c) persons who have injected illegal drugs; d) persons who have had numerous sexual partners, including male or female prostitutes; e) persons who have received blood clotting products before 1985; f) sex partners of infected persons or persons at increased risk; and g) infants born to infected mothers.

The risk of becoming infected is increased by having a sexual partner who is at increased risk of having contracted the AIDS virus (as identified previously), practicing sexual behavior that results in the exchange of body fluids (i.e., semen, vaginal secretions, blood), and using unsterile needles or paraphernalia to inject drugs.

Although no transmission from deep, open-mouth (i.e., "French") kissing has been documented, such kissing theoretically could transmit HIV from an infected to an uninfected person through direct exposure of mucous membranes to infected blood or saliva.

In the past, medical use of blood, such as transfusing blood and treating hemophiliacs with blood clotting products, has caused some people to become infected with HIV. However, since 1985 all donated blood has been tested to determine whether it is infected with HIV; moreover, all blood clotting products have been made from screened plasma and have been heated to destroy any HIV that might remain in the concentrate. Thus, the risk of becoming infected with HIV from blood transfusions and from blood clotting products is virtually eliminated. Cases of HIV infection caused by these medical uses of blood will continue to be diagnosed, however, among people who were infected by these means before 1985.

Persons who continue to engage in sexual intercourse with persons who are at increased risk or whose infection status is unknown should use a latex condom (not natural membrane) to reduce the likelihood of becoming infected. The latex condom must be applied properly and used from start to finish for every sexual act. Although a latex condom does not provide 100% protection—because it is possible for the condom to leak, break, or slip off—it provides the best protection for people who do not maintain a mutually monogamous relationship with an uninfected partner. Additional protection may be obtained by using spermicides that seem active against HIV and other sexually transmitted organisms in conjunction with condoms.

Behavior that prevents exposure to HIV also may prevent unintended pregnancies and exposure to the organisms that cause Chlamydia infection, gonorrhea, herpes, human papillomavirus, and syphilis.

Persons who believe they may be infected with the AIDS virus should take precautions not to infect others and to seek counseling and antibody testing to determine whether they are infected. If persons **are not** infected, counseling and testing can relieve unnecessary anxiety and reinforce the need to adopt or continue practices that reduce the risk of infection. If persons **are** infected, they should: a) take precautions to protect sexual partners from becoming infected; b) advise previous current sexual or drug-use partners to receive counseling and testing; c) take precautions against becoming pregnant; and d) seek medical care and counseling about other medical problems that may result from a weakened immunologic system.

> "Guidelines for Effective School Health Education to Prevent the Spread of AIDS," *Morbidity and Mortality Weekly Report,* 29 January 1988

6. Facts about birth control, (chapter 2) *not* as a recommendation but rather as the most responsible option if some students are proceeding to sexual intercourse or already having it, even though that is not right for them. These facts also should be directed toward peer counselors, to encourage their use by teenagers who are already sexually active and cannot be persuaded to change that behavior.

7. The choice of saying no is the best option. For help with how to respond to the pressures of their own desires, as well as the pressures of the opposite sex, refer

to *Smart Girls Don't and Guys Don't Either* by Kevin Leman, a book that is no longer in print but is available in many libraries. Another helpful book is *Why Wait?* by Josh McDowell. Role playing is often helpful, too.

    8. The positive expression of sexual intercourse in marriage (why and when married couples have sex).

V. Educate Single Adults (referring to chapter 13):
   A. To know the facts—What are the options?
   B. To know themselves, physically and emotionally
   C. To struggle with the reality of sexual desires versus sexual behaviors in light of their values
   D. To know their limits and make clear decisions regarding the appropriate degree of physical involvement
   E. To know their strengths and weaknesses
   F. To find joy in the choices they make

VI. Educate Premarital Couples regarding:
   A. Biblical affirmation of sexuality and sexual fulfillment in marriage. (See *The Gift of Sex,* chapters 3–4.)
   B. Preparing to make the emotional and relationship dimensions of sex work for them. To whatever extent they are physical with each other before marriage, they can assess their patterns of connecting and predict similar patterns with sex after marriage. (Read and discuss together *The Gift of Sex,* chapter 9–20.)
   C. Understanding their sexual response or lack of it. (In *The Gift of Sex,* individually do exercise 1 in chapter 5 and also read chapters 6, 7, and 8. Complete any individual exercises, but save joint ones for after marriage.)
   D. Learning how to give and receive pleasure for the sake of pleasure without demand. (Read chapter 13 in *The Gift of Sex* and complete exercises 8 and 9.)
   E. Communicating openly about themselves as sexual persons and about their expectations for sex in marriage. (See Table III at the end of this education model.)
   F. Preparing for their first sexual intercourse (refer to Table III at the end of this education model).
   G. Preparing for sexual intercourse after marriage when there has been sex before. Issues that need to be addressed are: recommending that the experienced one lead, minimizing

comparisons and demands to measure up, and experiencing forgiveness and release of guilt, etc.

H. Keeping the "spark" alive. (See chapter 6.)

Most of this content is presented in the Penner premarital video (90 minutes) available from Word, Inc.

Sex education is difficult for many. We bring to it the intensity of our own emotions and experience. We bring the attitudes that were developed in our own homes. Many times we are confused about what is appropriate to think, feel, and teach about sex.

May we continue to become more informed about our own beliefs, body functioning, sexual feelings, use of sexual-drive energies, responsible decision making, and sexual fulfillment as a gift from God.

Table I—Puberty Timetable

7–10 years old: *Sex hormones* begin to spurt three years before physical changes are obvious. This will lead to enormously increased production of testosterone in males and estrogen in females.

8–13 years: *Breast growth* begins; nipples swell a little. This usually occurs in one nipple before the other. It occurs three to four years before the girl's first menstruation. May occur in boys as well as girls. Boys' breast swelling goes away as their testicles begin to grow and produce more testosterone.

8–14 years: *Pubic hair* begins in girls. Enlargement of the labia and clitoris follows.

9.5–14.5 years: *Height spurt* occurs in girls—may be more gradual than in boys (feet tend to grow before height).

9.5–13.5 years: *Testicle growth* begins.

10–15 years: *Height spurt* starts in boys (feet tend to grow before height). *Pubic hair* begins in boys.

10–16.5 years: First *menstruation* for girls. Ovulation may occur before or after.

10.5–14.5 years: *Penis growth* starts.

11.5-15.5 years (or later): First *ejaculation* occurs about a year after penis growth starts, but this varies greatly. Orgasm can occur before ejaculation.

12–16 years: *Voice change* for boys.

12.5–16.5 years: *Penis growth* stops.

13.5–17 years: *Testicle growth* stops.

13.5–17 years: *Height spurt* stops for boys.

13–18 years: *Breast development* stops for girls.

Other changes that vary too greatly to list on the timetable:

Growth of underarm hair for boys and girls.

Growth of facial hair for boys.

Acne for some boys and girls.

Body shape takes on adult characteristics.

Table II Decision-Making Process (To follow the film *Running My Way*)

I. Define the problem
   A. What was the problem for Lisa?
   B. What was the problem for Sandy?
II. Identify the alternatives
   A. What were the alternatives for Lisa?
      1. She could not have sex.
      2. She could have had sex unprotected.
      3. She could have had sex protected.
      4. She could have a relationship with Tony on another level (including other forms of intimacy).
III. Identify the consequences of each alternative
   A. If she doesn't have sex, what is going to happen?
   B. If she does, what will happen?
   C. If she does, how will she feel?
IV. Gather data to predict your consequences accurately
   A. Have reliable information. (Biggest source of information is their peers—this is often misinformation.)

B. Be informed—as parents and adolescents, know how your bodies work.
C. What are kids' values?
V. State the values
   A. What were Lisa's values?
      1. Telling the truth was important.
      2. Having a boyfriend.
      3. Running.
      4. Carefulness about sharing her body.
   B. What were Sandy's, Ray's, and Tony's values?
VI. Make the decision
   A. Then try it in your mind. What will happen if I make this decision?
   B. Then actually act on the decision.
VII. Evaluate the decision
   A. Need to think, feel, and then act.
   B. What were the actual consequences?

Table III—Recommendations for Preparing for Marriage

Physical Preparations

For Women:

- Gynecological examination, including birth control, testing for sexually transmitted diseases and AIDS
- Stretching of the vagina using clean fingers or dilators
- PC muscle exercises (See page 61 of *The Gift of Sex*.)
- Genital self-exam (See page 57 of *The Gift of Sex*.)

For Men:

- Routine physical examination, including testing for sexually transmitted diseases and AIDS
- Genital self-exam (see page 66 of *The Gift of Sex*)
- Self-stimulation to ejaculation within twenty-four hours before intercourse (This is helpful to practice extending

ejaculation. See chapter 29 of *The Gift of Sex* and/or *P.E.: How to Overcome Premature Ejaculation* by Helen Singer Kaplan.)

Together:

- View the Penner premarital video.
- Plan to use a genital lubricant. Petroleum-based lubricants (which should not be used with rubber condoms or diaphragms) include Albolene, a facial cleanser, or Allercreme, a nonlanolin, nonalcohol lotion. Water-based lubricants include KY Jelly or Lubrifax. Natural oils, or other lubricants especially designed for sexual intercourse, such as Probe and Lubrin.
- Plan to proceed to intercourse *slowly*. Take time to enjoy all the pleasuring you have enjoyed together thus far—kissing, hugging, etc.
- Place no demands on each other, but thoroughly enjoy each other.
- Plan a time of quiet vagina (a time of resting quietly without thrusting) after entry, before and in between thrusting.

Emotional/Relational Preparation

Individually complete your responses to these questions and share them with each other, taking turns to be the one who shares while the other listens and reflects what he or she has heard and felt from the other partner.

> What did you learn about sex while you were growing up?
>
> What past experiences have you had that affect your sexuality today?
>
> Childhood exploratory play
>
> Self-stimulation
>
> Trauma—molestation, abuse, exposure, pornography, physical abuse

Dating—positive and negative experiences

What do you think your parents' sexual life was like?

What would you like your sexual life to be like? (Include frequency, initiation, sexual activities, romance, and preparation.)

For Further Study

For more detailed information about AIDS, including how to be tested for the HIV virus and where to seek counseling, contact your state or local health department.

Allgeier, Elizabeth Rice, Ph.D. "Research Notes." Psychology Department, Bowling Green State University, Bowling Green, Ohio.

Bingham, Mindy, Judy Edmondson, and Sandy Stryker. *Choices: A Teen Woman's Journal for Self-Awareness and Personal Planning.* Santa Barbara, Calif.: Advocacy Press, a division of the Girls Club of Greater Santa Barbara, 1987. (This book is distributed by Ingram Book Company—Bookpeople, LaVergne, Tennessee.)

————. *Challenges: A Young Man's Journal for Self-Awareness and Personal Planning.* Santa Barbara, Calif.: Advocacy Press, a division of the Girls Club of Greater Santa Barbara, 1984. (This book is distributed by Ingram Book Company—Bookpeople, LaVergne, Tennessee.)

Calderone, Mary S., M.D., and Eric W. Johnson *The Family Book About Sexuality.* New York: Harper and Row, 1990. (This is a secular book in which moral values need to be differentiated.)

Network Report, published by California Family Life Education. Fall 1981 to Summer 1991.

Gordon, Sol, Ph.D. "Sexuality Education in the 1980s—No More Retreats." *The Journal of Sex Education and Therapy,* 8, no. 2 (Fall/Winter 1982).

Gordon, Sol, Ph.D., and Judith Gordon, M.S.W. *Raising a Child Conservatively in a Sexually Permissive World.* New York: Simon & Schuster, 1989. (A secular approach.)

"Guidelines for Effective School Health Education to Prevent the Spread of AIDS." *Morbidity and Mortality Weekly Report,* 37, no. S-2 (19 January 1988). Available from the U.S. Department of Health and Human Services, Public Health Service, Centers for Disease Control, Atlanta, Ga. 30333.

Kaplan, Helen Singer. *P.E.: How to Overcome Premature Ejaculation.* New York: Brunner-Mazel, 1989.

Mast, C. K. *Sex Respect: The Option of True Sexual Freedom.* Bradley, Ill.: Project Respect, 1986.

McDowell, Josh, and Dick Day. *Why Wait?* San Bernardino, Calif.: Here's Life Publishers, 1987.

Nilsson, A. Lennart, Axel Ingelman-Sundberg, M.D., and Claes Wirsen, M.D. *A Child Is Born: The Drama of Life Before Birth.* Rev. ed. New York: Dell, 1989.

Nixon, Joan Lowery. *Before You Were Born.* Huntington, Ind.: Our Sunday Visitor, 1980.

Penner, Clifford, and Joyce J. Penner. *Premarital Video: The Gift of Sex.* 90 minutes. Word, Inc.

Risk and Responsibility: Teaching Sex Education in American Schools Today. New York: Alan Guttmacher Institute, 1989.

Schafly, Phyllis. "What's Wrong with Sex Education?" *The Phyllis Schafly Report,* 14, no. 7, sec. 1 (February 1981).

Part 4

Single Sexuality

13

Single, Sexual, and Sanctified

Life used to be uncomplicated. Sexuality for the single person was clearly defined. The old limerick put it this way;

> There was a young lady named Wilde
> Who kept herself quite undefiled,
> By thinking of Jesus
> and social diseases,
> And the fear of having a child.

It used to be so simple. After high school, you went to college and by the time you were twenty or twenty-one you had picked out the man or woman of your dreams. Then you married and did what your parents had done: work, start a family, and establish yourself in a job or location. Life was pretty clearly set.

It used to be so simple. Right was right, and wrong was wrong—and everyone knew the difference. There was no hazy morality. What was expected of the single Christian man or woman was clear.

Our world is no longer that simple. Whether we come from a rural part of the country or a metropolitan area, everyone has been bombarded by the cultural changes that are a result of the technological and medical advances of the past thirty years. Television has brought a variety of lifestyles right into our living rooms. Birth control has radically reduced the fear of having an illegitimate or unwanted child. Many Christian singles are actively, and often openly, sexually involved. Attitudes toward morality have changed. One thing that has gone full circle is the second point of the limerick—social diseases are again a major concern. Now with genital warts, herpes, and AIDS, disease is again a dreaded consequence.

Not only have moral and technological changes occurred, but the social structure has changed radically, too. We are no longer oriented around family, church, or community as we once were. Many times we exist in isolation from our neighbors. They provide no control. There has also been a significant increase in the number of women in the working world and the capability of the woman to function fully equal with a man (even though sometimes her salary still lags behind his). It is clearly possible for a woman to get along without a man. In addition, there are more single women than there are single men who are eligible for marriage. More single people are choosing to put off marriage, so the stigma of singleness is diminishing. All of these factors force us to take a fresh look at the subject of being single in these closing years of the twentieth century.

Who Is This Single Person?

Describing today's singles is no simpler than describing today's complex world. There are those who see themselves as temporarily single. This is the under-twenty-five age group of singles who graduated from high school, went off to work or college, and expect that they will be raising a family of their own. Many in the twenty-five to thirty-five range are focusing on professional goals without great thought or emphasis on marriage. Then there are those singles who intended to marry, but never did. These people can range all the way from their late twenties to the mid-seventies or older. The never-married group also includes some who chose not to marry (even if they had the opportunity) or some who chose the celibate life to give their energy to the call of God.

Those who are single as the result of divorce make up a large portion of the single world. Relatively few people marry with the anticipation of divorce, so singleness comes as a shocking intrusion into their life plans. There are many variations within the divorced group. There may be the young woman of twenty-two whose marriage lasted only eight months because her husband was violent with her. She got out of the marriage and feels rather scarred, but she is young and has her whole life before her. On the other hand, the divorce group also may include the thirty-eight-year-old husband whose wife left him with three kids. Now he is trying to be mother, father—and breadwinner, as well. Still others may have been divorced for fifteen or twenty years and have no hope or desire ever to marry again. Some couples lived together until the kids were through college and married, and then got a divorce as a statement of how unfulfilling life had been for them during those family-raising years.

The single group also includes those who are single because of the death of a beloved spouse. The widows and the widowers face the shock (often violent) of the trauma of death at an unexpected time. They now find themselves floundering among the singles. The feelings they report are different from those of other singles.

Sexual experience, viewpoints, and needs vary greatly for singles. For the twenty-one-year-old virgin, whether male or female, the sexual drive is quite different than it is for the divorced person of thirty-three whose sexual life has suddenly been shut off because of the loss of a spouse. Thus, it is important as we look at singleness and sexuality that we consider all variations, recognizing that there is no one simple answer that is readily applicable to all circumstances.

It is important for the authors to add a disclaimer here. We are not single, and we haven't been single for more than three decades! So we do not write about singleness out of our experience. Yes, we have talked with dozens, if not hundreds, of single people about their struggles, but that is different than writing from personal experience. We were married during our last years of college at age twenty-one, and have lived together now for more than a quarter of a century. We acknowledge that we write as outsiders, but trust that the insights gained from the open sharing of our single friends and clients will come close to defining the experience of those who are single. We hope it will be of some help in your life.

Painting the Singles Scene

Let's begin by attempting to get a realistic picture. There is an ever-increasing gap between the time when a young person's body is ready for sexual activity and the time when marriage is likely to occur.

If a young person is going to complete college or graduate school and then begin working, it may well be that he or she will put off marriage until the late twenties or even early thirties. Many of us encourage couples to wait until their mid-twenties to marry because the statistics show that younger marriages have a higher incidence of divorce than do later marriages. This makes sense. We change a great deal after leaving the parental home. As we grow older, we find ourselves to be more thoughtful in our choices. We know ourselves better.

This dilemma (of the body being ready for sexual activity but educational and societal influences pushing marriage later and later) leaves many young adults with ten to fifteen years of sexual readiness before marriage. While the sexual urges are at their peak, there is no acceptable outlet. Granted, many people agree with Charlie Shedd, who has called masturbation "God's gift to single people," but it is a gift with clearly limited potential for fulfillment. It takes care of the physical needs, but the emotional and spiritual dimension of sexual intimacy is absent.

Let us underscore the reality and vitality of every person's sexuality. We are sexual beings from even before birth. It is impossible for us not to be sexual. Our body functions sexually right from birth. A little boy has his first erection within minutes after birth, and a little girl has her first vaginal lubrication within hours after birth. We are sexual persons not only because of our physiology but also by the maleness and femaleness that is a part of who we are. As we move beyond puberty, we feel natural physical attraction to people of the opposite sex. That is how God designed us, so there is no way that we can be single and not be sexual. We *are* sexual, and that sexuality is confirmed not only by our physiology but also by our emotions and by our spirits.

Obviously, the single person has to take responsibility for how he or she expresses that sexuality. As the limerick at the beginning of this chapter indicated, conception, infection, and detection used to be the controls on singles' sexual activity. All three of these controls have changed radically. The easy availability of birth-control methods, especially the pill, has drastically altered the dating structure. The advent of the pill clearly is one of the benchmarks of modern social change. One can now safely engage in sexual activity without fear of impregnation, relatively speaking.

Next, while the moral attitudes about premarital sex may still be endorsed in our homes, churches, or society, modern birth control provides the possibility of private involvement without the fear of pregnancy. It does require a conscious choice on the part of the single person to be sexually active. That is a difficult decision for singles who believe sex outside of marriage is wrong. Thus, about 85 percent of first-time sexual experiences of single people are unplanned. Since they do not consciously decide that they are ready for sexual intercourse, the couple proceeds unprotected. Too often, the result is an unwanted pregnancy. Conception is an unnecessary dilemma for the single person. Birth control is readily available, but the conflict between sexual drives, social standards, and moral convictions keeps the person from actively confronting the decision of sexual behavior.

As mentioned earlier, infection is back in the picture in a deadly way. The incidence of sexually transmitted diseases rises every year. Infections are usually contracted outside of marriage. There is no cure for herpes and AIDS and the tedious, expensive medical process of eradicating precancerous genital warts can be life-changing. Thus, the thinking single person has to be much more cautious. Abstinence is again "in" on the high school and college campuses, at least as an option.

With the mobility and fragmentation of our society, "getting caught" while having intercourse is seldom an issue. Young people, even of high-school age, are often home by themselves for extended periods of time while both parents are working. There is the freedom to use the automobile, the truck camper, or the van. After high school, most young people live apart from their families in unrestricted settings. Hence, they are free to make their own sexual choices without detection.

While detection and conception are losing their power as sexual controls, society saturates the single person with sexuality.

Magazines, movies, videos, television, conversations—all promote an easy acceptance of not only sexual enticement, but also of sexual activity. This is available for all to see from an early age. Young people are talking in sexual terms in the elementary grades. Junior-high kids are very free in their language, and high-school students behave as if they are beyond the need for any kind of sexual education. This apparent openness and freedom surrounding sexuality should imply greater knowledge, and bode well for healthy sexual adjustment in later years. But it doesn't. While sex may saturate our world, accurate sexual knowledge and healthy decisions do not necessarily accompany freedom to use sexual language or to observe sexual activity on the screen.

Since the Christian community is a part of the world in which we live, its sexual practices for singles have changed as radically as those in society. Our research among single-adult groups has confirmed what others have reported: Sexual intercourse is an activity that many single Christians choose. This is occurring much more frequently than was true in times past. The justification varies greatly from one person to the other.

One twenty-six-year-old woman told us that, as a Christian, she had always felt she shouldn't be sexually active before marriage. But because she was not sure she was ever going to marry and since she was going to be responsible in her activity, she decided to make the choice to be involved totally—and not feel guilty about it.

In contrast, a thirty-four-year-old divorced woman reported being very distraught because of her sexual impulses and desires. These urges had been so regularly and satisfyingly fulfilled in her marriage that she found it too difficult to abstain from sex after her divorce. She continued to be sexually active, but told of feeling guilty for violating her belief that sex should only occur within marriage.

Both of these women claim to be committed Christians; both are involved sexually. But their responses to that involvement were completely different. These are typical examples of singles who are sexually involved.

There are also single people who choose not to be sexually involved outside of marriage. When this is a conscious choice with an alternative plan to keep sexual feelings alive and other intimacy needs fulfilled, contentment is possible. Both the sexually active and the sexually inactive single will experience times of frustration.

The Frustration of Being Single

The lack of physical, sexual fulfillment without the marriage commitment is an ongoing frustration for the single person of whatever age. There is that natural urge in each of us to connect in a vital way with another person, and when fulfilling that urge is limited or totally absent frustration occurs. Finding ways to minimize this frustration is an ongoing struggle for many single people. Some struggle with their sexual frustration on a daily or perhaps hourly basis, while others only wrestle with it occasionally.

If you feel continually frustrated physically, we encourage you to look at your life and see what you are doing that promotes this frustration. Do you spend time watching or reading sexually explicit material? That will certainly feed your frustration. Are you physically involved with a partner, getting highly aroused without orgasm or intercourse? This also will create physical frustration. Is your life empty, leaving you time to become obsessed with your sexual drives? Is self-stimulation an option? Obviously, there is a limit to the degree of fulfillment possible with oneself. Yes, an orgasm may be possible, but it may still leave you hungry for the intimacy of a relationship.

This lack of emotional intimacy is a common frustration of the single person. Every person needs the experience of close, vital, and meaningful relationships with parents, brothers, sisters, friends, persons of the same sex, or persons of the opposite sex. In adulthood, most of us need the additional bond of intimacy with one person of the opposite sex. This emotional attachment, although possible outside of marriage, is often missing for the single adult. Intimacy, closeness, and affection that meet those deeper, intangible needs can happen with people who are "just friends," or relatives. It can even happen within groups. Yet as we talk with single people, especially those who have been single for a number of years, we hear them speak of the hunger they feel for that vital connection with a single, "significant other."

Not only do single adults feel frustrations about sexual fulfillment and lack of emotional intimacy, they also may feel the frustration of not having a place in society. Most of society, with the exception of cosmopolitan collections of single people in major cities, is designed for married people and families. Thus, it's not surprising that many single adults feel unaccepted by their communities. The same thing happens in the church. If you look at the roster of church leaders in any major church, whether it be fundamentalist, evangelical, or more liberal, the great majority of the people on that roster will be married. Single people are rarely leaders in the Christian community, yet they make up a significant portion of society and church membership. Most social structures within the church community are not designed for single people. Even though many churches now offer singles groups and classes, single people often feel isolated with the other singles—away from the larger church family. So the single person often feels out of place and left out.

Being sexually active does not eliminate that sense of being alone within the social structure. In addition, you may live with the ongoing agony of guilt. The biblical expectation and guideline is rather clear: Sexual intercourse is reserved for marriage. If you are a believer and you desire to live by the standards of the Scriptures, then it is inevitable that you will struggle as you actively choose to go against what you believe.

You may have come to the point when you reconcile yourself to the fact that you are going to have sexual intercourse. Yet that underlying feeling of guilt may be a bur under your emotional saddle, keeping your emotions continually troubled. This does not mean you are not enjoying the sexual activity, it only means that you have not been able to find inner peace. You are not living by the standard to which you claim to be committed. There is tension or ambivalence within you. All of this frustration calls loudly for a *decision*.

Make a Decision: The Options

First, let's consider the choices single adults are making. Then we will look at how you go about making your decision.

Choice 1: Deny your sexual feelings. This may be one of the easiest choices to make, even though the long-term consequences are quite severe. All of us were created as sexual beings. Our Creator has ignited a sexual fire within us. To deny its power is to close down a vital dimension of ourselves. Long-term, we risk the consequence of being unable to rekindle those feelings when it is time to do so in marriage.

It is not uncommon for the young person who has either been raised in an emotionally/sexually unexpressive home to be unaware of sexual feelings. The single person who is intensely sexual may shut off those feelings because their power is frightening. Such a person may behave and feel as if he or she had no sexual feelings. This choice is understandable, but its detrimental consequences far outweigh its benefits.

We have worked with these consequences in young married couples who have no desire for one another. They just don't have the feelings! Sometimes one or both spouses report that they chose the route of denying their sexual feelings, believing this was what God wanted them to do before they were married. They hadn't separated their actions from their feelings. To be able to remain virgins, they had chosen to be asexual—only to discover, as they moved into marriage, that they continued to be asexual. The pain and the sense of being shortchanged are very powerful for these people because they had operated on the belief that if they did not let themselves be sexual before marriage, God would bless them with a free and abundant sexual life after marriage.

Sexuality does not work this way. It is an innate appetite, just like hunger. People can control how much they eat, just as they can control their sexual behavior. But when they shut down their appetites for food they become anorexic; likewise, if they turn off their sexual feelings, they become sexually apathetic. And this apathy sometimes continues beyond the point when they say "I do."

There is another consequence of denying sexual feelings. It happened, for example, to a young woman who had always been pushed sexually by men. Finally she met the man who would become her spouse. "He was such a gentleman. He really respected me," she said. It was such a relief not to be pushed. But the dilemma occurred after marriage. He continued to "respect" her; in fact, he *resisted* sex. Thus, after marriage, her husband's lack of sexual desire created great frustration, when, before marriage it had brought relief.

Be on the lookout for the denial of sexual feelings. Any couple moving toward marriage who has decided not to engage in sexual intercourse before marriage should experience that decision as a struggle. To maintain the boundaries you have chosen should be difficult. If it is not, you should take a long, hard look at yourselves and the relationship. In a close, loving relationship, abstinence should be a battle. Our bodies, our hearts, our emotions, our spirits—every ounce of our beings— urge us toward sexual union. If you are not aware of this urge, you may have denied your sexual feelings so long that it will be difficult for you to revive them. This will cause stress in your marriage—sometimes marriage-breaking stress.

Choice 2: Innocent involvement. Innocent involvement may grow out of ineffective attempts to deny sexual feelings or from failing to actively decide *not* to act on the feelings. If you are unable to accept your sexuality and yet continually find yourself going beyond your sexual limits, you set yourself up for involvement beyond your readiness. The sequence usually goes something like this: You meet a nice person and begin some casual, and then more serious, contact with him or her. You innocently send off many warm and inviting messages with no intention of acting upon them. You let yourself get into situations—in a car, your parents' home, your apartment, or even a motel—all the time convincing yourself that this is just a friendly contact that has no sexual purpose or intent.

Some couples even go so far as to bathe or sleep together without consciously intending to be involved sexually. As time together progresses, there is more and more physical involvement. You find yourself carried along, either by the urges in your body or your partner's body, and you end up making love. When it is all over, the rush of guilt and remorse is overwhelming. You commit to yourself and together that you will never do this again. You ask each other's forgiveness and you ask God's forgiveness. But two weeks later you find yourselves in identical circumstances.

The consequences of this pattern are very severe. First of all, since you can't get yourself to plan for it, no birth-control measures are taken, so you risk the chance of pregnancy.

Second, since you don't "intend" to do this, you don't provide yourself with the privacy that you need to really relax and enjoy it. You learn to have sexual experiences under tense circumstances, developing poor habits.

Third, since involvement isn't your intention, you develop a pattern of always connecting sexual activity with high risk. Later on in married life, you may still need risk as a part of your sexual experience to help you get the desired response of excitement.

Fourth, you violate your own standards, and thus you violate yourself. You experience guilt and the chronic internal ache that it brings. This sets you up for a future in which you may need to feel guilt as a part of your sexual arousal. As we do sexual therapy with couples, we hear stories about risk and guilt patterns that were established early in a relationship. These patterns are difficult to break.

Fifth, you may experience guilt in relation to God. If you are a Christian with a commitment to reserve sexual intercourse for marriage, then each time you violate that standard you will not only feel guilt in relation to yourself but also guilt in relation to God. Soon God and your sexuality become mutually exclusive. Innocent involvement is one of the most irresponsible and destructive patterns; it often leads to negative consequences later in marriage. We are not suggesting that you should "sin boldly," but we can say that from the perspective of marital and sexual adjustment, the next choice is clearly preferable to innocent involvement.

Choice 3: Chosen involvement. Some couples actively choose to complete their relationship with sexual intercourse, even though sex outside of marriage contradicts biblical teaching. They work to make peace with their standards and beliefs. They prepare for their sexual times together. They behave as if they were married. We encourage couples who are struggling with this particular choice to read Dr. Lewis B. Smedes's book, *Sex for Christians*.

The Bible is very clear that sex is for marriage. Those who choose to have sexual intercourse before marriage, yet accept the Bible as their standard for Christian living, often live with dissonance between their beliefs and their behavior. Others do not. Couples may bypass many other stages of intimacy if they jump into a total, sexual relationship. There may be a sense of vulnerability and insecurity without the trust-building commitment of marriage. There is no data to suggest that sex before marriage is an indication of how sex will be after marriage. The emotional dimension of sex before marriage is very different than that of sex after marriage. In fact, we have counseled a number of couples who claim to have had a very fulfilling sexual life before marriage, only to find it falling apart after marriage. Obedience, commitment, intimacy, and trust are all essential ingredients to a long-term happy sexual life.

Choice 4: Chosen abstinence. This is a healthy choice that fits the biblical directives on sexuality. It is least likely to lead to irresponsibility and guilt—but it is not easy! It is extremely difficult to choose to be a sexual person—aware of your feelings, knowing your impulses, responsive to kissing, touching, and caressing—and then choosing not to take your sexual desires to their natural conclusion. It is as conflict-laden as having a beautiful meal before you and choosing only to nibble at it rather than to heartily partake. For high-school or college-age young people who have chosen to limit their physical involvement to general hugging and kissing it is a boundary that is difficult but possible because it is consistent with where they are emotionally and developmentally.

As we can attest by our own experience and the experiences of many other couples, abstinence before marriage is possible. It is not a barrier to a fulfilling sexual life in marriage (as is often propagated by those who don't hold the biblical standard). For the thirty-year-olds who already have been active sexually, either unmarried or in marriage, and then choose abstinence, the internal pressure can be almost impossible. Once the floodgates of sexuality have been opened, incredible inner strength is required to hold back these urges. Abstinence is not easy to live with day after day and sometimes year after year. With these people, we want to be sympathetic and understanding, but we have not been through that struggle. The abstinence we practiced at age nineteen or twenty is not the same. We know couples, however, who have been able to maintain abstinence after being sexually involved, and they have done so joyfully.

When abstinence is the chosen route, it is important to plan for that. Do not set yourselves up to test the limits. Focus on all dimensions of the relationship. Emphasize activities and settings that are not tempting. Learn to enjoy physical intimacy within clearly defined limits that both of you respect. Richard J. Foster, in his book, *Money, Sex and Power,* deals very specifically with this whole subject. We recommend it!

Choice 5: Celibacy as a lifestyle. In 1 Corinthians 7:8–9 and 32–38 the Apostle Paul talks about the calling of celibacy. There is an important distinction to make between the lifestyles of chosen celibacy and chosen abstinence. Celibacy is for those who experience themselves as being called by God to stay single in order to serve humankind. It is very different than abstaining from sexual intercourse until marriage is possible. The apostle is saying that if you have your sexual desires well under control (not that you do not have any), and feel the distinct calling of God to serve, and you have an outlet for that calling, then celibacy may be your choice. We have known few people who fit into this category. They are people who choose a lifestyle of subjugating their sexual-drive energy and channeling it into outlets of service. Very few manage this well, but it is clearly one of the options.

Those are the choices. There may be some variations of these basic options, but every single person will fit roughly into one of these categories. Some singles may find themselves in one of these situations—but it's not by their choice. This is indeed a difficult and trying circumstance. If this is your circumstance, you need to make a decision about how you will make the most of who you are as a sexual person, given the reality of your situation.

Make a Decision: The Necessary Ingredients

Now that you know the options, how do you decide on the level of your sexual involvement as a Christian single person?

Know yourself. To be responsibly decisive about sexual activity requires self-awareness. Let's break that down into the various parts. First of all, you need to *know your own body.* How you feel about your body will have been influenced by the kind of touch and affirmation you received growing up. It is vital that you understand how your body works, what your needs are, how frequently you feel sexual urges, what kind of touch you desire, and how all dimensions of your sexuality converge to express the sexual you.

It is terribly important also to *know your emotions*. You may have grown up in a home where you learned to keep your feelings very much to yourself. If so, you don't find it comfortable to have others express their emotions, nor are you eager to share yours. Or you may have learned a style that is open and expressive. In fact, you need openness to feel trust.

A married couple came to us for sexual therapy. The man had grown up in a home in the Midwest with eight brothers and sisters, a very controlling, domineering mother, and a rather irresponsible father. He had learned that he wouldn't get hurt if he kept his feelings to himself, so that was the style he brought into marriage. His wife, on the other hand, had grown up in an expressive home. Feelings were the road to intimacy. She had great sexual passion while the man felt almost no need for sexual contact because he had learned to function independently from anyone else's response.

As you are making the choice about sexual behavior, you must understand your emotional needs in relation to that choice. How can you make your choice work for you, given who you are emotionally?

Know your value system. What do you believe? What is important to you? How do you feel about sharing your body with another person? You are responsible for your body. You are the only one who can decide when and to what degree you want to share it.

Whether you grew up in a home where you were taught that sex outside of marriage is sinful, whether that is a new belief for you, or whether you believe that rule doesn't apply to you today, it is essential that you come to peace with your beliefs. It may be helpful to test them with your Christian community and the Bible. The decision you make has to be congruent with what you believe. You can seek information, you can read books, you can hear sermons, you can listen to lectures and tapes, and you can receive letters from your mother, but ultimately the decision has to be based on your own convictions. Your mother won't be there when you feel those strong sexual urges in response to the person who makes you pulsate.

You have to make the decision. You can't count on anyone else at that particular moment. God's spirit can be with you and give you strength, but you have to want that spirit there as you struggle with your powerful urge. Single Christians need to be clear about their values and date only people who have similar values. Otherwise, they will find themselves pulled to be different than who they are.

A split value system can be a real dilemma. It tends to cause havoc within individuals (especially long-term), as they try to live out two sets of beliefs that cannot fit together.

Know your limits. Whenever we speak to single adults, we are asked, "How far is it OK to go? Where do we draw the line?" There is a temptation to quickly jump in and give an answer, to set a standard so that the questioner has been satisfied. We refuse to set the standard, other than the biblical one of intercourse within marriage (1 Cor. 7:1–2; 1 Thess. 4:3–7; Heb. 13:4; Matt. 15:18–20; Eph. 5:3; and 1 Cor. 6:9).

Once you accept the biblical calling, then you need to decide the level of involvement that will allow you to live a life consistent with your beliefs. That decision must be based upon clearly defined values, knowledge of your body's sexual responses, sexual-emotional awareness, and a discerning understanding of the levels of sexual involvement. These levels are:

Hand holding and hugging
Polite Kissing
Total mouth kissing
Intense, passionate hugging
Full-body rubbing with clothes on
Breast stimulation over clothes
Genital stimulation over clothes
Breast stimulation under clothes
Genital stimulation under clothes
Full-body pleasuring, no clothes
Oral/Genital stimulation
Sexual stimulation to orgasm
Intercourse

As explained earlier, when beliefs and behaviors conflict, guilt becomes linked with sexual arousal. This causes problems later in marriage because guilt and risk may then be needed to become aroused. So, for both emotional and spiritual well-being, your sexual decisions must reflect your spiritual and biblical standards.

Know your strengths and weaknesses. All of us gain strength from a variety of sources. If you need eight or ten hours of sleep to make wise decisions, then you must be responsible for getting that sleep before you decide. You may be someone who needs regular exercise to function properly. Know that drugs and alcohol reduce your capacity to say no. It may be that you find great strength in being together with other people who have commitments similar to yours—a Bible study group, a prayer group, a sharing and support group, a group with a mission, or an athletic, artistic, or political group. It is vital that you know where you get strength and what causes weakness. A source of strength for many individuals is a commitment to be accountable to one other person regarding their sexual behavior. Again, you must know yourself as you seek to live consistently with what you believe.

Questions Singles Ask

I find that I—and many of my single friends—live much of our lives in frustration. What can we do about this?

As we acknowledged earlier in this chapter, frustration for the single person can come from many different sources. Perhaps your frustration grows out of living as if life will begin when you find a mate. Or your frustration may be that your only contacts are people who have a different value system than yours and who set different limits than you do. You may find yourself continually sexually aroused, but always sexually frustrated. In all these circumstances, it is important to recognize that you *can* do something about it. Begin to live your life as it happens now, not as something you are waiting for. You can actively choose to be involved with those who live by the same values as you do. You can choose not to set yourself up to be perpetually frustrated. You can also choose to bring yourself relief through self-stimulation.

What about masturbation for the single, committed Christian?

Masturbation, at best, provides physical relief for the sexual urges and needs of the body until they can be relieved in a relationship with another person. If you have committed yourself to save sexual intercourse for marriage, then your only sexual outlet prior to marriage will either be through the intentional release from self-stimulation or through wet dreams (involuntary release during sleep) for men, and orgasmic release for women during sleep. As we understand the body, once it has reached puberty, it is designed to have regular sexual release. While not every person will experience the need for that release, most do. Self-stimulation provides that release without violating what we understand to be the biblical standard. As long as it is not an addictive obsession or associated with pornography, we find that masturbation does not cause turmoil in the individual's life, but rather brings relief. In fact, release through self-stimulation may help a single person adhere to his or her sexual boundaries when dating. When the sexual-drive needs have been taken care of before a date, the capacity for intimacy without sexual fulfillment will be easier.

Is it acceptable for a Christian to fantasize about sex?

From our perspective, whether you are a Christian or not, you have an imagination and that imagination is filled with a variety of images. This is how God created us to be different from the animals. Since you are a sexual being, some of those images will be sexual; there is no way around that. Sexual images will pass through our minds, unless all sexual feelings have been shut down. What we do with those sexual images will determine whether that fantasy moves into lust. So the answer is yes, fantasies or imagination about sexual subjects are very normal and natural. They become lustful when we are obsessed or enslaved by them, or when we would act on them if we could.

When should the boundaries in a relationship be set and who should set them?

Boundaries should be set at ten o'clock in the morning over a cup of coffee rather than eleven o'clock at night in the heat of passion. And *you* should set them. Determine your limits, independently, before you discuss them with your boyfriend or girlfriend.

Can a single person ever be fulfilled in the sense of intimacy?

It is important to recognize that there are many different expressions of intimacy. Different interests and involvements can make us feel intimate with one another. We can be open in sharing our feelings, which can bring close emotional intimacy. We can share extensively about our relationship with God, which will usually bring spiritual intimacy. We may focus on artistic expression—the enjoyment of a symphony or the appreciation of great art that encourages an aesthetic intimacy. We may be committed to tasks that bring us recreational or vocational intimacy. Yes, a single person can be fulfilled in many areas of intimacy. It is unlikely that your *sexual* intimacy needs will be met as a single person if you are choosing not to be involved in sexual intercourse before marriage. But that can well be compensated for by many other forms of intimacy.

If we hold very carefully to limiting our physical involvement before marriage, can we count on God's blessing after marriage?

God's commandments do not come as a bargain. In His Word, God does not say that if we follow certain guidelines we will have a happy or fulfilled life. It is a fact that many couples who have not had sexual intercourse before marriage have ended up very happy in their life together. On the other hand, many couples who did not even kiss before they were married have ended up very unhappy in their sexual life. We can also tell you about those who were totally involved sexually before marriage who ended up unhappy—and others who found great fulfillment. The level of premarital sexual involvement is not a predictor of future marital sexual fulfillment. So the reason for following the guidelines is not so that married life will be happy and fulfilling; instead, we have to trust that it is God's command and it will ultimately be for our best.

What do you think of two Christian singles of the opposite sex living together without being sexually involved if they intend to be married?

Frankly, we think it is very destructive. To live together, be "turned on to one another," and not be able to respond to those urges forces people to shut down their sexual feelings. When they marry, it may be almost impossible to get that sexual arousal and response turned back on. We have only known this to be a detrimental pattern and would not encourage it at all.

What if I never marry? Will I be an unfulfilled person never having experienced sexual intercourse?

If you have never experienced sexual intercourse, you are no less a person. Many wonderful people have gone through their whole lives unmarried, never having experienced a total sexual union. They are still great friends, servants, caregivers, and wonderful people of God.

For Further Study

Bird, Joseph, and Lois Bird. "Reasons You May Never Have Considered for Staying Single." *New Woman* (January/February 1982): 102–3.

Clarkson, Margaret. "Singleness: His Share for Me." *Christianity Today* (16 February 1979): 14–15.

Colgrove, Melba, Harold Bloomfield, and Peter Williams. *How to Survive the Loss of a Love.* New York: Bantam Books, 1984.

Forbes, Cheryl. "Let's Not Shackle the Single Life." *Christianity Today* (16 February 1979): 16–19.

*Foster, Richard J. *Money, Sex and Power.* San Francisco: Harper and Row, 1985.

Johnson, James R. "Toward a Biblical Approach to Masturbation." *Journal of Psychology and Theology,* 10, no. 2 (Summer 1982): 137–46.

Laury, G.V., M.D. "Myths About Masturbation Throughout the Ages." *Journal of Sex Education and Therapy,* 11, no. 5 (Summer 1979): 3–4.

Linton, Calvin D. "Dying to the God Who Is Me." *Christianity Today* (16 February 1979): 14–15.

Penner, Clifford L., Ph.D. "A Reaction to Johnson's Biblical Approach to Masturbation." *Journal of Psychology and Theology*, 10, no. 2 (Summer 1982): 146–49.

Smedes, Lewis B. *Sex for Christians*. Grand Rapids: William B. Eerdmans Publishing Co., 1976.

Smith, Harold Ivan. "Sex and Singleness the Second Time Around." *Christianity Today* (23 May 1979): 16–22.

Swindoll, Luci. *Wide My World; Narrow My Bed*. Portland, Oreg.: Multnomah Press, 1982.

*This book is no longer in print, but is available at many libraries.

Part 5

Handling Adult Sexuality in Special Situations

14

Sex and the Unconsummated Marriage

Four True Stories

Craig and Evelyn

Craig and Evelyn sat fidgeting as they began to unfold their story. They were a handsome couple in their late twenties; he was a college professor and she a nurse. Obviously, both were college graduates, and he had two advanced degrees. Evelyn had been reared on a farm in the Midwest with six brothers and sisters while Craig had just one sister and was from a large city on the West Coast. Both had grown up in loving and caring homes, but with little sexual information. As they tearfully told their story, we were gripped by the pain of three and a half years of marriage without consummation, without intercourse, without entry.

During their dating months, especially after engagement, they had difficulty controlling their sexual impulses. But being committed to wait for marriage, they held off having intercourse until their wedding night and honeymoon. With high expectations, they left the wedding celebration for a two-week vacation in the Caribbean. The excitement of being able to fulfill their love with each other engulfed them. Then came the disappointment. The first evening Craig had a firm erection for a long time, but when he attempted entry, it seemed like he was pushing against a brick wall. They tried again and again for the two weeks of their honeymoon, becoming more and more discouraged, yet convinced that they should be able to make it work.

After the honeymoon, Craig and Evelyn began married life together. The adjustment went smoothly. They worked well as a team, except sexually. The excitement and desire for each other's bodies waned as they would try to have intercourse, at first once or twice a week, then less and less frequently. By the time they saw us, they hadn't attempted anything sexual for several months. Originally, he was the initiator and they would both get aroused. Evelyn would experience nipple erection, vaginal lubrication, and even enjoy pleasurable stimulation, and yet somehow they could not manage to guide the penis into the vagina. After the years of trying unsuccessfully, Craig began to lose his erections as he attempted to penetrate. So now there were dual problems: an inability to penetrate and his inability to maintain an erection.

The natural question is: What would perpetuate a long-term dilemma like this when sex is supposed to be something so natural? Is it that difficult to get the penis into the vagina? Usually it isn't. But in this couple's case, several circumstances converged to conspire against them.

Evelyn had grown up in a strict Christian home. Her parents strongly disapproved of an older man she was dating. As she became more and more involved with him, she innocently or half-consciously let the physical involvement progress to the point where one time, in the car, he had penetrated her vaginally. She had screamed, jerked away, and shut out the experience from her memory. She broke up with the man and behaved as if the incident had never happened, broke up with the man. She never told Craig about this earlier experience. Now, whenever she engaged in sexual activity similar to that traumatic episode, her vagina would automatically tighten. The vaginal muscle would become so tense that Craig could not enter.

Craig had grown up in a very meticulous home where children were clearly taught to avoid all messiness. His mother had communicated the message that anything that had to do with the genital area was dirty or "yucky." It was very difficult for him to enjoy Evelyn's genitals because they were aversive to him. This was especially true as she would lubricate. Since he experienced her lubrication negatively, he stopped any genital touching once she began to respond. This interrupted any preparation that would have helped her relax for entry. He was very responsive, however, and so he initially had firm erections. As his efforts at entry failed, however, he began to experience impotence. By the time they sought help, this impotence occurred in virtually every attempt.

By now Evelyn was very down on herself, feeling miserable that she was not "normal," and Craig was feeling less and less like a man. Men are supposed to know how to do this, he believed, and he was not succeeding. Depression, hurt, and bitterness were permeating their relationship, which had been great in every other area. They had communicated effectively and really enjoyed each other. But the sexual area began to overshadow everything else, threatening their relationship.

Suzanne and Tom

Suzanne and Tom were also in their late twenties. Suzanne worked as a secretary for a local church, and Tom worked as a grocery store checker. When they came to see us they had been married six months. Before they were married they had thoroughly enjoyed rubbing their bodies against each other (fully clothed), and had often found themselves getting highly aroused. But on the honeymoon, at each attempt at entry, Tom would lose his erection and wouldn't be able to "do it." In subsequent attempts, as he would get an erection, he would attempt entry, but at the point of contact he would lose his erection. General love play and kissing did not bring him much arousal. Only oral stimulation got him firm enough to attempt entry.

Suzanne had been raised in a very prim-and-proper home in which sexual subjects were never discussed. The implied message was that sex is dirty, it is a pleasure that shouldn't be enjoyed, and it will be painful—and sure enough it was!

The longer Suzanne and Tom went on trying, the more frustrated and discouraged they became. Their experiences became briefer with less and less preparation. At first they tried once or twice a week, but as failure followed failure, their number of attempts diminished. Now even when they enjoyed love play together, they did not attempt intercourse.

Suzanne came to the marriage with relatively little experience and with conflict about the sexual pleasure they had experienced during dating. On the wedding night she was absolutely exhausted from all the family stress that centered around disagreements with her mother about the wedding.

Tom had developed the habit of masturbating during adolescence, but with a great deal of guilt. His particular approach had been to stimulate himself to ejaculation, often without a full erection. After ten years of practice, this pattern of sexual release without an erection was deeply ingrained. Yet Tom came to the wedding night without any anxiety about their performance. He knew how aroused Suzanne became when he stimulated her breasts and when they rubbed their bodies together. He had no fear or concern about how they would do together.

Fred and Carol

Fred and Carol were in their middle thirties. Fred was pastor of a growing suburban church. Carol, a social worker, counseled at a community mental-health center. They came for help regarding their unconsummated marriage. They had been married four months without sexual "success."

Carol had been married before and had been sexually active between her divorce and her marriage to Fred. After her divorce she had been traumatically raped, but felt that this should not be impacting her sexual experience with Fred since she had had sexual intercourse with other men after the rape.

Fred came from the opposite end of the experience spectrum. He had been raised in a rural community, had always been a bright student, and was dominated by his mother who had pushed him into pursuing education. She discouraged emotional expression and depreciated involvement with girls. Thus, Fred was shy. He did not go through the kiss-and-run stage of junior high. He had almost no dating experience and virtually no sexual awareness. At age fourteen, he had been part of a group of boys at a church camp who sat around, talked about sex, and stimulated themselves. He still harbored the guilt from this sexual experimentation. He had not been married before, had not had intercourse, and had experienced only limited physical contact with women.

On their wedding night he had been both excited and apprehensive. He was eager to be with Carol, but anxious because she had so much more sexual experience than he. He was naturally concerned that he wouldn't measure up. He was not able to keep an erection that night, and thereafter was impotent at the point of entry. Because of Carol's negative experiences with men, she brought a heavy load of anger into the marriage. After a few moments of stimulation, she would soon become bored and impatient.

Being an analytic type of person, Fred became a spectator. He began withdrawing from the pleasure of their experiences to watch what was happening. He became preoccupied with her needs. This only made him more and more anxious. By the time they came to us, his sexual desire was nonexistent and her frustration was at the breaking point. For her, his impotence was one more indication of men's incompetence. They both continued to function well in their chosen professions. Fred was very successful as a pastor, and was well respected, even admired, by his parishioners. Carol carried a full counseling load.

Joe and Elizabeth

By the time Joe and Elizabeth sought us out for sexual therapy, they had managed to consummate their marriage. But their story illustrates a pattern associated with pain for the woman and the unconsummated marriage.

Joe and Elizabeth had been active sexually after high school, but not to the point of intercourse. As their Christian commitment deepened, they made a decision that they would severely limit the degree of their sexual involvement before marriage. Both were eager on the wedding night because they anticipated that their sexual life would be wonderful. They had felt so much arousal during whatever physical play they had before marriage that they were totally shocked on their wedding night when they were unable to complete the sexual act. The reason for Joe's not being able to enter was Elizabeth's pain. Penetration was possible, but it was so severely painful that she drew back from it immediately. As is always true with pain, her desire diminished very quickly. A year after their marriage, the stated problem was her lack of desire. (The pain was identified in the assessment process.)

Sexuality was not discussed in Elizabeth's home when she was growing up. It was the "unmentionable" subject that brought a mixture of titters and frowns. Joe was a meticulous, if not obsessive, person. His career as an architect fit him nicely. He was very successful at his work. Since he was highly goal-oriented, it was difficult for him to back off from striving for intercourse, and this only elevated Elizabeth's resistance, pain, and eventual depression. By the time they saw us it had been eight months since they'd had intercourse.

What's the Problem?

When a couple is unable to consummate their marriage, one of four possible problems is present: bumbling, impotence, pain, or vaginismus. Let's talk about each of these problems.

Bumbling

If your lovemaking is a bumbling experience in which each of you feels like you don't know what you are doing, it would not be surprising to learn that you grew up in homes where there was a clear lack of physical affection and attention. It may be that you were not stroked, held on your parent's lap, patted, or wrestled with. As a result, you do not feel comfortable in physical contact with another person. Even if you enjoy touching and being touched, you may feel awkward in the way you touch. You probably avoided the usual kiss-and-run behavior of the typical early adolescent, and then didn't do much dating in high school. In our society, those activities have the positive effect of getting us through our awkwardness and on the way to confidently relating to a person of the opposite sex. When that confidence isn't gained during the developmental years, it must be learned in adulthood.

In a famous psychology experiment, often referred to as "Harlowe's Monkey Experiment," researchers isolated baby monkeys from their mothers, fed them from bottles, and kept them away from anything soft. When it came time for these monkeys to mate, they didn't know what to do. While humans are certainly more complicated than monkeys, the same is true for us. The couple who cannot get things to fit and work together usually needs education and practice making up for the lack of affection of childhood and the experimentation of junior and senior high-school years.

Impotence

The inability to achieve or maintain an erection is called impotence, or erectile dysfunction. We have written about this extensively in *The Gift of Sex,* which offers self-help steps. However, usually sexual therapy is required to reverse an established pattern of impotence. When erectile dysfunction is the reason for an unconsummated marriage and physical causes of impotence have been ruled out, it is usually due to anxiety about performance. (This was Fred's problem, described earlier.) Or it is a response to the inability to penetrate the woman, as was true for Craig, in another of the case studies we shared earlier. In a case like Craig's, impotence is considered secondary to the primary problem of vaginismus.

Pain

Pain is the underrated sexual troublemaker. There is no way a woman will enjoy the sexual experience if it produces pain. If it hurts every time the fingers are in contact with the vaginal opening or every time there is an attempt at entry, the woman is going to have an automatic tightening response. This will make entry more difficult and radically interrupt the sexual responsiveness of the woman. Both husbands and wives, as well as physicians, often play down the significant impact of pain on the sexual experience. First, there is the idea that the initial entry is supposed to hurt anyway. Then there is the myth that women make a bigger deal out of pain than is actually true. And finally, there is the expectation that the only cure for pain during intercourse is time and experience.

True, there is usually some pain at first entry, but for most women it is not severe. This will generally diminish after the first few times. This initial pain can be lessened by regular stretching of the vaginal opening before the first intercourse. Taking plenty of time to pleasure each other's body and using a lubricant will also minimize the discomfort of the first intercourse. Women can and do learn to tolerate intense pain, as evidenced by their stamina in bearing children. There is no evidence to support the idea that women exaggerate pain. Time and repeated painful experiences do not cure the problem. In fact, as pain goes on, there is less and less likelihood that it will be resolved; pain tends to perpetuate itself. The more pain, the more tightness; the more tightness, the more pain.

Pain during intercourse requires systematic intervention. The physical cause must be ascertained while the ability to relax and receive pleasure is being taught.

Vaginismus

The involuntary muscular tightening of the vagina is called vaginismus. The vaginal muscle can tighten to such a degree that it is impossible to insert even a small finger, let alone the penis. This constriction of the muscles in the vaginal outlet (the lower or outer third of the vagina) is a conditioned response to past trauma (like Evelyn's) or to ongoing pain or anxiety. The usual sequence is that sexual arousal occurs, causing blood and fluid to rush into the lower third of the vagina to form the orgasmic platform. But instead of the muscle being pliable, it is tense and rigid. The woman may continue to experience full sexual desire but without the possibility of entry.

The symbolism of vaginismus is clear. Even though it is an unconscious act, the woman is shutting out the man. She is protecting herself from painful past feelings. Sometimes the past cause is one specific traumatic event from the dating process, as in Evelyn's case, or from molestation or rape, as in Carol's example.

Vaginismus is not what we would think of as a disease, rather it is a response of tension that exhibits itself in the front or outer third of the vagina—the area of the pubococcygeus (PC) muscle.

It is a very treatable response. We encourage any woman who struggles with vaginismus to seek help now. You can learn to have control of that muscle and have enjoyable sexual intercourse. (For more detailed information, refer to chapter 14 in our book, *Counseling for Sexual Disorders*.)

Do What Comes Naturally!

No young couple goes into marriage expecting sexual problems. It always comes as a shock when sex doesn't work as it is supposed to. The shock comes because they may have had little instruction, and because they've heard a few off-the-cuff remarks that makes sex sound foolproof. A very common remark is, "Oh, don't worry about anything. Just go do what comes naturally!" If all of us had been raised out in the forest, running around naked as jay birds and living in completely natural settings, we might be able to follow this instruction and just "do what comes naturally." In our society, walking and talking come naturally to us, because we model what we see. But neither healthy sexual interaction nor intercourse is modeled for us. And in those instances where there is a struggle with consummating the marriage, unnatural events in the past may have created obstructions, preventing the individuals from freely expressing themselves sexually. For these couples, sex is not natural.

Just as perfect sex is expected to occur naturally, most couples also believe they should allow their problem to be resolved naturally; so they are hesitant to go for help. Hence, the Evelyns and Craigs waste three years trying to let their problem resolve naturally. Part of the investment in resolving the dilemma on their own is the couple's embarrassment to admit their unconsummated marriage. We would encourage any physicians who read this to be alert to any problem the new bride is trying to express. In every instance we have dealt with, the woman had tried to talk with her physician about it. But because of the woman's hesitancy and because of the physician's hurried schedule (and perhaps his or her insensitivity), the problem was never fully exposed or dealt with in the physician's office. We encourage doctors to ask specific questions that might reveal these problems as they do routine gynecological exams.

What to Do: Ten Steps to Consummation

1. See your physician. He or she can check that every-thing in and around the vagina is structurally OK. Have as much of a pelvic exam as is possible, given the tightness of the vaginal opening. Some women with vaginismus have no problem with the examination in the physician's office, but tighten up once there is arousal and attempt at entry with the penis. Others are tight all the time. The physician, while examining the woman, should have her tighten the vaginal muscle over his or her gloved finger and hold that for several seconds, then release the muscle. That tensing and releasing will often have the effect of freeing the vagina to greater openness. In most instances, it will be dis-covered that there is nothing physiologically wrong. We have written a detailed guide for therapists in *Counseling for Sexual Disorders.*

2. Practice PC muscle exercises. Four times each day, do twenty Kegel exercises, tightening and relaxing the vaginal muscles. For vaginismus, the relaxation part of these exercises is the most important. To learn to do the exercise, begin by sitting on the toilet and stopping and starting urination. To tighten, be-gin at the outer edge of the vagina. Squeeze the vagina tightly, hold to the count of three, and then relax—totally let go. Then imagine your vagina is an elevator. Start at the outer edge of the vagina and move in (or up). Tighten, as if going up the elevator, stopping to hold at each floor until you are on the fifth floor. Come down by letting out the tension at each floor. When you're at the bottom, the vagina should be completely relaxed. This will take time to learn. Your vagina has been tight for a long time. Relaxation won't happen immediately.

3. Use dilators. The physician or sex therapist should give clear instruction in the use of graduated sizes of penis-shaped dilators. Some are manufactured specifically for this purpose. If those are unavailable or too costly, sterilized syringe covers of varying thicknesses from the physician can function just as ad-equately. Before the smallest dilator is inserted, the woman should again tighten her vagina and hold it for three to five seconds, and then relax. Tightening first will allow greater relaxation of the muscles. A lubricant such as KY jelly, Allercreme, or Albolene should be applied to the dilator. For some women, it is easier to insert the dilator when alone. Others prefer having their husbands insert it. If the husband is to insert the dilator, the woman should guide the man as he gently inserts the smallest dilator into the vagina, being very careful not to cause any pain or distress. The woman will feel most comfortable if she can watch the process in a mirror. The dilator should be kept in the vagina for at least fifteen minutes—preferably an hour.

4. Enjoy pleasuring. While the dilator is in the vagina, the woman should be comfortably relaxed as the man pleasures her total body as set forth in *The Gift of Sex* or other books that describe sensate focus. Do not focus on arousal, but rather on pleasure—the skin-to-skin contact. Arousal may occur for the woman but that is incidental. The goal is to help her relax and enjoy pleasure while the dilator is in the vagina. This can be followed by the woman caressing and pleasuring her husband.

5. Communicate. It is vital that the spouses keep talking with each other. During the pleasuring times it would be best to focus on enjoying the touch and bodily sensations. Away from the pleasuring time, talk about fears, anxieties, concerns, and past experiences that seem to be connected with this involuntary vaginal closure. If communication is difficult for the couple, they should seek professional help.

6. Increase dilator size. The dilators should be used daily for twenty to forty minutes. When the husband is not around, the woman can insert them herself. It is always important to tighten the vaginal muscle and hold it for a few seconds and then relax before penetrating with the dilator. Continue to tighten and relax the PC muscle with the dilator in the vagina. The size of the dilators can increase quite quickly as the woman learns to relax her vaginal muscles. If it is possible to sleep with the dilator in place, that is even more helpful.

The goal is to move to the largest size possible as quickly as possible without causing pain. The ideal schedule is for the couple to have a daily pleasuring time with the dilator inserted.

When the woman inserts it on her own throughout the day, it would be best if she could just lie down and relax, listen to enjoyable music, read, or doze.

7. Insert fingers. After the woman is able to receive pleasure with a dilator in place, the couple can use the same procedure using fingers. The man can insert a finger or two into the vagina (after the woman has tensed and relaxed). Keep the fingers in the vagina for a few minutes without movement or thrusting. Once the woman has relaxed with a finger or two in the vagina, attempt slight movement. Allow the woman to guide; she needs to feel in control. At no point in the process should pain be allowed. If pain occurs, back off immediately. If pain persists with every attempt, wait until the woman has been able to tolerate larger dilators for longer periods of time.

8. Use the penis as a paintbrush. To paintbrush is to introduce the vagina to the penis without any demand for entry, so that the vagina can remain relaxed and receptive, even when the penis comes near. Both husband and wife can use the penis as a paintbrush to pleasure the woman's genitals. The penis can be flaccid or erect, it really doesn't matter. The penis is stroked over the clitoris, between the labia (lips), and across the opening of the vagina. There has to be a clear contract that entry will not be attempted. This is a trust-building step for moving toward intercourse.

9. Have intercourse with the woman in charge. When the woman has graduated to a dilator the size of the erect penis, the couple is ready to attempt entry. Begin with a time of mutual pleasuring. Have some focus on the woman's pleasure, as well as the man's, until there is a full erection. Keep in mind the assurance that if the woman has been able to insert a stiff, plastic object that is the size of the penis, then the penis, itself, will be much more comfortable since it is soft and pliable.

First, apply lubricant between the labia (lips) and on the penis. With the man lying on his back and the woman kneeling above him, the woman very gently pokes the penis into the vagina, just at the opening. She repeats the poking until that is comfortable. Then she inserts the penis a slight bit more each time until she is able to relax the vagina and guide in the penis fully. She should be sure to spread the lips so that they will not be pulled into the vaginal opening as insertion takes place.

The couple should move at a slow and comfortable pace. Only the tip of the penis might be inserted this first time. With each attempt, the penis should be inserted a little further.

Once full entry has taken place, it would be best to have a time of lying quietly together with the erect penis in the vagina—quiet vagina. This will help the man get used to being inside the vagina, and help the woman to relax the vaginal muscle. She may even want to tighten and hold the muscles for a few moments and then relax. When the woman is comfortable with the penis in the vagina and with gentle thrusting, then more vigorous activity can be attempted. The woman needs to be in control so that pain is avoided and comfort and pleasure are found.

10. Free intercourse experiences. Once consummation has occurred, the couple should repeat the process of pleasuring, tensing and relaxing the vaginal muscles, entry with the woman on top, quiet vagina, gentle thrusting, and then more vigorous experiences. They should continue this sequence until the two of them feel the barriers have clearly been overcome. Then they will be free to proceed to intercourse in any way they desire.

There Is Hope!

It is always a high risk to suggest 100 percent success. But with unconsummated marriages, we have never had a couple (who were both willing to work with the problem) continue through the therapy process who were not able to achieve intercourse happily and successfully. Any failures that have occurred are those who stopped therapy before the process was completed. With an unconsummated marriage, success is easy to define. There either is entry of the penis into the vagina or there is not. Our message to you is that you *can* be successful. It may seem discouraging right now, but it is possible to get past the barriers. Do not give up! Our bodies were designed for sexual union. It is almost always possible to consummate a marriage. Yours is no exception!

For Further Study

Kaplan, Helen Singer, M.D., Ph.D. "Vaginismus." In *The New Sex Therapy*. New York: Brunner-Mazel, 1974.

Masters, William H., and Virginia E. Johnson. *Human Sexual Inadequacy*. New York: Bantam, 1981.

Penner, Joyce J., and Clifford L. Penner. *Counseling for Sexual Disorders*. Dallas: Word, 1990.

15

Sex and the In-Laws

What does sex have to do with the in-laws? An awful lot! As we have worked in sexual therapy for many years, we've been impressed with how frequently the parents' influence impacts what is happening sexually in a couple's life. This influence may be affecting the son or daughter by their actual physical presence in the community or by their presence in the home of the married couple. Or their influence may be the attitudes they instilled in their son or daughter during childhood that continue to impact his or her adult life.

To our knowledge, no one has previously addressed the issue of the in-laws' effect on the sexual relationship of a married couple. But we believe it is an issue that needs attention.

First, we will explore the impact the in-laws have on a newly married couple. Then we'll look at how sexual adjustment throughout married life continues to be affected by parental influence. The effect of visiting the parents' home and long visits from parents will be addressed. Finally, we'll discuss the impact of a parent living in the home with the couple, especially when that parent has a long-term illness.

Newlyweds and the In-Laws

Marsha was in a real dilemma. Her husband wanted to leave for the honeymoon immediately after the wedding, but Marsha's mother insisted they stay around for a few days since so many relatives had traveled such a great distance to come to the wedding. It wouldn't "be fair" to these relatives not to give them a chance to visit with the newly married couple. Mother had planned several special events honoring the newlyweds. As Greg and Marsha tried to resolve this dilemma, Mother's wishes continually dominated the discussion. It finally became clear that there was another motive influencing the decision. Mother wanted to protect her daughter, to keep her nearby, to be sure she was all right and was not being "used" by her new husband.

Newlyweds need a private opportunity to become adjusted to living with each other both relationally and sexually. The parents' influence that was predominant during childhood is over. Now the children need to be left on their own. If they are old enough and responsible enough to marry, they are old enough and responsible enough to find their way sexually. This will be true throughout the rest of their lives.

It is difficult for some parents to let go of their children, to allow them to be responsible for themselves and make their own mistakes. Yet if the bride and groom are going to bond and grow as a couple, they need the freedom to do that. So, regardless of how tempting it is to become involved in their lives, parents need to move into the background. If you are the parent of married children, let them know you care and are available to them as they need you. Then stay out of their lives, except to enjoy them. You are no longer responsible!

The one exception would be if abuse, or any other harmful behavior, occurs in the children's marriage. If you get the sense that your child or in-law is being abused, and he or she is immobilized, you may need to take action. Offer your assistance to find protection or professional counsel.

Parental Influence Causes Sexual Turmoil

When a couple comes for sexual therapy and reports the main problem to be one or more parents, it is usually a case of a very close but unhealthy attachment between parents and child that has continued beyond the marriage ceremony. This influence takes the form of a collusion of the parent and the married child. When they carry on as special allies, the other spouse inevitably feels left out and depreciated. The stereotype for this connection occurs between mother and daughter, but we have also seen it between mother and son.

This is not a sexual problem. Rather, it is a dependency problem. Resolving it requires helping the adult child recognize the importance of his or her marriage separately from his or her parents. When the Bible talks about leaving mother and father and cleaving to one's spouse, that is exactly what it means. In the last two decades some teaching in the Christian community has seemed to foster lifelong obedience to parents. This is both unscriptural and destructive.

Visiting Parents' Home

Many of us did not grow up with sexual openness in the home. Therefore, we have difficulty allowing ourselves to be sexual when our parents are around. It is particularly difficult to let ourselves be sexual in our parents' home. When this happens, the other spouse must recognize that a genuine inhibition occurs because of restrictions that are unspoken but clearly felt. This isn't a fantasy; it may be directly communicated by the parents. It can show up in behaviors such as parents coming to talk with their child in the couple's room at bedtime, or walking into their room without knocking, or continuing to behave as they might have when their child was young. There may be no recognition that the adult child is now a married person who needs to have his or her privacy respected. If the visit is a longer one, this will become somewhat frustrating for the couple. They may decide to go to a motel for a day so that they can bring joy to one another with freedom.

It can be terribly disruptive when parents are excessively interested in the newlyweds' sexual activity. The young couple can't be natural or spontaneous. In one situation, a husband of one month walked into the bathroom next door to the bedroom where he and his wife were sleeping to discover his mother-in-law there in the dark, bent over the furnace vent. She was attempting to hear what was going on in the newlyweds' bedroom!

There may be other inhibitions that have nothing to do with the parents' attitudes or behaviors. Here again, so much depends on the kind of openness that was present in the family while the child was growing up. The new bride may find that she is inhibited around her in-laws and her own parents because she is not used to being overtly sexual. This also may be true for the new husband.

It is most important that the couple discuss the subject openly and establish guidelines about how they want to function. They should be as clear as possible about those guidelines to their parents. It is best if the two of them make their relationship a priority.

If it is possible for you to make sex an enjoyable game, you can add some extra excitement and titillation to your love-making experience by playfully accenting the fact that you are doing something a little bit naughty under the nose of your parents. This can add a special spark. Some of the most intense times that a couple can experience are those when they feel very aroused and rambunctious, yet have to make love in complete silence. It can build an incredibly positive tension that brings extra fulfillment.

They're Coming for the Whole Winter

A couple has just established themselves in a marriage and they are trying to work out their communication differences, as well as their sexual life. Then Mom and Dad call to announce they're free for a couple of months, so they would like to spend some time with the couple. Serious stress can result from having to adapt to two other people around the home. This is especially so when the two people happen to be parents who have a powerful impact on how the couple behaves and feels. To minimize such an interruption, make sure you keep your relationship a priority. Work together to keep those old childhood feelings from getting in the way of your togetherness. If you find that one or both of you is inhibited or has lost your sexual appetite when your parents are around, talk about it, plan dates for yourselves, or sneak away at lunch. Do anything to keep your relationship alive and well while you also enjoy the visit from the parents.

Grandma Is Moving In

The need for adult children to care for their own parents usually occurs about the time their children leave the nest, just when the couple is finally free to be alone. While this is occurring less and less in our society, it is still a reality for many couples. Perhaps Father has died, and Mother is not able to care for herself either physically or financially. You have an extra room, so it makes good sense for her to move in with you. It is the loving, responsible thing to do. But it may also wreak havoc with your sexual intimacy and change your living patterns. Bedtime may be interrupted. Time alone at home may be almost impossible to find. The biggest effect of all may be the emotional impact on either or both of you.

One husband told us what happened when his mother-in-law moved in. His wife and mother-in-law had never gotten along since his wife was twelve. But the mother's inability to care for herself and their available space led to this move. The mother and daughter were in such continual stress that the husband and wife had almost no sexual life. There was no energy left for sexual experiences. In another situation, a wife told us that ever since her mother-in-law had moved in, her husband hadn't had any interest in her sexually, but was always doting on the mother. These marriage-wrecking circumstances need to be taken very seriously! They are best anticipated before the move takes place, and must be dealt with openly and honestly between the couple. Professional help may be necessary.

Long-term Care of a Parent

When a parent is ill and has to be cared for, the couple endures additional added stress and physical and emotional challenges. This can drain off sexual energy just as much as a newborn child or remodeling the house. It is often difficult for the adult child of the sick and elderly parent to actually perceive the effect. He or she may need the objective words of a friend or counselor to recognize what is happening.

Conclusion

In conclusion, let us say a word on behalf of the parents of the married couple. Most parents have no intention of meddling or disrupting their child's marriage. Their influence on the married couple is a continuation of some habits that have been established long ago. Adult children want to be loving and caring to their elders, including their parents, but it is important to recognize that their primary commitment has to be to their own wife or husband and their family—then to their parents.

We are reminded of the couple who lived in the family home, taking care of her mother. They were unable to establish a successful sexual life until the mother left for another city. They were on the verge of divorce before she left, yet suddenly they found new life and fulfillment with each other once they were without the inhibiting influence of a third party.

It is an extremely difficult thing to have three or four adults sharing a home. The impact on a couple's sexual life can be very powerful and its influence should not be taken lightly. Openness, honesty, and flexibility are the only way to survive as you work this out together.

16

Sex and Illness

Our sexual relationships and how we feel about ourselves as sexual persons will be affected by illness. Any stress that demands our emotional and physical energy will use up sexual-drive energy. Illness is no exception. That is true whether the illness strikes one of us, one of our children, or a parent for whom we feel responsible.

The Stress of Parenting the Child Who Is Ill

It is not unusual for parents of a terminally or chronically ill child to find their marriage crumbling. At the time when they most need each other, the demands of the situation get in the way of being able to relax and enjoy each other. The "spark" gets smothered with the emotional pain and fatigue of medical tests, waiting for results, hospitalization, surgeries, and wakeful nights. It's no wonder they no longer desire one another sexually! Yet many never connect their loss of feeling for each other with the illness of their child.

As Cindy told us her experience with this situation, tears coursed down her cheeks. The first two and a half years of her marriage had been happily normal, with sexual satisfaction for both of them. After their first daughter was born, the frequency of their lovemaking had decreased, and her husband, David, complained occasionally. After Melissa (their second daughter) arrived, they never reestablished their sexual life.

The problem intensified when Melissa was two months old and doctors discovered she had a severe kidney problem. Trying to cope with the problem, Cindy was always tired, overworked, and preoccupied with Melissa's condition. When she wasn't running to a doctor's office or waiting outside the operating room, she was trying to catch up with her normal duties as wife and mother. She never felt like making love any more.

David had tried to understand but grew increasingly frustrated and distant. It seemed that they shared almost no close moments now, except times to talk about Melissa—or to argue. Both David and Cindy experienced their difficulty as a loss of love for each other, rather than the result of a distracting stress.

The Stress of Caring for a Parent Who Is Ill

A similar distracting effect happens when spouses find themselves responsible to care for an aging or sick parent. This is especially draining when the parent is in the couple's home. Our society and lifestyle do not equip couples for caring for members of their extended families. So they find themselves torn between the guilt of not giving enough to Mom or Dad, yet not wanting their own family and marriage to suffer.

The struggle really is between the command in Genesis 2:24 to leave one's father and mother and cleave to one's wife in sexual union, and the wisdom offered by Paul in Ephesians 6:1–3 that honoring our parents will bring us long life upon the earth. Given Scripture's high view of the marriage relationship, we believe it would not be God's intention for us to sacrifice our marriage to care for our parents. But within the context of building our immediate family, we must make certain that aging or sick parents are cared for and loved. We need to find a balance between the priority of the marriage and the responsibility to parents.

When One of the Spouses Is Ill

The external stress of caring for a sick child or parent drains physical and emotional energy from our sexual relationship. However, maintaining the sense of ourselves as total, complete men and women is most tested when one of the spouses is afflicted with illness.

Maintaining sexual wholeness during illness is particularly difficult in our society, which connects sexual satisfaction with the act of intercourse—with an emphasis on erection for the man and orgasm for the woman.

When one of the spouses is experiencing physical impairment, finding sexual fulfillment is possible if the couple are able to broaden their view of what encompasses satisfying sexual expression. Sexuality involves body, soul, spirit, and emotions. We can't limit our sexual expression to intercourse or orgasm.

As we have said throughout this book, our sexuality is present at birth. This is evident emotionally, relationally, and physically. Mothers and fathers of newborn babies will hold and relate differently to children of each sex. The parent's maleness or femaleness interacts with the maleness or femaleness of the child. Physically, a little boy has his first erection within minutes of birth and a little girl lubricates vaginally within twenty-four hours of birth.

These natural body responses continue throughout adult life, *unless* interrupted by an illness that inhibits the physical, sexual response of the body. Adult men have erections and adult women lubricate vaginally every eighty to ninety minutes while they sleep. So our sexuality remains within us.

Because our sexuality *is* so basic, it is not something that can be taken away. Frequently, we hear, "I just don't think I'm a sexual person. As far as I'm concerned, sex could go away forever." Or as Cindy ended up feeling, "God gave sexual capacity to every woman except me."

Even if we feel no desire for sexual intimacy, experience no sexual arousal, believe we don't have the capacity for release, or live in a body that has been invaded by disease, impaired functioning, weakness, or pain, *nothing* can take away the fact that we *are* sexual persons. You are and always will be a man or woman with sexual needs and potential. That fact, and all the emotions that go along with it, continues to provide us with the full credentials to maintain sexual intimacy to the end of life.

We may be stripped of all the external elements of genital sexuality that we see promoted through the media. But we can never be stripped of our maleness and femaleness. Thus, some form of satisfying sexual expression is necessary to maintain an intimate, warm, loving relationship. That is a God-given capacity in every person. Even Cindy, through the process of sexual therapy, discovered that to be true for her. She found that all the sexual enjoyment she could have with David had been smothered by the stress caused by Melissa's illness.

Factors That Interfere with Sexual Fulfillment When There Is Illness

If our sexuality and the capacity for satisfying, intimate sexual experience is a given for all of us, what gets in the way of this expression when illness invades the family?

1. Physical Demands of the Illness. It is normal for the physical, energy demands of an illness to consume all of one's drive for sexual intercourse. That is true whether you are the patient or the caretaker. Since we tend to limit our view of the sexual drive to going to bed with someone, we don't pursue alternative methods of sexual intimacy.

It is important to know that our sexual drive provides us with energy for all of life: (a) getting things done, achieving, being productive, (b) emotional intensity, (c) the desire for touch and bodily pleasure, and (d) the energy for sexual arousal and release.

Since sexual drive is primary to *all* of life's energy, the need for physical intimacy and affirmation remains, even when the drive for intercourse has been used up by the demands of adapting to the stresses of illness. Learning to be close, to touch, care, and soak in the pleasure of each other's bodies without demand to feel exotic sexuality, to get turned on, or to have a climax can be a great strength to the relationship during this stressful time.

2. Emotional Stress. Unfortunately, just as physical stress can keep a couple apart, emotional stress caused by illness frequently forms a wedge between two people. This comes at the time they most need to be affirmed by each other. The negative emotions can take the form of guilt, blame, anger, helplessness, feeling left out, uncared for, or unloved. David experienced most of these feelings both because of Cindy's lack of sexual interest and because of his own difficulty accepting Melissa's poor health.

When we suffer the loss of health in ourselves, spouse, or child, we will grieve that loss just as we grieve when someone dies. The grief process will not require as much of us as when we lose a loved one, because the loss isn't as total. Nevertheless, loss of health *is* a loss and we *will* experience the whole set of emotions that go along with facing that loss. When we recognize that these are normal and necessary feelings, we can freely share them with each other.

It is not unusual, however, for even the most psychologically aware to find that their grief, their emotional pain, is creating a distance between the two of them.

When Kristine, our youngest child, was two months old, we started to supplement her breastfeeding with baby cereals. She reacted with intense abdominal stress that caused her to awaken anywhere from five to ten times a night. As we continued to work with various doctors and try new foods, this pattern of awakening, plus frequent illness, continued until she was two years old. During this two-year process, we became more and more fatigued.

But in addition, we went through the intense emotional reactions of having produced a child with a physical problem. We felt that God was giving us more stress than we could handle, that our lifestyle commitment to our two other children and our professional calling just didn't allow room to deal with a sick child. We felt the typical guilt-blame syndrome: "If only we wouldn't have started solid foods so early, if we had been calmer, if only. . . ." On and on the thoughts would flow.

The most distancing came between us in handling Kristine's waking up at night. That kept us apart sexually. The baby didn't awaken at night with an infant's normal short-lived crying that one could decide to ignore. It could involve up to forty-five minutes of intense screaming due to her distended, bloated abdomen. There was no doubt that Kristine was in pain and needed a caring person with her. Even though we knew one of us needed to be with her and there was no way we could feel angry with her, there *was* anger at having to get up. We took out that anger on each other.

This anger surfaced in both active and passive forms. When we were most exhausted, we would argue about who had been up the most times, or we might pretend we were asleep, hoping the other one would get up. Many times each of us would feel angry at the other for not taking enough of the responsibility. With the distancing effect of that wearing-down process, our sexual times became fewer and farther between. Thus, the one area where we *could* have found renewal with each other wasn't even working for us. At that point we sought outside help.

When the physical drain and emotional strain of illness begins to interfere with the *strengths* of a relationship, a third party is usually needed. No matter how great the marriage is and how satisfying the sexual life has been, no marriage can easily survive the endless stress that comes with a long illness. Couples in this situation need outside support and objectivity. A psychotherapist can help guide them through the emotional problems the situation has stirred up. A counselor can assist in expressing the hurts and needs in a way that enlists each partner's care and love, rather than creating distance.

An outside facilitator of any type, professional or friend, can help the couple sort out some way to find relief from the demands of their situation, and get some time for each other. Time is needed to communicate effectively and to touch and love each other physically.

When the emotional reaction to illness begins to pull the couple apart, there may be a snowballing effect. The anger keeps them apart sexually; then not being together sexually causes them to be short-tempered with each other so more anger is felt and expressed—thus creating more distance. You can see the dilemma. This negative pattern must be interrupted.

3. Bodily Disfigurement. Bodily disfigurement or impairment may keep spouses from wanting to be sexual. How we feel about our bodies, i.e., our body images, has a critical effect on our ability to open ourselves to each other and be vulnerable, physically and emotionally.

When we are dissatisfied with our bodies, our feelings about ourselves may be uncertain, or even negative. We may feel undeserving or unworthy of receiving or giving sexual pleasure. If that is the case, the person who has been marred will need much affirmation in order to risk sexual intimacy. That requires both genuine acceptance of the physical change and security in the relationship. When the spouse is able to give, concerns about the body image may be broken through.

Many times, the spouse may also have difficulty with the disfigurement. For example, when a woman has had a mastectomy (removal of a breast), her husband may have a difficult time accepting her as a sexual person, even as she has trouble accepting herself this way. Each person and each couple is unique in their reaction. For some men and women, breasts have little to do with their view of sexuality; for others, they are the key.

For a wife, it may be particularly trying if the man's disfigurement or impairment means he has to be passive while she must become the sexually active one.

Other consequences of disfigurement that make it difficult for the spouse to respond sexually include major alterations in physical appearance that are visually difficult to face. Other times, body odors and changes in the texture of the skin are negative to touch.

When either or both spouses react to a bodily change with lack of acceptance, those negative feelings will interrupt sexual satisfaction. Outside help may be necessary. Someone may be available who has experienced the same body change, such as a person from an ostomy group. A professional therapist or counselor may be enlisted. Or the two of you may do some self-help body image work together (see page 52 in *The Gift of Sex*). There is always a way to maintain some level of comfortable sexual intimacy, but it requires willingness to work toward that goal.

4. Physical Pain. Physical pain will cause a person to pull inward. This is a self-protective response to help him or her cope with the pain. In pulling away and allowing his or her body to survive or heal, the person will avoid sexual contact and emotional intimacy. Each of us has different needs at that point. Some of us simply need space to be left alone. Others find that the security of just having someone close by them can help reduce the intensity of the pain. For other people, the distraction and relaxation of touch helps relieve the pain, as well as providing a way of maintaining sexual closeness and gratification.

5. Lack of Sexual Function. In addition to the physical and emotional demands an illness brings to the sexual life, there are sometimes specific changes in the body's ability to respond sexually. These can result from the disease, itself, or from a negative side effect of the treatments used for the disease.

For example, when a spouse has multiple sclerosis, there is actual scarring and damage to the nervous system. A person with MS may experience loss of sensation or lack of sexual response in the genitals. That doesn't mean the person is no longer sexual or the couple's sexual relationship has to stop. However, it does mean adjustments will need to be made.

What are the sexual dysfunctions a person might experience as the result of the disease or its treatment?

For a woman, it may be the inability to get aroused. She doesn't get turned on or sexually excited. There is little or no vaginal lubrication or nipple erection when she is sexually stimulated. The normal vasocongestion of blood and fluid rushing into the sexual parts when they are stimulated is not happening.

The other complication the woman may experience is the inability to have an orgasm. The reflex action that automatically gets triggered when sexual arousal intensifies to a certain point does not occur. It feels like getting ready for a sneeze and never letting go.

For the man, difficulty or inability to get or keep an erection can be a serious loss for the couple, since sexual intercourse may not be possible. This definitely requires openness to learning new ways to find sexual satisfaction together.

Retarded ejaculations, difficulty or inability to ejaculate, is the same as when a woman is unable to be orgasmic. Even though the man desires release and receives more than sufficient stimulation, the orgasmic reflex does not get triggered. This can be frustrating, but is usually not as devastating as impotence, unless the couple wishes to get pregnant.

It is important to be aware that these difficulties with arousal or release for men and women that can be the result of a disease or its treatment are also common dysfunctions of people *without* physical disease. Therefore, if you are experiencing interruption of your body's normal sexual response, seek out a medical doctor who is competent to treat both your particular disease and the sexual disorders it can cause. Or the physician may consult with a sexual therapist about how to best treat your problem.

The best resource book in this situation is the *Textbook of Sexual Medicine* by Robert C. Kolodny, William H. Masters, and Virginia E. Johnson. Unfortunately, the book is no longer in print, but it is available at many medical libraries. Your difficulty should be evaluated to determine if it is a reversible interruption in the physiology or if it is an emotional barrier that has surfaced which may require sexual therapy. The *Textbook of Sexual Medicine* deals in detail with physical disorders and their effect on sexual functioning.

For our purposes, we would like to list various physical difficulties and treatments that are likely to interfere with sexual functioning. We don't expect this list to tell you if your sexual dysfunction has a *physical* basis, but we hope it will help you determine if that might be true for you.

Disorders That Interfere with Sexual Function

1. Endocrine Disorders. The endocrine system is the body's regulator. It works through our hormones and neuro-transmitters. Because hormones greatly affect our sexual drive and responsiveness, and the sexual response is triggered by messages transmitted through the nervous system, it is logical that the endocrine function is the key to sexual response. Therefore, diseases of the endocrine system, such as diabetes, thyroid dysfunction, pituitary problems, and sex-hormone disease, are frequent and typical causes of sexual dysfunction.

2. Cardiovascular Disease. The emotional reaction to a heart attack is usually the reason for sexual dysfunction, not the physical changes in the body. There are cardiovascular disorders that can *physically* affect sexual functioning. When the disease usurps all the energy the system can produce, there will not be enough cardiac capacity left for a full sexual response. When the disease limits the blood flow to the pelvis, the natural responses of erection and vaginal lubrication will be hindered. Generally, however, sexual activity is a good cardiovascular stimulant.

3. Disease of the Reproductive Organs. Any disease of the external genitals of the man (penis) and woman (vulva) are likely to cause pain or difficulty with sexual intercourse. This is true whether the disease is venereal in nature, a structural difficulty from birth, the result of childbirth for the woman, injury for the man, or surgical removal of a tumor. Internal disorders of the reproductive tract that cause problems include urinary-tract infections or problems with the prostate gland in the man and diseases of the vagina and uterus in the woman. The effects of these changes on sexual functioning may be either physically or emotionally based. Renal (kidney) failure causes a high incidence of inability to function sexually due to the physical changes in the body.

4. Alcoholism. The chronic abuse of alcohol causes sexual dysfunction by inhibiting the production of the sex hormones, as well as by diminishing the normal sexual response. The other medical complications of liver disease, anemia, and so forth add to the difficulty.

5. Neurologic Disorders. Like the endocrine system, the nervous system is an integral part of the sexual response. Disorders of this system are likely to interfere with the ability to respond sexually. This *can* be true for brain tumors or injury, multiple sclerosis, cerebral palsy, muscular dystrophy, myasthenia gravis, poliomyelitis, and spinal-cord injuries. For details about the effect of each of these disorders, please check the *Textbook of Sexual*

Medicine. More information is available from Northwest Regional Spinal Cord Injury Center in the Seattle, Washington, area. There are other such resource agencies throughout the country.

6. Malignancies. The sexual needs of the cancer patient have often been overlooked. In addition to the emotional impact of cancer on the marriage relationship, the growth or tumor, itself, may physically interfere with sexual functioning. The debilitating effects of the disease may make response difficult or impossible. Drugs, surgery, and radiation can also cause sexual problems. Again, specific information is needed for each situation to assess the physical or emotional effects of such a disease process on a specific person's sexual functioning.

Treatments That Interfere with Sexual Function

1. Surgeries. An operation can physically interfere with the sexual response when nerves are severed that control sexual body responses, when genital pain is a result of the surgery, or when there is loss of genital sensation. The emotional sexual interference caused by an operation is usually due to body-image disturbance.

2. Drugs. Both prescribed medications and street drugs may be potent sexual inhibitors. But their effects vary greatly from one individual to another. Prescription drugs that reportedly interfere sometimes with sexual functioning are listed here:

> Diuretic and non-diuretic blood-pressure lowering agents
>
> Hormones (enhance or hinder)
>
> Steroids
>
> Tranquilizers and sedatives, especially barbiturates
>
> Anti-depressants
>
> Anti-cholinergic drugs used for gastrointestinal disorders
>
> Digitalis (for cardiac problems)
>
> Antihistamines (for allergies)

3. Radiation Therapy. Radiation therapy has a high percentage of reported interruption of sexual feelings and responsiveness. This may be a temporary effect that reverses when the radiation treatments are discontinued.

4. Chemotherapy. Little is known about the side effects on sexual functioning of the chemotherapeutic agents currently used to control cancer. There are some reports of dysfunctioning caused by certain of these chemical agents.

Keeping Close During Turmoil

When there is a physical interruption of the body's sexual response pattern due to a disease or its treatment, look for an alternate form of sexual intimacy that brings satisfaction and a feeling of closeness to both.

What can be done to keep the sexual relationship alive when there is little time or energy for each other, or when functioning is not there? What helped David and Cindy reconnect?

Crises shake up our usual systems. Patterns are changed. Feelings are different. What was once solid is now fluid, yet moldable. That is why a period of crisis can be a time when we allow our relationship to deteriorate, or it can be a time when we can make it even stronger than it was before. We will not be as set in our ways, so new growth is more possible.

David and Cindy not only regained what the stress of their situation had taken away, they added new closeness. David was a high-powered businessman who had not participated in home life. He assumed a new role in the children's bedtime routine and joined outings with the children, assuming more of the burden for Melissa. Cindy and David had never fought seriously, but neither had they communicated feelings and needs. The therapy process opened up a new world of knowing each other deeply.

Ten essential ingredients of our work with Cindy and David helped make the difference for them. Perhaps they will help you, also.

1. Identify the problem. Recognize the havoc this illness is playing on your relationship. Don't blame yourselves or each other. Give the relationship a chance.

2. Build communication. Above all, get help to be able to hear each other. Take time to communicate. Tell each other what you would like, both relationally and sexually. Find out and share what feels good and is possible. Set aside a period to experiment with touch, even though time will be hard to find. Tell each other what kind of touch turns you on. You might want to take turns sitting in each other's laps and guiding each other's hands as a way of communicating what is pleasurable (see Non-Demand Touching Experience in *The Gift of Sex,* page 145). Both verbal and touch communication are essential to growing together.

3. Schedule time together. Take time for the two of you to be together *without* any demand or expectation of sexual intercourse, sexual arousal, or release. Togetherness allows the possibility for sexual interest to build. It also provides a forum for finding mutual enjoyment with each other. This might be a two- to three-hour block of time once or twice a week to do something together that costs little or no money, but is free of your usual responsibilities.

4. Learn about yourselves sexually. Start by becoming familiar with the physical and emotional dimensions of the sexual experience. The sexual response has been measured and described by Masters and Johnson. Others have added to that knowledge base from their experiences as sexual therapists. We have written about all dimensions of the sexual relationship in *The Gift of Sex.* The two of you may find it helpful to read that book aloud to each other.

5. Learn to give and receive pleasure. Learn to touch and to enjoy the warmth of each other's body. Communicate feelings of love without pressure to please or to respond. These can open new worlds of enjoyment. This is true for any couple, but especially important for the couple who is under stress. To learn this, you might start by giving each other a foot and hand caress when you are both freshly bathed. Take turns being the giver and receiver. The primary focus should be soaking in pleasure for both the pleasurer and the receiver. When you are the one doing the touching, you might find it helpful to think of discovering your spouse's hands and feet through your fingertips. This same type of pleasuring can be learned with a facial caress and a total-body caress. Sexual arousal is not the intention or purpose of such experiences, but may be enjoyed if it should occur. (See *The Gift of Sex,* pages 143, 145, 274.)

6. Take responsibility for your own sexual response. Many of the tensions and demands of a sexual encounter are relieved when each person assumes responsibility for knowing and communicating his or her needs for touch, arousal, or release. Make a mutual decision that each of you will assume the responsibility to go after what feels good, counting on the other to let you know if what you are doing is violating or feels negative in any way. Then you will find an enjoyment of each other's body that is mutually satisfying, yet takes into account the illness factor.

This system can include the freedom to exaggerate natural desires and body responses to heighten the experience, and to direct your partner to provide the touch for which your body is hungering. When we assume the responsibility for our own sexual needs, this directing of each other need not be taken as a putdown. Rather, it is a message that communicates what the other wouldn't be expected to know. We are the best experts on our *own* sexual needs.

7. Plan for creativity and fun. If there is any time we need to be able to laugh together, it is when we are stressed or feel self-conscious about our bodies. Take turns planning your scheduled times together. Vary the setting and the activity. Include a little surprise and maybe a favorite treat. Sometimes the stress of the situation will leave us feeling empty of ideas. There are many good sex books filled with fresh ideas available. Feel free to go to one of these to add some spark.

8. Distract from anxieties and demands. When we are physically drained or feeling unsure of our bodies or their responses, we may avoid physical closeness. We are afraid we will fail. However, if our only goal is to find mutual enjoyment together, then *there is no way to fail.*

Yet fears and demands tend to surface. The most effective way for dealing with these anxieties is to talk about them at their onset. It's very helpful to be able to say, "I'm avoiding you. I just can't get into this. I'm so tired. I don't think I'll be good for any-thing." Then perhaps the other spouse can accept that and re-spond with something like, "That's OK. I'm not in much better shape. What *would* feel good?" or, "That's OK. I'm feeling pretty good. Maybe I could just enjoy stroking and holding you, if that would feel all right." Distracting from the demand to perform by saying what you feel can provide incredible relief, especially when the spouse is able to receive the message for what it is meant to be.

9. Experiment with alternative methods of sexual en-joyment. Other methods of finding sexual satisfaction may be necessary when sexual intercourse is not possible. It may be necessary to enjoy the intimacy of being together and having a full sexual release through kissing, breast stimulation, general body caressing, manual stimulation, or oral-genital stimulation, but only when that is an acceptable sexual activity for both. A vibrator may be incorporated as a substitute or addition to an erect penis when the man doesn't experience this as a threat. A lubricant can be used by the woman when vaginal lubrication is not occurring.

When sexual arousal isn't happening, the focus on mutual body pleasure for the enjoyment of the touch can maintain the sexual closeness. When there is plenty of stimulation with lots of arousal but the orgasmic reflex isn't working, the best solution seems to be to take time to hold and affirm. Allow the sexual intensity to dissipate slowly as you enjoy the physical and emo-tional closeness.

An experimental approach to your individual situation will probably lead to new ideas you have never encountered. Take courage and have fun!

10. Maximize your general health. The ability to main-tain a satisfying sexual relationship throughout a stressful illness is greatly enhanced when the rest of one's health is at its best. Daily exercise has been shown to decrease stress reactions con-siderably, and adequate sleep always makes the world look a lot brighter.

Eating smaller, more frequent meals can keep the energy level on a more consistent basis. A snack between meals or at bedtime may be the most effective way to put this into effect. Eliminate sugar, white flour, and added salt. Increase fresh fruits, vegetables, whole grains, and proteins of all sorts to enhance nutrition unless your illness or its treatment would require something different. Eight to ten glasses of water a day is great for the system, too.

Details of your specific nutritional needs should be worked out with a professional in your area. That could be a physician, a biochemist, or a nutritionist. Avoid getting caught up in a fad diet. Good general health is a great asset in positively coping with illness in yourself or a family member.

Conclusion

Sexuality is closely linked with physical appearance and performance. When illness affects physical appearance and sexual performance, it is necessary to unlink them and still find sexual enjoyment. You can do it! It is the only way to maintain your sense of well-being as a whole, sexual person who can enjoy all the intimacy of a marriage relationship.

Keep in mind these guidelines for sexuality for the physically handicapped that were suggested by T. P. Anderson and T. M. Cole in an article in *Postgraduate Medicine:*

> A stiff penis does not make a solid relationship, nor does a wet vagina.
>
> Urinary incontinence does not mean genital incompetence.
>
> Absence of sensation does not mean absence of feelings.
>
> Inability to move does not mean inability to please.
>
> The presence of deformities does not mean the absence of sexual desire.
>
> Inability to perform does not mean the inability to enjoy.
>
> Loss of genitals does not mean the loss of sexuality.

Take courage, have fun, and enjoy the gift of each other!

For Further Study

Anderson, T. P., and T. M. Cole. "Sexual Counseling of the Physically Disabled." *Postgraduate Medicine,* 58 (1975): 117–23.

Kaplan, Helen Singer, M.D., Ph.D. *The New Sex Therapy.* New York: Brunner-Mazel, 1974. See chaps. 4–5.

*Kolodny, Robert C., et al. *Textbook of Human Sexuality for Nurses.* Boston: Little, Brown, and Co., 1979. See chaps. 5–11.

*Kolodny, Robert C., William H. Masters, and Virginia E. Johnson. *Textbook of Sexual Medicine.* Boston: Little, Brown, and Co., 1979. See chaps. 7–14.

*This book is no longer in print but is still available in many medical libraries.

17

Sex and Aging

The old can do anything the young can do—it just takes them longer.

An eighty-four-year-old man sits before us seeking sexual therapy. He has been married to his seventy-nine-year-old wife for fifty-four years. Since he is no longer experiencing the joy and pleasure they once shared, he asks, "Am I just too old for sex? Should I give up on the possibility of enjoying my wife like I used to?" His wife had always enjoyed sex, too, but recently seemed to be less interested, reportedly because of the difficulty he was experiencing. He isn't concerned about intercourse and orgasm. It's the intimacy he misses. He says he feels rather ridiculous coming for sexual therapy at his age. But on the other hand, he asks, why not? We couldn't agree more!

A sixty-five-year-old woman calls us on a talk show and tearfully expresses her concern that the sex life she and her husband used to enjoy has disappeared. Her husband visited his physician two years ago, and when he complained about slower sexual responses, the physician laughed and said, "What do you expect? You're sixty-six years old, aren't you?" Ever since then her husband had been less and less interested in initiating sexual activity and had a very defeated attitude about their diminishing sex life.

An elderly couple from the East Coast (who didn't give their ages) heard us on a nationwide radio broadcast. They wrote to ask us a typical advice-column question. They believed that their children assumed that they, their parents, were no longer sexual. When sexual contact between the couple was implied, a derogatory attitude surfaced suggesting that sex among old folks is weird and a little perverted. The couple was seeking our opinion on this matter.

In a society that worships youth, and either depreciates or disregards the elderly, it is not uncommon to encounter the attitude that sexual activity among the "older set" is suspect or strange. The older male interested in sex may be perceived as "a dirty old man," and the woman as someone to be pitied for showing the first signs of senility and regressing to her youth. Since sex is so highly connected with the virility and beauty of youth, it is no wonder that some people assume sexuality disappears as the skin wrinkles and sags, the brown spots increase, the hair lightens or falls out, and agility diminishes. If youth and sexuality are highly correlated, it only makes sense that as we age, sexuality will decrease and when we are old it will have vanished. Fortunately for all of us, this is a myth.

However, as is true with most myths, there is a slice of truth in this view. It is true that our sexual powers peak in young adulthood. It is also true that conception is most possible in young adulthood. There is usually greater frequency of sexual activity among the young. But it is not true that sexual interest disappears with the process of aging.

Another part of the myth was begun by the Greek philosophers, who taught that each of us is dealt a certain amount of sexual energy or virility. This must be conserved and parceled out carefully, lest one's sexuality be spent before life is over. In 1919, H. W. Long authored a book entitled *Sane Sex Life and Sane Sex Living*. This book was to be sold only to the medical profession. In it the author wrote very openly for his time, but his words reflect the attitude that sexuality must be carefully dealt out throughout life.

Here is an excerpt from his section on sex and aging:

> The question is sometimes asked as to how late in life the sex organs can function pleasurably and wholesomely for the

parties concerned. And here, as elsewhere, the reply can only be that it all depends on the individual. But this is true: that, as a rule, the status of the individual during the years of active life will persist, even to old age, if the sex functions are used and not abused. There is no function of the body, however, that will "go to pieces" quicker, and ever after be a wreck, as will the sex organs, if they are not treated rightly.

And this works both ways: If too rigorously held in check, if denied all functioning whatever, the parts atrophy, to the detriment of the whole nature, physical, mental, and spiritual. The body will become "dried up," the sex organs shriveled, and a corresponding shrinking of the whole man or woman, in all parts of the being, is very apt to follow.

On the other hand, an excess of sex-functioning will soon deprive the individual of all such power whatsoever. A man will, in his comparatively early life, lose the power of erection, or tumescence entirely, as a result of excess, either by masturbation or from too frequent coitus; and on the part of the woman, many unfortunate conditions are liable to arise. However, for reasons that have already been stated, a woman who is strongly sexed, and of a pronounced amorous nature, can maintain even great excess of sex exercise without suffering such ill results as would befall a man who should so indulge. That is, an excessively passionate wife can far sooner wear the life out of a husband who is only moderately amorous, than can an abnormally passionate husband wear out a moderately amorous wife.

But if the sex nature of the husband and wife are well cared for during years of active life, neither too much restrained or too profusely exercised, the functioning power of the sex organs will remain, even to old age, with all their pleasure-giving powers and sensations intact. This is a wonderful physiological fact, which leads to a conclusion, as follows:

This fact of the staying qualities of the power of sex functioning, even to old age, is the supreme proof of the fact that sex, in the human family, serves the purpose other than reproduction! . . .

If a wife is a normal woman, sexually, and has neither abused her sex nature nor had it abused or neglected, and is a well woman, she will enjoy coitus as much after she has passed her three score and ten date in her life as she did before! She may not care to engage in the act as frequently as in her younger days; but if she is well courted by her old lover, all the joys of former days are still hers, to as great a degree as ever. And what is true of her is true of her husband, if he is well preserved, as she is, and has never abused himself or been abused.

This is a reward of virtue, for old lovers, that pays a big premium on righteous sex-action in early years!

H. W. Long, M.D., *Sane Sex Life and Sane Sex Living,* 1919

This long quote depicts beautifully the old, mythical claims that if one "indulges" oneself too frequently, all the potential for sexual response will be used up. Husbands and wives were encouraged to experience frequent sexual activity but to limit the number of times that they actually came to orgasm lest they spend themselves in their youth. It is obvious from Dr. Long's report that in the early part of this century, our knowledge about sexual functioning was at a most primitive level.

This concept of having a limited number of sexual responses was the reason for teaching that frequent self-stimulation was a form of self-abuse. In addition, sexual release for a man was thought to make him weaker. Hence, the rule was established that a man should not ejaculate before competing in a sport or going into battle. Thus it seems to follow that if people had been excessively sexually active, they would have used up their share of sexual responses. Since Masters and Johnson's research, however, we now know that we all have an unlimited ability to respond sexually. There is some truth, however, in Dr. Long's 1919 teaching about too little use. When the sexual anatomy is not used, atrophy does occur.

What effect does aging have on sexuality? There is an implicit stance in our culture against older-adult sexuality. We find it difficult to imagine our parents or older people being sexual. For some people, the idea of the married senior citizen having intercourse is repulsive. They imagine that sexual urges lessen with age. Yet we know that romance and sexual experience are a very common part of the lives of the elderly in homes for the elderly. Let's look at what actually does happen to us as we age.

Menopausal Changes for Women

For the woman, the reproductive years are marked by the onset of menstrual periods in early adolescence and terminated by the cessation of menstruation as a result of menopause. Menopause usually occurs when women are in their fifties, but it can occur as early as the thirties or as late as the sixties. For the woman in menopause there is a decrease in the production of estrogen and progesterone—the female hormones that increased noticeably during puberty. They nudged, then catapulted, the little girl into womanhood, setting off her reproductive functioning. Estrogen and progesterone have a major role in keeping up the monthly production and release of an egg and the repetition of regular menstruation. This process changes as these hormones decrease. As is true with most physical patterns, women differ significantly in their menopausal experiences. Some hardly notice the changes, others have moderate symptoms, while still others experience severe reactions over a period of years. The differences can be either physical, emotional, or both.

Hot flashes are the most common reaction that causes women discomfort. These sweeping waves of heat can flood the woman's body in a moment, and may occur several times a day or night. Some experience them only occasionally. For others, stress or anxiety triggers the hot flashes.

When you begin to experience hot flashes, prepare for them. Choose absorbent-fiber clothes that can be loosened. Whenever possible, don't wear pantyhose. Usually a woman can lessen a hot flash by quickly removing as many blankets or as much clothing as is appropriate.

Other physical symptoms may include general aches and pains, numbness in the extremities, or irritating skin sensations. Some women notice that a small amount of urine is leaked during intense sneezing or laughing. This happens because of the relaxation of the muscles and the change in the tissues due to the lowered hormonal levels. There is a rather simple remedy for this. Practice tightening and relaxing the pubococcygeus (PC) muscle around the vagina and the urethra. These Kegel exercises have many benefits, so we would encourage their regular use.

For those who are not familiar with these exercises, they are really quite simple. While sitting on the toilet urinating, spread your legs and practice stopping and starting urination. Learn to hold those stops for two or three seconds, and then relax for two or three seconds. If you are out of condition, you may need to do several hundred of these exercises per day, but once your muscles are in good tone, fifty to a hundred will keep you in good shape. Find some natural cue in your environment that gives you the reminder to practice, such as doing dishes, answering the telephone, or waiting for a traffic light to change. (For further information, refer to chapter 5.)

While some women gain weight during menopause, most find it is the distribution of their weight that changes. It is most common for the body shape to become fuller and rounder. These extra fat cells come on the scene to produce estrogen that is necessary to the body.

Emotional reactions such as depression, anxiety, nervousness, irritability, sleep disturbance, and unpredictable and erratic mood swings can be a part of menopause. For some women, the small things in life that normally would have been taken in stride are suddenly elevated into an overwhelming crisis. Tears come easily. For others, there may be an increase in tension headaches. Extreme fatigue, shortness of breath, dizziness, lightheadedness, heart palpitations, nausea, bowel disturbances, constipation, or diarrhea can all be symptoms of menopause.

For many women, the first emotional sign of approaching menopause may be a noticeable lessening of self-esteem. It is puberty in reverse. When hormones are fluctuating, the woman's feelings about herself vary also. She feels less secure. There may be changes in the woman's view of herself and her femininity. With her child-production potential coming to an end, she may feel an overwhelming sense of loss or uselessness.

An acquaintance of ours in her mid-forties struggled through eight months of depression and a lack of zest for life, until someone finally asked her if she might be menopausal. She headed right to the doctor, got a shot of hormones and B12, and felt like a new person in several hours. The positive response to the hormonal replacement confirmed her menopausal condition.

When life has had disappointments, the losses of menopause will be exaggerated. For example, a woman who was unable to bear children may relive the grief she has worked through earlier in life.

The initial physical changes of menopause often include irregular menstruation and very heavy flow, resulting in anemia. This may be accompanied by pelvic congestion syndrome. Because of the swelling of the uterus and other tissues, the woman's abdomen protrudes and she may experience a feeling of fullness, bowel changes, and hemorrhoids.

To minimize the negative symptoms and to maximize coping positively with the changes of menopause, it is important to consult a physician. It is also vital to recognize that these are passing symptoms and won't last forever. Life will settle down. The physical and emotional fluctuations will not continue for the rest of your life.

Hormonal-replacement therapy is highly recommended for most women, but not all. While estrogen-replacement therapy was linked with endometrial cancer, the addition of progesterone ten to fourteen days per month eliminated that connection. In fact, women are likely to be healthier after menopause if they take hormones. Hormone-replacement therapy improves the heart and circulation, keeps the bones from deteriorating, and will probably keep women living longer than if they did not take hormones.

If a woman still has her uterus, she should take progesterone with estrogen. After a hysterectomy, progesterone is optional. Most doctors do not prescribe it after the woman no longer has her uterus.

The following plan is recommended to prevent negative symptoms and maximize health during and after menopause.

Health Plan During Menopause

Exercise

1. Exercise the upper body for thirty minutes three times per week using weights or some other form of resistance
2. Walk daily

3. Practice PC-muscle (Kegel) exercises; do two hundred repetitions per day. (For instructions, see the Menopausal Changes for Women section in this chapter and the section on Enhancing Sex after Bringing Baby Home in chapter 5.)

Nutrition

1. Your diet should include high-calcium, whole-grain foods; fresh fruits and vegetables; low salt; low protein (protein stimulates excretion of calcium). It should be low in fat (30 percent of total calories), low in sugar, and include six to eight glasses of water per day.
2. Modest or no alcohol consumption
3. No caffeine
4. No smoking
5. Calcium supplement (calcium carbonate is the form that is best absorbed): up to 1,000 to 1,500 milligrams daily
6. Vitamin D: 400 international units and limited exposure to the sun to help the body utilize the vitamin D

For Vaginal Irritation

Take oatmeal baths and use lubricants and estrogen cream around the opening of the vagina and inside the vagina.

For Hot Flashes

Estrogen-replacement therapy (lowest dose possible to relieve symptoms). Your physician will probably start you with 0.625 milligram of estrogen orally, or with estraderm 0.05 (the patch).

If estrogen-replacement is not recommended for you, you may ask your physician whether he or she would consider trying the following to relieve the hot flashes:

• Medroxyprogesterone acetate

- Ergot alkaloids (Bellergal)—questionable
- Clonidine—may lower blood pressure significantly

For General Well-Being

1. Yoga, relaxation techniques, or meditation
2. Counseling
3. Frequent sexual release

If possible, keep ovaries (they produce androgens) into your eighties. If ovaries must be removed, you may ask about using testosterone (1–2 percent) vaginal cream every other day or low-dosage testosterone patches. This would need to be prescribed by your physician.

Keep your uterus if it is not diseased or causing symptoms. If the absence of your uterus has reduced sexual pleasure, try to remember the past feelings and create those feelings mentally. For most women, removal of the uterus has no effect on their sexual pleasure.

To Prevent Metabolic Consequences

To relieve menopausal symptoms and prevent metabolic consequences of osteoporosis and atherosclerosis, estrogens and progesterones are the preferred medical treatment when they are not contraindicated.

Alternative Therapy

This plan should be managed by your physician. Your awareness of available options will help you be an active participant in making decisions for your treatment.

The following options may be suggested when hormonal replacement is contraindicated due to cancer, blood clots, or undiagnosed vaginal bleeding:

1. Androgens can be used for hot flashes, night sweats, or other psychogenic disturbances. They help libido, well-

being, and depression.

2. Follow other options listed for hot flashes.
3. Use a calcium channel blocker such as verapamil HCL (Calan by Searle).
4. Calcium up to 1500 to 2000 milligrams daily.
5. Calcitanin by injection three times per week.

There are many positive benefits to menopause: There is no more menstruation. There may be an increase in energy. Much of life is ahead. You still have a long time to be productive. This may be an ideal time to reevaluate your life and make plans for your future. Many women make a major contribution to society after menopause. Life is not over!

What If I've Had a Hysterectomy?

If you have had a hysterectomy with the removal of two ovaries, you will experience a surgical menopause. When the ovaries have been removed, the production of estrogen will have been suddenly lowered. Many physicians will give the woman an injection of estrogen when she is still in surgery, so there is no experience of sudden estrogen loss. If only the uterus has been removed, menopause should occur gradually as the ovaries decrease hormonal production just as that would occur for a woman who still has her uterus. Some of the symptoms of menopause will not be experienced by the woman who has her ovaries, but not her uterus. She will have no bleeding and no pelvic or uterine congestion.

Changes of Aging for Men

In contrast to what happens to women, there is no cessation of fertility or reproductive capacity for men. Fertility continues to be a possibility throughout life, even though the sperm count and the potential for healthy reproduction decreases with age. The male hormone testosterone not only decreases significantly from age sixty on, but its effectiveness in the body is also decreased because of changes in other circulation hormones. In response to these changes, some men experience what would be similar to menopause in women—this is called male climacteric. It may produce similar symptoms such as depression, listlessness, decreased appetite, diminishing libido, erectile dysfunctions, loss of potency, physical weakness, fatigue, or irritability. While these symptoms may be due to other causes, it is generally assumed that when four of these are present, it is possible that the man is experiencing a male climacteric.

This condition is treatable by prescribing testosterone. A reversal of the symptoms should be evident in a period of two months or they are assumed to be caused by something other than the hormonal change. While menopause is inevitable for all women, the climacteric response is not noticeable for all men.

It is relatively common for men to suffer from prostate swelling, infection, or tumors as they age. The prostate gland surrounds the junction of the vas deferens (the tube that brings the sperm and seminal fluid from the testes) and the outlet from the urinary bladder. Any man living to age eighty has a one in ten chance, or 10 percent probability, of requiring surgery for the removal of a prostatic tumor. While in the past prostatic surgery would damage the nerves and end sexual functioning, new surgical techniques offer the possibility for men to continue to function after the prostatectomy. Some will experience a retrograde ejaculation which means that the sperm and seminal fluid are forced back into the bladder. But the sensations of pleasure and arousal, and even some of the pleasures of ejaculation, continue.

It should be emphasized that prostatectomies do not inevitably lead to impotence, although there is a high probability. Impotence has to do with the inability to achieve and maintain an erection, not ejaculation. If it is not possible for a man to experience an enjoyable erection after this surgery, he should determine with his physician if this is a permanent consequence of the surgery. If not, he should go for sexual therapy. If it is related to the surgery, the loss of that ability will be felt deeply. A penile prosthesis (implant) is a viable option. Learning to enjoy sex without erection, careful discussions with the physician, and a loving, cooperative wife will help the transition after prostatic surgery to be most positive.

Sexual Changes for Men

A man can continue to function sexually throughout his whole life. There are reports of men in their nineties who function sexually. But even as the rest of the body begins to slow down with age, so does the man's sexual response. The old saying we shared at the beginning of this chapter is literally true for men: "The old can do anything that the young can do, it just takes them longer." Five changes are most common.

1. Now it takes direct physical stimulation to get an erection. In his youth, the man may have come to every sexual experience already aroused. This arousal triggered his initiation of sex. Or he may have gotten an erection when he saw his wife's nude body. As he gets older, however, he starts needing stimulation to get an erection. This has been an issue of such concern to some men that they have sought sexual therapy to remedy the dilemma. A steelworker and his eager wife came to our clinic seeking help with what they described as "impotence." As we listened to their story, we discovered that the real dilemma was that the man, who thought of himself as a "real man," had always come to the sexual experience already aroused. In recent years he had been noticing that he was experiencing less arousal. Because, for him, an erection was a prerequisite to taking sexual initiative, he had radically reduced the frequency of his initiation. If his wife initiated intercourse when he wasn't aroused, he drew away lest he be shamed by coming to the marital bed without being fully responsive.

This is a myth that develops rather naturally. In their twenties, men respond at even the hint of a sexual possibility. As they age, this changes and becomes a most unrealistic demand. It can bring great pleasure to have the woman participate in bringing about the arousal by direct stimulation. Yes, it does require direct stimulation of the penis and it may take longer to get an erection as a man gets older. But for many couples, this change doubles their pleasure. As they age, women and men become more similar in their responses. Wives are usually thrilled that husbands have slowed down their pace; so it doubles the couple's fun.

2. After a man reaches sixty, he may find that his erections are not as firm as they once were. He will still become erect, be able to enter, and experience full sexual pleasure, but his penis may not be as hard.

3. His ejaculations are likely to be less intense. This is probably related to the reduction in the volume of seminal fluid produced, as well as diminishing muscle tone. While the eighteen-year-old "spurts" his ejaculation, the sixty-year-old "dribbles." That does not make it less enjoyable, unless the sixty-year-old demands an eighteen-year-old "spurt" of himself. Then he sets himself up for disappointment.

4. There may not be a need to ejaculate with each sexual experience. Beginning around age forty, some men find that they can be fully satisfied in their sexual experiences without an ejaculation. Ejaculation is likely to be inhibited if alcohol has been consumed shortly before the sexual experience. But most men report that the lack of ejaculation is not frustrating for them. They end up fully satisfied.

5. A man will need a longer time of abstinence between sexual experiences as he ages. This period is referred to as the "refractory" period and is the length of time between one erection and ejaculation and the next. This may be experienced as a diminished desire level, but it is not to be seen as a lack of sexual desire.

If the man is aware of these changes and accepts that they need not interfere with sexual functioning, he can continue with a satisfying sex life as long as he desires. If, on the other hand, he becomes anxious about these changes, or is unaware of their normalcy, then they may seriously impair his desire or potency. The anxiety about the changes, not the changes themselves, affects sexual functioning. This small bit of knowledge can make a major difference in the later years of sexual experience. Once the anxious habit of impotence develops, it is difficult to reverse. Avoiding the development of that anxious habit can save a couple much stress as they age together.

Sexual Changes for Women

For women, sexual changes as the result of aging are less noticeable than is true of men. Small reductions in the responsiveness of the breasts, the sexual flush, and the engorgement or the expansiveness of the vagina may be noticeable to the researcher, but not to the woman, herself. However, two physical sexual responses are noticeably affected by aging in the woman. These are a decrease in vaginal lubrication and a thinning of the vaginal wall. The walls get thin because of the diminishing estrogen production. This can actually hasten the atrophy referred to by the 1919 physician, Dr. Long. But atrophy (a marked decrease in muscle and muscle tone) will occur mainly because of lack of use. Estrogen-replacement therapy and/or estrogen creams help restore the vaginal wall and lubrication. During sexual intercourse, other lubricants can be used to reduce irritation and friction. Exercise is the most effective method to keep good vaginal blood circulation and enhance natural lubrication. Thus, the PC (Kegel) exercises described earlier in this chapter and in chapter 5 are vital.

While there are obvious physical changes that affect the sexual functioning of the aging couple, these need not interrupt their sexual life. Rather, they need to be recognized and adjusted for as they occur in each couple's life.

Desire and Frequency Changes with Aging

The data are just now beginning to be gathered regarding the sexual habits of the aging population. The Kinsey Reports, the research of Masters and Johnson, or the Consumer Union Report (*Love, Sex, and Aging* by Edward M. Brecher and the editors of *Consumer Reports*) are common resources. Since these data have been voluntarily collected, they are not regarded as scientific research. But the data do give us a sense of how some of the older population is thinking and behaving.

First of all, it is interesting to note that women often report the decreases in their sexual activity and interest as they get older, but they usually attribute this to some change in the man, such as his decreased desire, illness, or impotence. On the other hand, as men report their decrease of sexual interest, they usually blame themselves for the same reasons that the women blame them. Also, women who take estrogen report a higher sexual interest level and greater sexual enjoyment. Statistically, there may be a decrease in desire or frequency as the aging process goes on, but there is usually an increase in the positiveness with which the sexual activity is experienced. This should be a loud message of hope for couples. It is true throughout life—sexual enjoyment can never be measured by quantity but always by quality.

Why the decrease in frequency? Let us look carefully at some of the factors that cause decreasing sexual desire as men and women age.

1. Physical problems will lessen desire. Any physical problem is likely to decrease sexual desire. For example, heart disease and alcoholism can affect both men and women. While there are no reasons to stop sexual activity because of a heart condition, the fear that sexual excitement will further exaggerate the difficulties inhibits sexual fulfillment for many. Alcohol is a depressant; it decreases sexual appetite. While one drink may reduce inhibitions and allow people to be freer sexually, more than one drink usually deadens their sexual awareness. This effect increases with age. After a few drinks, older adults are more likely to want to go to sleep than to have sex. In general, sexual energy will probably decrease slightly with age, just as our energy for life lessens.

2. Social expectations of sexual functioning are reduced. Couples function less frequently and experience less desire as they age because of reduced social expectations. When old people get the message that they should not be sexual, they *feel* less sexual. It becomes a self-fulfilling prophecy. Their sexual urges may elicit feelings of strangeness, so they shut off those feelings and operate within the norms they feel society sets up for them.

3. A previous low desire level throughout the early- and mid-adult years is likely to continue in older age. When desire has been lacking it is not usually reversed as a couple moves into their sixth, seventh, and eighth decades.

4. Boredom, routine, lack of creativity, or lack of experimentation will bring about a decrease in desire with age. Sex becomes uninteresting. If a couple is going to keep their sexual life alive for forty to sixty years, it will take creativity and experimentation.

5. The couple perceives an inability to function due to impotence in the man.

The main physical culprits for men are diabetes and high blood pressure. While diabetes can also affect the woman's sexual response, it mainly impairs the nerve endings that help bring about and maintain erections for the male. The medications used to reduce and control blood pressure can have a serious impact on the man's potency. Blood pressure medications are designed to function as vasal dilators, relaxers of the blood vessels. For a man to maintain an erection he needs just the opposite, that is, vasal constriction.

If you have noticed a shift in your sexual responsiveness since taking blood pressure medication, discuss this with your physician. Adjustments can be made in dosage or in the type of medication so that it may not affect your erectile response.

Impotence is the most common reason for aging couples' decrease in sexual involvement. It is not an inevitable consequence of aging, and it can be reversed; but the man may need sex therapy.

6. Lack of activity diminishes desire. The surest guarantee to keep the sexual life alive over the years is to keep active. This is one situation where the "use-it-or-lose-it" adage is accurate. Through lack of use there is atrophy in the vagina, which seems to shrivel; and through lack of use it becomes more and more difficult for the man to get an erection. This is particularly true in one special set of circumstances described by Masters and Johnson as the widower's syndrome.

The Widower's Syndrome

The situation is predictable. A couple enjoys a normal sexual life. Then, sometime during her fifties or early sixties the wife is stricken with cancer, severe heart problems, or a stroke.

The husband dutifully and lovingly takes care of her for a few years, and then she dies. He mourns for a year or two, then becomes connected with another woman.

At the point when he attempts a sexual relationship, whether before or after marriage, he is slow or unable to respond. At first this may not cause much anxiety, but as repeated efforts fail, a fear that he has lost his sexual potential creeps in (even though his libido, or sexual interest, is still high). While there are variations to this sequence, it is so common that widowers need to be alerted. Be aware that when there has been a full sexual life and then a cessation (even if masturbation continues during the interim), it may take some time to regain the normal sexual functioning that was there before the catastrophe struck. This could also apply to the man who experiences a long-term illness with lack of sexual activity or when a divorce occurs late in life.

Professional help may be necessary, although we have known several couples who understood this syndrome and resolved it on their own. They came together lovingly and without demand, and gradually experienced full sexual responsiveness. When a man who is experiencing the widower's syndrome has a wife who can totally enjoy him without demanding a response and without expecting intercourse, over time he will regain an erectile responsiveness. This is clearly one circumstance where change is possible.

Keeping Sex Alive Over the Years

As you move toward the last third of your life, it is crucial that you be prepared for the changes that will take place. Certain physical, emotional, and sexual response changes are inevitable. You need to be prepared for them. Beyond that, there are many ways the older couple can bring an extra measure of joy and fulfillment into their sexual lives. You are past the childbearing years, free of the fear of pregnancy, and, for that matter, free of the fear that the kids are going to walk in or hear you.

In *Love, Sex, and Aging,* Edward Brecher lists ten factors that contribute to long-term sexual satisfaction and marital happiness:

1. Ongoing sexual intercourse.

2. Mutual sexual enjoyment.

3. Frequency of intercourse is not nearly as important as having and *enjoying* sex with a spouse.

4. Contentment with the frequency of intercourse.

5. Regular orgasmic responsiveness by both spouses.

6. Ability to discuss the sexual activity.

7. A high interest in sex.

8. Easy sexual arousal.

9. Mutual sexual initiation.

10. Enjoyment of a variety of sexual activities.

If you are reading this at a time when you still have some years until you call yourself elderly, now would be a good time to evaluate yourself on these ten issues. How are you doing? This research strongly suggests that if you want to live a long, full, and satisfying married life, it is important to work on the sexual aspect of your life together. It is a large and significant dimension that will keep your relationship vital for years.

If you are elderly and want to keep sex alive, begin by bringing something new to your sexual experiences. Whether this is a new setting, a new touch, a new activity, or a new openness, creativity will enliven your sex life. Perhaps nudity has been uncomfortable—this may be the time to break down that barrier. Older couples often enjoy breast stimulation and find that this is a great source of pleasure for both the man and the woman. Some couples get into more scrotal and clitoral stimulation during their later years. All of these will add spark and break down barriers.

Experiment with activities that you have avoided in the past, such as oral-genital stimulation. Go at this gradually. When there is no disease present and when the sexual organs are freshly washed, this can be most satisfying for the older couple.

If the man responds more slowly, with occasional impotence, this would be a good time to practice the technique of stuffing a partially erect penis into the vagina rather than having to have a full, firm erection. Sometimes this is easier in the side-by-side position or in any position that works for the two of you. Similarly, the woman may want to use extra lubricants as she ages to compensate for the decrease in lubrication.

Finding better times for lovemaking may also add spark. Many older couples have discovered that sex in the morning, when they are well rested, gives them a very positive start to their day and finds them at their physical best with each other. This will usually also allow more time for touching and cuddling, which seems to become more important with age.

Keep the sexual responsiveness alive by yourself. Women can practice the tightening and relaxing of the PC muscle. We have not talked about men exercising their PC muscle, but that can be helpful also. They can practice these exercises the same way we've described for women, by starting and stopping urination and by using the other PC exercises outlined in chapters 5 and 17. Some self-stimulation, with or without orgasm, also may enhance responsiveness. Older couples seem to incorporate the use of fantasy on a regular basis. Many times these fantasies are of the couple's own special circumstances or memorable experiences of earlier days. What a great way to let the past enhance the present, as events from days gone by are used to bring added life now! Some spouses get creative with each other, sharing fantasies of pleasure and joy that bring them closer, even as they heighten the turn-on.

Finally . . .

The message is clear. Procreation may be for the young, but sex is for the young *and* the old. Our sexuality does not die until we die. There is something beautiful about two people enjoying the touching contact in their fading years just as they did in their blooming years. Perhaps this poem by an anonymous seventy-four-year-old wife says it best.

Finding the Fountain

The slim young man I married
Has slowly gone to pot;

With wrinkled face and graying pate,
Slender he is not!
And when I meet a mirror,
I find a haggard crone;
I can't believe the face I see
Can really be my own!

But when we seek our bed each night,
The wrinkles melt away:
Our flesh is firm, our kisses warm,
Our ardent hearts are gay!
The Fountain of Eternal Youth
Is not so far to find:
Two things you need—a double bed,
A spouse who's true and kind!

> Used by permission from Edward M. Brecher and
> the editors of Consumer Reports, *Love, Sex and
> Aging: A Consumer Union Report* (Boston: Little,
> Brown, and Co., 1984), 379.

May you, too, experience this joy as you find continued pleasure in your marital bed—though it be well advanced in years.

For Further Study

Brecher, Edward M., and the editors of Consumer Reports. *Love, Sex, and Aging: A Consumer Union Report.* Boston: Little, Brown, and Co., 1984.

Gambrell, R. Don, Jr., M.D. *Estrogen Replacement Therapy.* Amityville, N.Y.: Essential Medical Information Systems, 1989.

Greenwood, Sadja. *Menopause Naturally.* Volcano, Calif.: Volcano Press, 1989.

Kaplan, Helen Singer, M.D., Ph.D. "The Effects of Age on Sexuality." In *The New Sex Therapy.* New York: Brunner-Mazel, 1974.

*Kolodny, Robert C., et al. "Geriatric Sexuality." In *The Textbook of Human Sexuality for Nurses.* Boston: Little, Brown, and Co., 1979.

*Kolodny, Robert C., William H. Masters, and Virginia E. Johnson. "Geriatric Sexuality." In *The Textbook of Sexual Medicine*. Boston: Little, Brown, and Co., 1979.

London, Steve, and H. Jane Chihal. *Menopause: Clinical Concepts*. Amityville, N.Y.: Essential Medical Information Systems, 1989.

Long, H. W., M.D. *Sane Sex Life and Sane Sex Living*. New York: Eugenics Publishing Co., 1919. (No longer available, but cited in this chapter for historical perspective.)

McIlhaney, Joe S., Jr. *1250 Health-Care Questions Women Ask*. Grand Rapids: Baker Book House, 1988.

Williams, Warwick. *Rekindling Desire: Bringing Your Sexual Relationship to Life*. Oakland, Calif.: New Harbinger Publications, 1988.

*This book is no longer in print but is still available in many medical libraries.

Part 6

Tough Sexual Issues

18

Sexual Molestation and Abuse

"I have absolutely no interest in sex! In fact, every time I get into a sexual experience, my head starts screaming, 'No! No! No!' If sex could go away forever and I knew that he could be happy without it—I'd never do it again."

This was the opening comment from Lynette, a pleasant woman in her middle twenties who was seeking our professional help. As her story unfolded, we discovered that she had been raised in what seemed, from the outside, like a fine Christian home. Her father, an attorney, had always been a church leader: deacon, trustee, or elder. He was a close friend of the pastor. Lynette's mother was more the quiet, reclusive type. She seemed to brood a lot and hence was not that close to Lynette. Her father had ruled with a steady, firm hand. The children respected and feared him.

As each of the three daughters (including Lynette) reached puberty, their father took on the task of providing them with sex education. However, this education went far beyond the usual lecture and discussion accompanied by some pictures from a textbook. He not only took liberties with their bodies, but also insisted on their involvement with his. This started a pattern that continued until Lynette put a stop to it when she had her first boyfriend at age sixteen. While intercourse had

never been attempted by her father, the regular genital stimulation over a period of three years left her confused and withdrawn. Beyond insisting on her cooperation, Lynette's father
was never forceful. At first, his touching was a little strange but
felt good—and it was so affirming to get that much touching
attention from her father, who otherwise was austere and distant. But as time went on, the strangeness became discomfort.
Then the discomfort turned into guilt, the pleasure grew into
distaste, and trust became revulsion.

Gathering accurate data about sexual abuse is very difficult. There is no way to be sure that the results of any survey
represent the truth. It is usually assumed that the information
we do gather is an underestimate of the actual extent of the
problem. We assume this because many do not remember or
do not want to recall the abusing events. Others choose not
to risk responding factually because of the emotional trauma
associated with revealing what is usually a secret. Many times
the abused children have been threatened with severe consequences if they ever reveal the secret. Sharing the facts and
details stirs up old feelings that most would rather leave buried. While boys are also frequently the victims of sexual abuse,
the great majority of information available is from women. For
this reason, we will refer mainly to girls or women as the
abused ones.

Sexual abuse impacts the lives of a massive segment of the
population. It is estimated that one-third of the population has
been affected by incest or molestation. Eighty percent of the
violators are known to the victims, with 40 percent being fathers
or stepfathers. In 41 percent of the cases there are repeated of-
fenses.

What do we mean by sexual abuse, incest, or molestation?
Sexual abuse refers to any form of sexual contact or conversation
in which the child is sexually exploited for the purpose of
bringing sexual gratification to the exploiter. This could take the
form of exploratory or stimulating contact with the child or it
could involve requesting and demanding manual or oral stimulation from the child. It could be much less direct. Suggestive or
derogatory talk can be very harmful. Even when no physical
contact has occurred, the impact can be powerful.

Janice serves as an example of this. She and her husband came to us with the complaint that she lacked sexual drive. She was always resistant to his advances. When Janice was a young adolescent visiting her best girlfriend's home, this girlfriend's father found ways to isolate her and exhibit himself to her (while she was in the swimming pool or back yard). He would do it in a way that made it appear to be an innocent event, yet she knew he was intentionally "coming on" to her. This happened on repeated occasions without any physical contact. The images of these experiences still impacted her sexual life thirty years later.

If the perpetrator is part of the family, especially a father or stepfather, this behavior is called incest. When it is not initiated by a relative, all forms of sexual abuse except intercourse are referred to as molestation. Sexual intercourse with a minor is rape.

The Violator

The sexual abuser may be the fourteen- or fifteen-year-old brother experimenting with the five- or ten-year-old sister. His hormones are encouraging his natural sexual curiosity and feelings, but his behavior is not appropriate. He is taking advantage of the younger child to fulfill his needs. While he clearly understands that this behavior is unacceptable, the excitement, newness, and intrigue of the experience urge him on. Usually it begins with mild genital exploration, then moves to more involved play as the incidents are repeated. This activity may begin very innocently but gradually become a pattern accompanied by threats, coercion, and sometimes physical force or violence. These boys do not necessarily grow up to be adult abusers, especially if the pattern is broken before it becomes a habit. The pattern can be broken by learning to handle sexual feelings in acceptable ways (see chapter 11).

Often these boys lack the normal heterosexual social skills that would allow them to do their sexual experimentation with girls of their own age. Frequently they are unsupervised in the home and left in charge of the younger children. The young sibling or cousin may desire attention or affection from someone who usually pays no attention to her. So she is caught in the conflict between the need for attention, and her feelings of shame and guilt for the behavior involved.

The older the violator the greater the likelihood that a compulsive pattern has developed. It is also more likely that the individual, himself, is a troubled person and part of a troubled family. Abusers are usually unhappy people who do not find themselves fulfilled in any relationship. This is true both in terms of outside friendships and the marriage relationship. While this unhappiness may take the form of depression, it can just as likely turn to hostility. This is why it is not uncommon to find that physical abuse occurs in the same family where there is sexual abuse. Those who do the abusing, whether it be of their own children or those of someone else, tend to be men who experience feelings with a great deal of intensity and have never learned emotional control. They have not developed acceptable channels for their emotional expression. In this way they tend to be emotionally immature.

As we grow up, we are expected to learn control of our inner impulses. The sexual offender usually lacks control of these urges. Thus, the forces inside him drive him to abusive behavior.

The abuser has often learned this behavior from both his mother and his father. The violator has, in many instances, been abused by his father. Perhaps he did not experience his mother as a supportive presence affirming him as a boy or protecting him from the inappropriate anger of his father. So he falls into the compulsive pattern that has been modeled for him, even as he doubts himself as a man. Most abusers will, at various moments, face their abusive behavior and chastise themselves for it, determining never to repeat the activity—only to find themselves engaged in it again. This self-doubt is as repetitive as the abuse. In many circumstances, it is fueled by alcohol and this reduces the capacity to control behavior and exaggerates emotional reactions.

The abusive male is generally a part of a troubled marriage marked by difficulty with communication, minimal levels of intimacy, and lack of sexual fulfillment. In fact, this may be one of the rationalizations used as a justification for his behavior. He can claim that he is the way he is because his wife is not providing him with what he needs and deserves.

This brings us to another important point. Society, in the past and to some extent at the present, depicts children as the parents' possessions. The abusive father will often justify his sexual activity as clearly within his rights. He will claim that he is not being unfaithful to his wife—he is not involved in an adulterous relationship—because he is not going outside the family. This distortion is all part of the rationalization that allows the man to justify his ongoing abusive behavior.

There are those sociopathic men who evidently have regard only for their own wishes and desires. They care little for the havoc and emotional destruction they wreak upon their victims. We are reminded of a situation from the Midwest in which an uncle repeatedly raped and threatened his eleven-year-old niece, radically impacting the next thirty-five years of her life. He did this with total disregard for her feelings. The following Sunday he could stand up and teach his Sunday school class as usual, with no apparent discomfort at the incongruity.

While it is easy and natural to feel only disgust and disdain for the violators, and while it is rare for them to come forward and actively seek healing, it is important for us to remember that they are persons, too. Usually they are acting out of a very troubled world. This is by no means an excuse, but rather should be seen as an impetus for us to be active in bringing an end to these destructive situations by finding both control and help. This is a call for understanding and compassion as we deal with the violators, even as we take swift action to bring an end to their destructive behavior.

The Victim

No one stereotype describes all the victims of sexual abuse. A question often arises as to why one child out of a family might be singled out for the abuse. In many instances it is the oldest daughter. It may also be the softer, more compliant, less verbal child. Whether she becomes that way as a result of the abuse or was that way to begin with is not clear. But we do know that once the abuse begins, it has a tendency to make that child quieter and more withdrawn. In retrospect, in looking at the disposition of these victims, it is difficult to determine whether these emotional characteristics are the cause or an effect.

The kind of person the sexually violated woman becomes depends not only on the violation but also on the traits with which she was born and other environmental factors. Some of these women turn out tough, and others turn out timid. This would seem to be contradictory, yet both possibilities grow out of the same experience. The woman who goes the tough route is usually saying, "I'm never going to let anyone get to me again. No one can hurt me, especially a man." She is a fighter who believes, "This is the only way to stay safe." Underneath the tough exterior we usually find a scared, hurt person who has learned to put up a brave front. It is a shallow presentation.

On the other hand, timidity is probably the more natural response. The timid one tries to be unobtrusive, to slip into the woodwork so that she will not draw attention to herself by how she walks, talks, or dresses. One woman talked about how she always dressed with several layers of loose clothing so that her body would not be seen by anyone, thus it would never elicit a sexual response. Panic set in when the response came in spite of all this.

Some abused children become very promiscuous in their adolescent and early-adult years. Having been used as a sexual object, that is how they view themselves. It becomes a compulsion for them to repeat that event in search of satisfying love. They seek the perfect experience, but never find it. Sometimes this behavior even leads to prostitution.

It is not uncommon for the sexually abused woman to at least seriously consider, and perhaps even experiment with, homosexual activity. When the experience with men has always been hurtful and violating, and when she has never felt a full sense of love and acceptance from her mother, it is not surprising for a young woman to search for fulfillment with other women. It seems to be the only place of hope.

Some sexually abused women become habitual, anxious people-pleasers. They feel it is their responsibility to make everyone in their world fulfilled and happy. This is a heavy burden. It is the only way they know to gain love and attention.

Having begun this behavior as children during sexual abuse, they accept it as a way of life. This ongoing pattern of living life for others is a great source of disappointment since they never get what they need.

Darlene saw no value in herself unless she could be fulfilling the needs of others, even her abusive father. As the eldest daughter, she was responsible for the younger children. Her mother was emotionally immature and unable to cope with her husband. Now, as an adult, Darlene finds herself continually on the giving side of every relationship. Inside she is crying out for someone to take care of and love her, but she always seems to choose friends who need her and are verbal about their needs. So she goes on, starved for the love that never came her way as a child, and it eludes her even now.

Some victims become "spaced-out." This can take them to a psychotic point, but most often it is manifested by an emotional shutdown. Nothing affects them in a positive or a negative direction. They live life with little or no show of emotion. Responses such as this usually grow out of severe abuse that was violent in nature.

At what age does incest usually occur? It happens to children of every age, even infants. We have dealt with adults who were abused at all ages from the two-year-old toddler to the seventeen-year-old adolescent. Different patterns occur with children at various ages. Whether the abuse goes to the point of intercourse and begins at age five or at age fifteen, it is a devastating event that alters the life of the victim. This is true whether the victim is a boy or a girl and whether the violator is an adult man or a woman.

The abuse may not always be physical. The impact is just as powerful if the abuse is verbal, emotional, by innuendo, or exposure. Intrusive medical procedures in the genital area (such as catheterizations or enemas), performed insensitively at critical stages of development have the same impact as direct physical abuse.

Bear in mind that boys are also victims, and their abusers can be men or women. We have heard too many stories from men about molestation by a trusted leader at a camp-out. So be sure to teach your boys as well as your girls about appropriate and unacceptable touch.

Consequences of Abuse

Denial

When the perpetrator is known to the victim, the most common response is denial. This denial is not only to others, but also to oneself. It is not uncommon for us to deal with a woman who displays all of the symptoms of abuse, but reports no recollection whatsoever. In one instance it took a full year of weekly psychotherapy before the woman was able to acknowledge that her memory block was related to the abuse she had experienced from her brother thirty years earlier. It was not that she was consciously hiding this from us or attempting to deceive us. It was just not a part of her memory.

Even when abuse is recalled, it may be only a vague recollection. The victim has put the event out of her mind as a possibility. Children have an incredible capacity to deny what they can't handle. Women will talk about a vague feeling that something happened. Still others will have clear memories, but because they have made a commitment to the violator and to themselves, they will never share the memories with anyone. To come out in the open with the story of their abuse is a most traumatic event. Secret commitments such as these are amazingly powerful; there is something magical about them. Women who hold these secrets have convinced themselves that if they never tell anyone about the incident(s), the negative consequences promised them by the violator will never occur. They see it as a form of magical protection.

Lucy had been threatened that if she ever told anyone about what had happened to her she would be put in an insane asylum for life, severe harm would befall her family, and no one would believe her story about the abuser. Years later, as Lucy shared the pain of her devastation, she continued to feel (even though she didn't believe it) that somehow this man had the power to influence good or evil, depending on whether she kept the contract she had made with him. Hearing such stories, it becomes understandable why a victim would not want to share the secret no matter how painful, and keep it locked up for a whole lifetime.

The denial usually extends to the spouse, as well. A married couple will share many secrets, believing they know everything about each other, yet the abusive event may go untold for years. The wife fears that if her husband knew what had happened to her, if he knew that she was "damaged goods," he wouldn't want anything to do with her. She fears the loss of his respect and love. Maybe he would even desert her. While this desertion rarely occurs, it is still a powerfully traumatic event to share past abuse with a spouse.

Why deny? For children, the sexual violation may have been the only source of affection in their world. The mother may not have been very affectionate; the father may have given them little attention. Suddenly, someone was interested. He gave gifts. He touched. He was not violent and so, in a desperate way, a need was met.

This experience sets up an unresolvable conflict for children. On the one hand, they feel all of the negative consequences of the event, including the guilt and self-depreciation. On the other hand, they are being touched where it feels good. They are receiving attention and affection. The only way to handle this conflict is to engage in denial.

We have had some women report to us that as children they would pretend to be asleep, with a mixed hope that this might make the abuser go away and not do what he came to do. It also made them feel less responsible for whatever went on. The conflict of childhood sexual abuse often makes it almost impossible for victims to totally enjoy the sexual experience in adulthood.

Fear is another impetus to denial. The fears of a child are usually only vaguely defined. They fear what is happening to them. They also fear what might happen, not only to themselves but also to their families, if someone found out. They fear they would be placed in a foster home, that Mother would be extremely angry or Father would show his anger through violence. The experience is ridden with fear.

Denial protects the self-image since any inappropriate sexual contact from an older person makes the abused child feel different, strange, and unusual. It invariably alters the child's self-image. The denial serves as a way of keeping this image intact so the child can pretend that this segment of his or her life is not really a part of him or her. Abused children try to behave like normal kids, only confronting the abuse when they are at home. Thus, denial protects their public self-image. It is very important for all children to believe that their parents are good, caring, loving, wonderful people. When parents do not behave in this manner, the child will deny the reality to protect the image of having good, normal parents like everyone else.

Denial is a basic form of defense against undesirable thoughts, feelings, and experiences. It should never be seen as lying or deception but rather as a coping mechanism that helps the child survive what he or she is unable to deal with overtly and directly.

Distortion

Distortion takes place in almost every circumstance of abuse by a familiar person. A four-year-old girl reported to her parents that she and the fifteen-year-old male babysitter from next door had a secret. They were doing something that Mom and Dad would really like. They would be proud of her because it was something that moms and dads did when they loved each other. As the story unfolded in bits and pieces (even though the child had been warned not to tell), the reality was that this fifteen-year-old neighbor had convinced the four-year-old that what they were doing was loving and good.

In the movie *The Color Purple,* the main character talks about men having to "do their business." This was a way of changing something painful and devastating into an event that was normal and tolerable. Distortion of this nature is not at all uncommon, particularly in cases of repeated abuse.

A woman in her early forties who was finally dealing with abuse reported that her father had begun intercourse with her when she was five years old. She remembers thinking that this was a normal event that probably occurred in all families. This is what fathers do with little girls, she assumed. This becomes part of the line used by violators to convince children that the "loving" activity is a natural expression of family affection. Early in the experience the violators encourage distortion by suggesting that what is going on is a normal occurrence. They tell the child she will learn to accept this activity and that it is happening to other children, as well.

Not only do the victims make the activity normal in their minds, they also distort the extent of the involvement. This makes it less painful and dramatic. Victims will say things like, "Well, he didn't hurt me," or, "It wasn't that often," or "It only occurred on weekends." They will do anything to diminish the extent and significance of the involvement. *I'm sure that there are lots of people who had it worse than I,* they think. The distortion helps minimize the event and, thus, the pain.

Justifying the violator's actions is another form of distortion. The violator will often participate in this by talking as if the behavior is justified. One stepfather continually referred to his nine-year-old daughter as having such a sexy body that she really needed what he was doing for her. Often the justification comes in terms of what the mother is not providing. The violator will complain that the mother doesn't "put out" for him. The child will go along with these distortions in an attempt to make sense out of the events.

If the violation includes pain or violence, then the justification is that the child made him angry, so it is really the child's fault. The child distorts this by bearing the responsibility for the abuser's action. The result can be overwhelming, debilitating guilt that plagues the child throughout life. Even though the adult is responsible for the action, the child experiences herself as being responsible. Hence, she feels guilty.

Even when victims do not overtly believe the activity is their fault, that huge sense of guilt says they have done something wrong. Often it is easier for the children to blame themselves than to put the responsibility where it belongs: on the older, abusive adult.

To cope with painful abuse, a more severe distortion takes place. The girl may learn a form of detachment from that pain by having it spread out over her whole body rather than just feeling it in the location of the pain. This coping style, while necessary at the moment, tends to establish a pattern of detachment from pain—or even from life. It then becomes an ongoing part of the child's personality. As the child grows up, this detachment invariably causes emotional havoc in adulthood.

Difficulty

Virtually every adult who was sexually violated as a child will have difficulties in life. Lack of trust is usually the biggest of these. When trust has been so severely violated, it is extremely difficult to rebuild. No excuses, no talking, no explanation, no extenuating circumstances can take away the damage. An additional trauma occurs in some instances, making the distrust even more severe. A child may seek out someone she trusts for help to stop the abuse, only to find that the person doesn't believe her or doesn't do anything even if he or she does believe. This is hopelessly devastating. Sometimes the child is violated again by the adult she thought she could trust. A thirteen-year-old girl, Virginia, had been repeatedly molested sexually by her two older brothers. As these experiences overwhelmed her, she decided to talk to her very special male piano teacher. Within a period of about three months, he was initiating sexual activity between himself and her, thus smashing her trust one more time. It was fifteen years before she risked sharing herself and trusting again.

When the protector becomes the abuser, it leaves the child in a severe state of helplessness, powerlessness, and mistrust. It is as if her world has been turned upside down. The very one who was supposed to protect her from danger has become the feared one. Trust is broken and confusion sets in, even when only one incident occurs. Adults sometimes diminish the significance of a single incident of incest or molestation, but one incident can so radically alter a child's view of the world that it will affect him or her for life. When these trusted ones become the source of pain and confusion, it is as difficult to rebuild trust as it is to rebuild a broken egg. Abuse leaves a permanent scar, so the individual will always have a struggle with trusting another person.

Abuse also destroys the victim's self-worth. A child's ego is not developed enough to be able to see the violator as a sick person. The more powerful impact is on how the child sees herself. In their book, *Betrayal of Innocence: Incest and Its Devastation,* Susan Forward and Craig Buck quote an incest victim as she describes how she feels about herself. This is a common self-concept of the victim of abuse. She says, "Think of the lowest thing in the world. Whatever it is, I'm lower." The victim of abuse has an incredibly low view of herself. Her self-worth can be so low that she does not want to live. Suicidal impulses are common, especially for the victim of incest. These impulses reflect how worthless the individual feels.

Drugs, alcohol, enemas, laxatives, overeating, undereating, dangerous or foolhardy activities may all be a part of the self-destructive pattern. This grows out of a two-sided feeling. On the one hand, there is the feeling, *I'm not worth anything anyway, so who cares?* On the other side is, *If I can put up with all this, I am invincible and can tolerate anything.*

Our daughter, Julene, who is now working toward her Ph.D. in psychology, found that addictive behavior of all sorts is highly correlated with sexual abuse. When she looked at those for whom sexual and physical abuse were combined, addictions were found in as many as 69 percent of the victims.

A lack of confidence in her capabilities will often accompany the victim's self-depreciating stance. She may be bright, talented, beautiful, or capable in many areas, but she will not have internal confidence about herself. She will feel flawed. No matter how she feels on the outside, inside she is putting herself down, depreciating who she is.

Victims of sexual abuse deeply feel that they are unworthy of love. Obviously, they believe, if someone misused them so callously, how can they be worthy of loving? In adult life, abuse victims may find themselves repeating their childhood patterns. They connect themselves with men who are cold, distant, physically or sexually abusive, and emotionally neglectful. It is not uncommon for a woman who was abused as a child to marry a man who abuses her children, just as she was abused. While it is never intentional, this kind of lifestyle perpetuates the low self-image.

Feeling "different" than everyone else is another difficulty. This is especially true for victims during their early-adolescent years when it is so important for them to feel normal and part of their peer group. Once there has been abuse, the girl usually feels set apart from everyone. This feeling of separateness occurs even with the very young.

Denise came to us at age forty with some severe sexual barriers in her marriage. As we were gathering her history, she shared her story for the first time. She had grown up in up-state New York. When she turned three, her mother found it necessary to go to work; she left Denise with a neighbor for childcare. The eighteen-year-old son of the caretaker was around the home and was often left to care for Denise and her sister. Over time, a pattern of molestation and exploration of both girls was established by the young man. From the age of three, Denise felt different. She felt she knew something that other kids didn't know. There was a small sense of pride, but also great self-disdain and sadness. Having had this experience set her apart from everyone else. Since that time it had always been difficult for her to feel normal.

Intimacy

Intimacy is another difficult area for the abused person because he or she has a natural tendency to keep a safe distance from everyone. Victims of abuse feel "dirty." A piece of themselves has to be kept a secret. So they close themselves off completely from others. They find it difficult to form deep, lasting relationships. This is true whether they are children, adolescents, or adults.

The sexual relationship in marriage is particularly difficult for the victim of abuse. One of the major causes of sexual dilemmas for women is a history of sexual abuse. Though abuse has a powerful impact on the sex life, it is frequently not thought of as the cause for the problems that are experienced. The abused girl may be very sexual during her courting years. But once the relationship moves into the intimacy of marriage, where sex is expected, the interest falls off with relative rapidity. Yet there is a sense of the woman being very sexual. Needless to say, this leaves the husband extremely frustrated. This frustration becomes the impetus for seeking help.

An important word to the husband: Some men feel the wife is blowing this whole experience of abuse out of proportion. On the contrary, the impact of abuse on the sexual freedom of a woman is devastating. She cannot just "decide" to put it in her past. It needs to be taken with extreme seriousness. Even if there has been only one incident, it may radically impact her sexual life. Being tough about it and telling her to shape up and get over this problem only makes it worse. She reexperiences the pain and rejection with each such response. The most helpful stance is to be supportive and caring, but strong in taking the lead to get help.

Physical symptoms

Victims of abuse live with chronic physical complaints. In *Betrayal of Innocence: Incest and Its Devastation,* Susan Forward reports that migraine headaches were present in about half of the people she counseled. Of course, not everyone who has migraines is or was a victim of sexual abuse! However, frequently when there has been sexual abuse, one of the consequences may be regular migraine headaches. Various other kinds of skin, gastrointestinal, or gynecological ailments are physical manifestations of the distress that the violated person experiences.

Perhaps the best way to sum up the consequences of abuse is to emphasize that these are the resulting patterns of abuse that have not been resolved. As victims confront the incest or abuse, change takes place. Victims do not have to live with these consequences for the rest of their lives. It is important to emphasize this.

Where Was Mother?

Whenever abuse is an ongoing pattern, both the victim and the violator will be communicating signals that should alert the rest of the family to the problem. In about a fifth of the cases, the mother or the rest of the family is completely unaware that anything is going on. In only a few instances is there active and knowing participation on the part of other adults in the family. Often there is an unconscious participation either out of ignorance, fear, or anger.

When a mother senses that something is going on between her child and an adult family member, she may feel powerless. Confrontation frightens her. Remember, she was probably a victim of childhood abuse, too. She fears she will be unable to stop the behavior, even if she does confront it. Mainly, facing it is too painful.

We found this to be true of the mother of a missionary wife. The mother had sexually abused her daughter over a period of years. The father was the passive one, while the mother was the stronger of the two. He mildly raised questions about the mother's activity but never confronted it directly. Eventually, he had left her for other reasons.

The silent one is often the submissive one. Most frequently, the wife is submissive. The daughter learns submission from the mother. She learns not to stand up to the patriarchal authority.

Sometimes the mother contributes passively by neglecting her husband, thus pushing father and daughter into circumstances where sexual behavior could easily develop. She may have serious difficulty being affectionate with her husband and the rest of the family. She may have emotional or physical difficulties that make it almost impossible for her to participate actively in the emotional or functional life of the family. In several instances we have seen that abuse occurred during a time of extensive illness on the part of the mother.

The victims of sexual abuse may be both enraged and disillusioned by mother's neglect of them. If she cared, they feel, she would have done something about it. Once the abuse is discovered, mothers experience extreme guilt and inadequacy. Yet they often direct their anger at the child rather than at the abuser, especially if he is her husband, father, brother, or son.

In those circumstances where mother is completely unaware and then discovers the abuse, she needs to be loving, caring, supportive, decisive, and strong. Quick action is necessary to check out the physical health of the child and provide for the child's safety. Having the mother help the child work through the emotional trauma can be a life-changing event for the victim. This is very difficult for most mothers to do. We want to encourage each one of you who find yourself in this circumstance to take a clear, strong stand. Seek supportive help, whether it is from your doctor, your minister, or a professional therapist.

Getting Over the Abuse

A one-time molestation by a stranger can be faced and overcome with relative ease. Valerie came to us with a strong block toward anything sexual. While being very attractive and even sexual in appearance, she could not find it within herself to respond to her husband. As therapy progressed it surfaced that at the age of thirteen she had been violated by a physician. With blatant disregard for her person and her tender age, the physician had callously catheterized her for a kidney problem while making sordid comments about her virginity to her mother. This traumatic experience had been forgotten until it surfaced in discussions with her mother. Within two weeks of the new awareness, she had worked through the scars from the event and was responding vigorously and enthusiastically to her husband.

It would be wonderful to be able to claim that all incest and molestation barriers are dealt with that easily. Unfortunately, this is an exception. Alice's story is in sharp contrast. Her father molested her over a period of six years. She struggled for months after the memory had surfaced before she could talk about her sexual feelings at all. It was not until two years after the therapy process began that sexual responsiveness was possible for her.

Just recognizing that sexual abuse occurred and facing the memories are usually not enough. The memories must be shared with someone the victim can trust, who will not be judgmental, and who will be able to care without giving advice. The sharing process seems to be absolutely essential as a way of freeing oneself from the bondage of the violation. It is necessary to share some of the details and the extent of the abuse. But it is particularly important to share the feelings, the self-concept, and the pain. Many times we find that inviting a woman to write her memories and then share them is very helpful. As new memories come along, they can be added to her journal of writings and then put back on the shelf. It is one way of getting the pain out of her system. Working through *The Courage to Heal* book and workbook by Ellen Bass and Laura Davis is a helpful way to deal with the pain systematically.

Whenever we have experienced a severe loss, such as the loss of innocence in childhood, there is a grief process to go through. When that grieving is delayed from the childhood event to the adult process, all kinds of baggage gets attached. Thus, the process can be painful and laborious. As with most grieving, when we survive the disbelief and distortion and can get to the anger, there is an overwhelming sense of rage. Fear of this rage may be part of the reason why it takes so long to face it. So much anger is stored up inside the violated person, he or she fears its release.

Fear is another powerful emotion experienced as the incest or molestation is being dealt with. The fear can be a gripping, terrifying, trembling apprehension that all those threats made long ago will still materialize. The abuse, violence, or even death that was threatened overpowers the emotions of the victim as she reveals the secret. Thus it's clear that a major part of the grieving process is dealing with the anger, the rage, and the fear.

When shame and guilt have been a part of life for ten, twenty, or thirty years, they are not easily overcome. Getting over shame and guilt requires a recognition of the patterns of being a victim. Patterns of promiscuity, timidity, or self-debasement all are an outgrowth of the abuse and need to be faced in the process of going beyond the devastation.

While some victims work through all these feelings with a helpful spouse, pastor, or friend, others need to seek a professional counselor as they begin to tiptoe and then run through this minefield of emotions. The therapist would best be someone experienced in helping people through the grief and pain of sexual abuse. The therapy process is designed to help victims face the truth and reality of what went on in their lives. Part of facing the truth is letting go of the hopes and dreams that somehow they can still have "the daddy" they longed for all those years. Hopes and dreams die hard. Group therapy is most effective in helping women abused as children move through the abuse.

Forgiving and forgetting is such a difficult process. In his book, *Forgive and Forget,* Dr. Lewis B. Smedes talks about healing the hurts we don't deserve. He explains that while it may be our intention to forgive at a given moment, forgiving is a process that happens over a lifetime. While hate weighs us down and eats at our souls, we should never demand instant forgiveness of ourselves. Letting go of the pain and hate has to be a gradual process.

What about confronting the violator? This is an issue that needs to be addressed carefully. In many instances, confronting the violator only causes more turmoil because of the violator's denial or anger. In other cases, healing is possible. We have worked in two specific instances where a very special healing took place within a family as the violator was confronted, the anger heard, the pain shared, forgiveness sought, and relief experienced. We would be most hesitant to cite this as the norm, though. To encourage the abused person to confront someone she has feared all her life may set her up for further trauma. Before suggesting such a confrontation, we need to be very sure that both individuals are strong enough to handle it.

We do find that as the victim can recognize who is responsible and stop blaming herself, deliverance is possible. She needs to share out loud, go through the grief process, experience the anger, fear, shame, and guilt. She needs to let go of the hopes and dreams, face the truth, and begin the process of forgiving and forgetting. Then relief can come. Healing does take place. Reversal of lifetime consequences is possible. Sexual happiness can become a part of life. This seldom happens in an instant. It usually doesn't occur as a result of a quoted Bible verse or a quick prayer. It is like dealing with a cancer that has spread throughout a victim's body and needs to be removed one small speck at a time. But relief is possible, and we would encourage you to seek that relief with all the determination, strength, and energy you can muster.

Interrupting Abuse: Looking for Clues

While we, as parents, do not want to be paranoid in watching for abuse, we must be on the alert for any indications of it. Obvious physical symptoms, such as blood or excessive vaginal discharge in the panties, should be investigated. Marked increase in fearful and hesitant behavior should lead a parent to at least suspect incest or molestation. Sometimes a child will change and become very withdrawn.

One patient reported that she had been happily playing at a family gathering when she was accosted and molested in a bathroom off a back bedroom. From that point on she sat quietly beside her mother for the rest of the event. Her mother, who was not very sensitive to emotional variations, thought her daughter was getting sick but did not notice that she had no fever, was not throwing up, or demonstrating any other symptoms of illness.

This kind of withdrawn behavior may take the form of pulling away from friends or activities with a loss of normal enthusiasm. Taken to the extreme, it may even mean going into hiding where the child shuts herself off from the rest of the world in her room, the basement, or up in a tree far away from everyone else.

Sudden sleep disturbance—crying out at night, bad dreams, renewed bed-wetting—can also be a sign that something is amiss. Sudden accumulation of money or candy that has no reasonable explanation is also a warning signal. There are many individual ways that a child might demonstrate emotional turmoil, so it is crucial that we parents remain sensitive to any emotional or behavioral changes. Obviously, there are many other reasons besides abuse for these behaviors. We should not expect the symptoms to be the same from one child to another. One may lose her appetite while another may start eating more than ever. We need to be sensitive to individual differences in reacting to stress.

What do you do if you suspect abuse? Begin by asking some indirect questions that give your child opportunity for response. Start spending extra time with her. Always listen with an ear toward feelings. Listen when she is talking with her friends. Watch how she plays with her dolls. If she is older, even pay attention to what kind of doodles she draws with her pencil. If you keep suspecting and don't get anything from her by the indirect manner, then confront her directly. Ask, "Has anybody been touching you in a way that has made you feel uncomfortable?" The most likely response will be a denial, but even the way the denial is expressed can give a clue as to whether there is any factual basis for your suspicions. If your suspicion becomes confirmed, reassure your child that she is not the one responsible for what has happened. Be sure she knows that you are available to help. You definitely want to know about what happened. Encourage her to tell you about it in whatever way she can. If it's easier for her to write it rather than tell you directly, give her the permission to do so. Assure her that you will not be angry with her but that you care deeply and want to protect her from harm.

If you know that abuse has happened, deal with it directly. Give the child the chance to talk and work it through. Give her time and let her express her feelings. Introduce the topic when there is opportunity to talk. So many parents disregard their child's hints and clues because they don't want to face the problem.

While teaching a seminar in the Northwest, we heard a frightening story. The daughter of the leading women's Bible study teacher in the church had been molested in the stairway of the education building. The incident was dealt with as a spiritual issue. This mother believed God would take care of the pain. They prayed to forgive the man and decided it would not be talked about again. While this may sound like a wonderfully spiritual example, we would have great fear for the consequences. As this nine-year-old child grows into adulthood, the failure to face the trauma realistically will undoubtedly impact her powerfully. Abuse must be dealt with whether or not we are comfortable with it.

If you are in a helping profession and have opportunity to recognize sexual abuse, know what your responsibilities are to report these situations, and follow the law to protect the innocent. While the temporary effects may be very jarring to the family, the process is crucial to let the child know that there is somebody out there in the world who cares and will act to protect her. Follow through. Make certain that the action taken is helpful, rather than destructive. Stay involved!

The subject of sexual abuse is one that we would like to avoid. Yet we do a disservice to everyone (especially innocent children) by failing to confront these issues head on. We must deal with them realistically and become agents of intervention to the ones whose innocence has been violated. We must stand up with a message of healing and hope.

For Further Study

Abramson, Paul R. *Sarah: A Sexual Biography*. Albany: State University of New York Press, 1984.

Bass, Ellen, and Laura Davis. *The Courage to Heal: A Guide for Women Survivors of Child Sexual Abuse*. New York: Harper and Row, 1988.

Buhler, Rich. *Pain and Pretending: You Can Be Free from the Hurts of the Past*. Nashville: Thomas Nelson Publishers, 1988.

Forward, Susan, M.S.W., and Craig Buck. *Betrayal of Innocence: Incest and Its Devastation*. New York: Penguin Books, 1978.

Frank, Jan. *A Door of Hope*. San Bernardino, Calif.: Here's Life Publishers, 1987.

Hancock, Maxine, and Karen Burton Mains. *Child Sexual Abuse: A Hope for Healing*. Wheaton, Ill.: Harold Shaw Publishers, 1987.

Herman, Judith Lewis. *Father-Daughter Incest*. Cambridge, Mass.: Harvard University Press, 1982.

*Kolodny, Robert C., et al. "Rape." In *Textbook of Human Sexuality for Nurses*. Boston: Little, Brown, and Co., 1979.

*Kolodny, Robert C., William H. Masters, Virginia E. Johnson. "Rape." In *Textbook of Sexual Medicine*. Boston: Little, Brown, and Co., 1979.

Penner, Julene M. *Childhood Sexual Abuse: A Risk Factor for Addictive Behavior in Adulthood*. Honors Thesis, Harvard University, 1990.

Smedes, Lewis B. *Forgive and Forget: Healing the Hurt We Don't Deserve*. San Francisco: Harper and Row, 1984.

*This book is no longer in print but is available in many medical libraries.

19

Sexual Infections

Yuck! Who wants to learn about sexual infections? Our focus in this book has been to present a wholesome view of sexuality, as God intended, especially in a handbook for the family. Yet the reality is that we live in a world filled with fallible human beings. There are germs in this world. Some of those germs are spread through sexual intercourse and cause illness. Sexually transmitted diseases (STDs) are those infections that are transmitted through sexual contact.

The havoc of AIDS, the pain of herpes, and the rampant spread of genital warts have alerted all of us to the seriousness of sexually transmitted diseases. Yet even simple, annoying genital infections that sometimes occur between a husband and a wife in a monogamous relationship can cause incredible stress.

Being informed is essential! This is not just the doctor's area, it is yours. After all, your body and your life are affected when infections invade. You need to be a partner in the medical process. Be aware of your own body and its reactions. Read everything available on the subject. Seek medical help to correct situations that might make you more susceptible to infections and to diagnose and treat symptoms already present. Be an active participant. Share any information that might add to or disagree with the physician's suggestions. It is your body!

Urinary Infections

Bladder Infections

Frequently labeled honeymoon cystitis, a bladder infection, or urethritis, an infection of the tube that carries urine from the bladder to outside the body, are among the most common female diseases. About 85 percent of women experience them. These occur frequently because the opening to the urinary tract is so close to the opening of the vagina—which is close to the opening to the anus, which is highly contaminated. Thus, infection-causing organisms can easily spread from the anal opening to the vaginal opening and on to the bladder opening. Sometimes contamination happens through wiping after toileting. This is the reason little girls should be taught to wipe from front to back. Most often, however, these urinary infections are contracted during sexual intercourse.

Because cystitis or urethritis is so common in new sexual relationships, we have sometimes suggested that honeymooners take prescribed medication along, particularly if they are going far away from home where consultation with their local physician would be difficult. The pain of cystitis can hit suddenly and be unbearable. Yet it can be relieved by medication almost as quickly as its onset.

We were in Hawaii on vacation several years ago when Joyce developed a bladder infection. In a matter of a few hours, this progressed from frequent urination to extreme pain. We attempted calling her gynecologist to have a prescription called in to the local pharmacy, only to discover that there were no pharmacies open on that side of the island after 5 P.M. on Friday until Monday morning. In addition, no physician licensed outside of the Hawaiian Islands was allowed to prescribe. While Cliff located a physician who would write a prescription, found a pharmacy that was open, and made a two-hour drive to get the needed remedy, Joyce soaked in a hot tub and drank water and cranberry juice, trying to get some relief. Not much relief was gained, however, until after the medication was taken. Then, within an hour, the intense pain was totally relieved.

There is a dilemma for the physician who prescribes a medication for cystitis before a urinary culture is taken. For Joyce's situation and for much of "honeymoon cystitis," that solution works fine. It's a once- or twice-in-a-lifetime infection that is easily corrected with antibiotics and doesn't recur. Not all women have it that easy.

A different type of bladder "infection" is *interstitial cystitis,* often referred to as *painful bladder syndrome.* It has been researched and written about by a woman urologist, Dr. Larrian Gillespie, who was frustrated by the typical medical approach to women who suffer from chronic painful bladders. What she discovered is that these women do not show bacteria present in their urine as do the women whose cystitis is easily relieved by antibiotics. In fact, when antibiotics are given to these women without first taking a urine culture to determine if bacteria are present, the antibiotics actually make the situation worse. The antibiotics "wipe off" the protective surface of the bladder and are one of the causes of interstitial cystitis, a disease in which the membrane lining of the bladder is destroyed. Because the protective lining is absent, the urine burns the bladder surface, like an acid burn, and eventually the bladder is no longer able to expand and contract. This obviously causes pain.

In fact, the symptoms for interstitial cystitis are the same as those of a bacterial cystitis: frequency of urination, burning pain, and cramps. The difference is the urinary tests show no bacteria, so antibiotics are not the treatment.

Dr. Gillespie has used Rhimo50 (a steroid), an experimental drug approved by the FDA only for this purpose, and sodium bicarbonate (baking soda) to reverse the acidity and allow the bladder cells to regenerate. DMSO, an industrial solution, also has been used. Scientists in the urology department of the San Diego Medical Center are currently researching treatment for the excruciating dilemma that has baffled many urologists. Dr. Naomi McCormick, Ph.D., in the psychology department at State University of New York at Plattsburgh, offers support to women who struggle with painful sex as a result of interstitial cystitis.

When all medical treatment has failed to relieve what seems to be chronic bladder infections, we recommend a "home remedy" we have found to be very effective. We cannot take credit for the idea. It was brought to us by women who have come to us for help. They have reported to us that after years of medical treatment, other women told them about this remedy, so they tried it—and it worked! Since reading the research by Dr. Gillespie, we assume the remedy works because it restores the natural flora of the entrance to the bladder and counteracts the infectious agents or irritations in the vagina. It also restores the acid-base balance of the woman's genitals. But these are only guesses. We claim no well-researched, scientific basis for this recommendation. Use it only with medical consent or when all other medical help has failed to correct the problem. We use the same approach for vaginitis when there is no infection present. And we find chronic bladder pain and vaginal irritation are often reported as occurring together. All these problems come to our attention because they lead to sexual dysfunction. Since we have been recommending this, we have also seen it recommended for vaginitis by Sylvia Close, a midwife who wrote from England.

This is the plan:

1. Eliminate or severely reduce sugar and artificial sweeteners in your diet. Unprocessed honey may be used in limited amounts.

2. If you are a sugar craver (many of these women are) or have hypoglycemic-type symptoms such as light-headedness between meals, eat fresh fruits (apples are best) and protein (yogurt, meat, cheese) between meals and a protein at bedtime.

3. Increase fresh fruits and vegetables. In fact, try to stick with fresh foods in general so that you eliminate chemical additives that are irritating to some people.

4. Take an all-purpose vitamin-mineral supplement that is high in the B vitamins.

5. The key recommendation is the use of natural, *unsweetened* plain yogurt. Apply it between the labia (lips), to the opening of the vagina, and insert it on a tampon in the vagina. It needs to be applied at least daily. Several times a day is even more effective. In addition, eat plenty of natural, unsweetened yogurt. It helps restore the normal bacteria and the acid-base balance throughout the body. If you can't

tolerate the taste, stir in a little unfiltered, frozen apple-juice concentrate and some cinnamon or fresh fruit.

We had been very hesitant about giving such unfounded recommendations until we received a desperate letter from a woman who had heard us on Dr. James Dobson's "Focus on the Family" radio broadcast.

She had been married five years and had never had sexual intercourse without contracting bladder pain. During those five years, she had continuous and excruciating bladder pain and even blood in the urine. She had consulted her family doctor first, then several urologists, several gynecologists, and finally the top urologist in her state. She and her husband followed a prescribed routine before and after every incidence of sexual intercourse. Their genitals and hands had to be freshly washed with soap and water, she was to urinate before and immediately after sexual intercourse, he was to use a condom to prevent the transfer of organisms from him, and she was to take antibiotics for a certain amount of time after each intercourse. She was now on continuous antibiotic treatment, but with no success. The physicians didn't have anything more to recommend. Her marriage was stressed, even though her husband was extremely understanding and cooperative. Her feelings about sex and herself were so negative that the relationship was suffering.

By the time we responded to her letter with a telephone call, she was suicidal. She was in terrible pain, hopeless and helpless, feeling guilty for not wanting sex with her husband.

We validated that all the traditional medical approaches had been tried and were being utilized. Then to give some hope, but not feeling that confident, we suggested our plan. By the way, we also determined that she was a sugar craver and had been told to cut down on sugar by her physician because of some hypoglycemic tendencies. She had recently had a glucose-tolerance test.

About three months later we received a note from her, thanking us for saving her life and her marriage. She said she had been pain-free for three months and also free of the "infection." She had begun using our program immediately after the call. She had not discontinued any of the medical prescriptions.

Sex was now a part of her life that she positively anticipated. She saw herself as a "normal woman" for the first time.

It was that experience that nudged us into deciding to share with you this "home remedy" plan for persistent, unsuccessfully treated bladder pain. To the best of our knowledge, it can do no harm, even though medically it is uncomfortable for us to publicize a program that has no scientific validation. Dr. Gillespie recommends a different dietary plan; either method is worth a try.

Painful urination and painful intercourse are not a "cross you have to bear." Bring Dr. Gillespie's information to your physician. (You may request more information from her through the American Foundation for Pain Research, 120 S. Spalding Drive, No. 210, Beverly Hills, Calif. 90212.) Or you can try our plan, or contact the Interstitial Cystitis Association, P.O. Box 1553, Madison Square Station, New York, N.Y. 10159 (telephone 212-979-6057). Keep seeking the help you need until you find it. If you encounter your first bladder-infection symptoms, ask your physician to do a urine culture before he or she starts you on your first dose of antibiotics. A urine culture will not be accurate if it's done after you have started antibiotics. The urine sample can be taken and antibiotics started (in the case of severe pain) before the results of the culture are determined. If no bacteria are present in the urine, the antibiotics should be stopped and other treatment pursued.

Genital Infections

In their natural state, the genitals are clean; the penis and the vagina are primarily free of disease-producing microorganisms. The clear, colorless, odorless secretions keep the genitals comfortably moist. Bacteria are present in the vagina, but these are friendly bacteria that help the body fight off infections. Sometimes women are found to have a few pathogens, disease-producing microorganisms, but with no other indications of infection. It is believed that the genitals can become contaminated from the anus or by other means. But when a person is in a healthy state, the pathogens may be warded off or lie dormant.

Genital infection may be caused by a fungus, a virus, or bacteria. The infection occurs because of an increase in the disease-producing microorganisms present in the genitals. These pathogens are most often sexually transmitted, although they may also invade the area after surgery or trauma. A person is more likely to acquire a genital infection when the environment of the genitals becomes unfavorable. For some reason the acid-base balance changes, the friendly bacteria of the vagina are destroyed, or the mucous membranes are sluggish. The conditions that may make a person susceptible to genital infections include taking the contraceptive pill or douching and altering the normal vaginal environment, taking antibiotics and destroying the friendly bacteria, or being generally run down or in ill health.

Can genital infections be avoided? Prevention can be enhanced by good health habits. A healthy body is a great protection against infections. Keep it healthy by adhering to the following guidelines.

Learn to lower the stress in your body. Taking charge of your life so that it works for you and learning to use relaxation techniques for those times when life gets the best of you emotionally are both beneficial. Time management, scheduling, prioritizing commitments are all a part of reducing stress. It helps to alternately tense and relax muscles until you can let your body feel limp as a rag doll. Then fill your lungs with air, breathe in through your nose and blow out in short breaths through your lips until you can't blow out any more. Or you can breathe slowly and deeply.

Understand nutrition. The effect of nutrition on the body is a wide-open field of study. Follow a diet that is varied and loaded with fruits, vegetables, and other fresh foods such as the whole grains and complex carbohydrates. Eat foods low in sugar and additives. There is controversy about whether the best sources of protein are plant sources (like soya and nuts) or animal sources (meats and dairy products). A balance of both is probably best. Avoiding red meats high in saturated fats is believed to have long-term benefit for the body. The latest medical advice is to keep your overall diet low in fat.

Practice careful hygiene. This is another protective measure. Being freshly washed before sexual intercourse reduces the possibility of contaminating the genitals from the anal opening. Girls and women need to learn to wipe from front to back, as we mentioned earlier. Since germs grow fastest in a warm, moist atmosphere, it is best to wear underwear that allows circulation of air (cotton rather than synthetics) and keeps the genitals clean and dry. Drying thoroughly after bathing is critical. Sometimes a blow-dryer set on low heat can be used to dry the genitals. Urinating before and after intercourse has been recommended as a technique to keep the genitals clear of infection since urine is sterile and acid, thus discouraging infections that like an alkaline environment. Condoms used for sexual intercourse can provide a barrier against invasive microorganisms, although they are not completely failsafe. Anal sex should be avoided because the rectum is full of germs that can cause infection of the genitals.

Since most genital infections are sexually transmitted, the most reliable of prevention is *sexual abstinence*. Since that is not ideal for most of us, the next best prevention method is the monogamous relationship of marriage.

Vaginal irritation, or vaginitis, joins bladder infections in causing havoc in sexual relationships. Sometimes these irritations may be caused by infection, other times by aging, allergic responses, or acid-base imbalances that are difficult to correct. Whatever the cause, the physical discomfort of vaginal irritation— the burning, itching, and tenderness—make sexual activity undesirable. That is why this is the most common genital "infection" reported in our offices. The symptoms must always be diagnosed and be treated by a physician for both the woman and her sexual partner. When no infection can be identified, but the symptoms persist, we recommend the plan for interstitial cystitis described earlier in this chapter. The use of plain, unsweetened yogurt is surprisingly soothing and healing. Apply it immediately for irritation.

Most often the infectious causes of vaginitis are Trichomonas (a parasite), Candida albicans (a fungus), and Hemophilus vaginalis, or gardnerella, (a bacterium). Symptoms include a change in the consistency, color, and smell of the vaginal discharge, as well as itching and burning sensations. Candida can be treated with terconazole, an antifungal agent. Trichomonas and gardnerella are treated with a prescription drug such as Flagyl (metronidazole).

Viral infections are the cause of *genital warts* and *herpes.* Both are highly contagious and have long-term effects. The warts, a precancerous condition, occur in both men and women, and are caused by Human Papilloma Virus (HPV) viruses. These viruses may be carried by a person and transmitted sexually long before they are detected or causing any symptoms. Even though they are painless, they are itchy and irritating, and they *are* a precancerous condition. All sexual partners of the affected person should be identified and treated. HPV infection has reached epidemic proportions. It may be the most common STD in the United States today. These viruses definitely are killing more women than AIDS. Their treatment can be expensive and extended over long time periods.

The blister-like sores of herpes can occur on the vulva or cervix of the woman and on the penis of the man. When they are caused by the herpes simplex virus type I (the cold-sore virus that usually occurs in or near the mouth and nose), they are relatively harmless. The more serious virus is the herpes simplex virus type II, which is associated with the genital area; it affects the whole body and never seems to leave. It can be a debilitating disease, in addition to causing incredible genital pain. The person suffers from general symptoms similar to any other viral infections, like the flu. But once a person is infected with herpes virus, the symptoms recur throughout his or her life. Zovirax (oral acyclovir), a prescription medication, can be given to lessen the severity of the outbreaks, but at this point there is no cure. It is essential that a pregnant woman report herpes to her physician. Active herpes at the time of delivery may cause damage to the newborn infant, and risk viral encephalitis, which can be fatal to the infant.

The age-old bacterial infections of gonorrhea and syphilis may seem to have disappeared with the national concern for herpes and AIDS. But like termites in a house, they fester and destroy the lives of their victims when not treated. Unfortunately, the antibiotics that have been effectively used to treat these infections are not as effective as they were previously. Gonorrhea, referred to as the clap or drip, is an extremely serious bacterial infection. Some of these bacteria have become resistant to the penicillin that used to cure them. These bacteria are transmitted during sexual intercourse. The symptoms of a burning sensation during urination and a greenish, smelly discharge can occur within three weeks of being infected. The dilemma is that 75 percent of infected women are asymptomatic carriers—they show no signs of being infected, yet they can transmit the disease to their sexual partners. The infection is not always limited to the genitals. It can travel into the uterus and the uterine tubes in the woman and throughout the body in both men and women, causing cardiac infections, brain infections, arthritis, and skin lesions. Should a woman be infected and untreated when her baby is born, the baby's eyes are subject to infection with the gonorrhea organism.

Before AIDS, *syphilis* was considered the most serious of all sexually transmitted diseases. It is transmitted from one person to another by direct contact. Ten to ninety days after contact, a chancre develops somewhere on the genitals, or on the cervix of the woman, or elsewhere in the body. This is the first or primary stage. Most women are not aware of this stage of the disease, so they go untreated unless the syphilis is detected by a blood test. If untreated, syphilis passes through secondary, latent, and tertiary stages. The secondary stage is characterized by a rash on the feet and hands, lack of appetite for food, fever, and sore throat. The disease circulates to every part of the body through the bloodstream.

The latent stage begins when the secondary stage symptoms recede. This is a hidden stage which can last as long as twenty years. It can be diagnosed by a blood test, treated, and stopped.

The tertiary stage is irreversible. The person is no longer infectious but the disease may have affected any or all of the vital organs of the body. Thus, the person may have brain damage, heart disease, spinal-cord damage, and blindness. This damage may demonstrate itself with severe mental disturbance, lack of coordination of voluntary movement (the syphilis shuffle), and general paralysis. If a pregnant woman is infected with syphilis, her unborn baby is at a great risk of being infected.

What about AIDS? It is one of the major health-care issues of our time, and the disease is on the increase. Until a cure is found or sexual caution is practiced, more and more people are going to be affected by it. Research will be continually supplying us with new information.

Acquired Immune Deficiency Syndrome (AIDS) slipped into medical awareness in 1981. The rapid increase in the number of cases and the frightening fatality rate continue to surpass the scientific data available. What we know now is that the AIDS patient's normal defense system against disease or invading foreign organisms is not working. In fact, the immune system is attacking the person's own body, rather than fighting off the invasion of infectious organisms and malignancies.

The HIV virus has been identified as the cause of AIDS. The virus causes this defect in the body's immune system by invading and then multiplying within the white blood cells, called the T-cells (T-lymphocytes). In fact, the Centers for Disease Control announced that as of January 1992, anyone with a decreased T-cell count of 200 will be diagnosed has having AIDS. The average life expectancy is predicted to be seven years from diagnosis.

We know that transmission of AIDS occurs through direct contact of body secretions, especially blood, semen, and vaginal secretions (fluids rich in T-lymphocytes). Sexual contact is the primary method of transmission. In the United States, about two-thirds of AIDS patients are homosexual or bisexual men. Transmission does occur heterosexually, however, most commonly from male to female. About 5 percent of AIDS patients are heterosexual. The risk increases with the number of sexual partners. The AIDS virus is also transmitted by blood-to-blood contact, such as through shared needles in IV drug abuse and through transfusions of blood products or blood from infected donors. (Blood products are a minimal risk at this time because of upgraded screening procedures.) About 20 percent of AIDS patients are intravenous drug abusers. The third way AIDS is transmitted is from mother to child during pregnancy and childbirth. There is no evidence at this time that the disease can be contracted through casual contact.

Once people are exposed to the AIDS virus, they progress through four stages, as described by the Centers for Disease Control. Shortly after infection (days or weeks), mononucleosis-like symptoms may occur. The AIDS victim has swollen glands and constant low-grade to high fever. About half of the infected persons experience these symptoms before Stage II sets in. Stage II is asymptomatic. This stage may last for several years. Stage III shows itself with enlargement of the lymph nodes (persistent generalized lymphadenopathy). These symptoms can come and go for three to five years before other, more serious disease appears. AIDS is most often diagnosed in its fourth stage.

AIDS is a severe immune deficiency, so that the person develops opportunistic infections—infections that a healthy person would be able to fight off. These infections can be bacterial, viral, fungal, and protozoal. It is the multiple infectious diseases that cause death for the victims of AIDS. The outlook is dreadful.

How can we protect ourselves against AIDS? It is natural for us to be anxious about a life-threatening disease that is connected with our sexuality. Sometimes when we are afraid we fail to get the facts clear. It is important to know that the AIDS virus is not spread through the air. It requires direct contact with body secretions or blood. We cannot breathe it in. That is why casual social contact with an AIDS victim is not of concern. The research also shows that AIDS is not likely to be communicated through saliva as in kissing. If the victim should have blood in the saliva, that would be dangerous. Obviously, direct contact should be avoided with blood, semen, vaginal secretion, and open wounds. It is not transmitted by contact with feces, nasal secretion, sputum, sweat, tears, urine, or vomitus, unless these fluids contain visible blood, according to *Contraceptive Technology 1990–1992,* page 72.

The only way to be certain of not being infected sexually is to avoid the contact with seminal fluid, blood, or vaginal secretions of someone who might have been exposed to the AIDS virus. How can we be sure of protecting ourselves from someone who has been exposed? One way that certainly reinforces biblical teaching is to have sexual contact only with one person and to know that you are that person's only sexual partner. Another way is to use a barrier in all sexual contacts so as to avoid exposing your body to any secretions that might be contaminated with the AIDS virus. Condoms used with the spermicide nonoxynol-9 have been shown to lessen the transmission of the AIDS virus. Nevertheless, there really is no "safe sex" when one partner is carrying the AIDS virus. The virus is much smaller than sperm. One can contract AIDS any day of the month. A woman can get pregnant only a few days of each month. Yet about 10 percent of women using condoms get pregnant. How much more likely one would be to contract AIDS, even when using condoms. If condoms are being used to protect against STDs, they must be used before any genital contact whatsoever!

Because AIDS may not develop until six months or up to five years after exposure, the only way to be sure that we are not involved with someone carrying the AIDS virus is to have the person tested for AIDS. There is, however, much controversy about who should be tested and when the test would be sure to be accurate. A marriage relationship in which neither spouse has ever strayed or been involved sexually before marriage is sexually the only safe protection against AIDS.

Other genital infections that are sexually transmitted have not been discussed here. Dr. Joe McIlhaney's book, *Sexuality and Sexually Transmitted Diseases,* is an excellent resource for both extensive information and for challenging attitudes that are necessary to change today's frightening increase in both the magnitude and the severity of sexually transmitted diseases, particularly in our young people.

For Further Study

Bennett, Jo Anne. "AIDS: Epidemology Update." *American Journal of Nursing,* 85, no. 9 (September 1985): 968–72.

Brackett, James W. *Condom Info Guide.* Durant, Okla.: Essential Medical Information Systems, 1988.

Close, Sylvia. *Sex During Pregnancy and After Childbirth.* San Bernardino, Calif.: Borgo Press, 1986.

Gillespie, Larrian. *You Don't Have to Live with Cystitis.* New York: Avon Books, 1988.

Hatcher, Robert A., M.D., et al. *Contraceptive Technology 1990–1992.* 15th rev. ed. New York: Irvington Publishers, 1990. 91–130.

Keeling, Richard P., M.D. "AIDS on Campus: What You Should Know." *Reports, The Journal of the Association of Universities and Colleges,* 28, no. 2 (March/April 1986): 24–28.

McCormick, Naomi B., Ph.D. and Robert K. Vinson, M.D. "Interstitial Cystitis: How Women Cope." *Urologic Nursing,* 9, no. 4 (April–June 1989): 11–17.

————. "Sexual Difficulties Experienced by Women with Interstitial Cystitis," *Women and Sex Therapy.* The Halworth Press, 1988.

McIlhaney, Joe S., Jr., M.D. *Sexuality and Sexually Transmitted Diseases.* Grand Rapids: Baker Book House, 1990.

Tseng, C. Howard, M.D., Ph.D., T. Guilas Villanueva, M.D., and Alvin Powell, M.D. *Sexually Transmitted Diseases.* Saratoga: R&E Publishers, 1987.

20

Sexual Addictions

The setting is a lovely middle-class home with a family of five. The children are all doing well in school. The mother is involved in the church and community. Father is a successful executive. One Sunday, the mother goes to church by herself because the father says he isn't feeling well. The kids are all gone for the weekend. Mother decides not to stay for the class that she usually attends after the morning worship service and so arrives home an hour earlier than expected. She walks into the bathroom to find her shocked husband dressed in women's clothes and a raving red wig, makeup, and jewelry. A piece of her dies right at that moment. Shock, horror, and despair blast both of them.

A missionary, home on furlough from Africa, is arrested for exposing himself to some teenage girls at the local public swimming pool. He has been a "faithful servant" for the past twenty years, a loving family man, and a caring and concerned minister of the gospel. His career is virtually ruined.

A seminary student writes from the Midwest, concerned that we are the only people with whom he can talk because we are far away and don't know him. He is planning a life of service in the church, but is plagued by a habit over which he cannot gain control. Once a week he acts on the compulsion to pick up a prostitute. He doesn't always complete the act, but he takes it to the point of being with the woman without clothes on in her room. How can he continue to "serve God," he asks, while he is carrying on in this manner?

A wife discovers a cache of pornographic photos and magazines stored in the garage. They range over a twenty-year period, are well worn and carefully filed. It had always seemed to her that her husband was a prude. He had been so vocal about his disdain for this type of material and the people who used it.

A gospel singer, who has had a very effective ministry, sits in tears as she tells about her inability to stop the habit of getting involved sexually with strange men in every city she visits. She grew up in a home with relatively little warmth and care. A sensitive and concerned youth pastor had recognized her talents and encouraged her to pursue them. As she did, she became well known and went on the road; but "the road" only led her deeper and deeper into a habit that had begun at age eighteen, almost by accident. She is now convinced that there is no way she can break the habit, and she lives in continual fear that she will be discovered. The woman is torn apart inside by the inconsistency of her public ministry and message, and the real life that she leads.

The wife of a local church leader sobs out her story of pain and despair as she tells how her husband, who is superintendent of the primary Sunday school department in a large evangelical church, has been discovered to be molesting his own three- and five-year-old daughters. Always so caring and loving with children, he seems like such a sensitive man. He gives so much of himself to the children under his care and is such a loving father, adored by everyone, including his own children. Now the wife is in a heart-wrenching dilemma as to what she should do. One side of her says she should leave him to protect her children from him. The other side feels that she would be taking a very important and special person away from her children and herself. The economic factors only make it worse. What should she do?

Each of these true stories represents a world of dilemmas now thought of as sexual addictions. In the past we have always referred to these as perversions, deviations, self-gratification, or sin. They may be all of those, but while getting control of the behaviors it is helpful to understand them as addictions. Usually those engaged in these behaviors despise themselves and their activities. They feel they can't gain control of the behavior. They cannot stop what they are doing. It is as if they are driven to it, acting as if they were on remote control. Their situation is similar to that of the alcoholic who has to have a drink, or the drug addict who must get a fix.

The New York Times (16 October 1984) reported this new understanding of addictive sexual behaviors, which has been voiced by many authorities. About six years ago, we also came to the conclusion from our own practice that these behaviors should be looked on as addictions. The repetitive pattern and lack of cure convinced us. An individual would get control of the behavior, and then a year or two later find himself or herself right back into it. We observed the "out-of-control" quality of the behavior, and the desperation that was felt by the individual as he or she tried to get control. A few years later, we discovered the 1983 book *Out of the Shadows* by Patrick Carnes. The author had developed a detailed theory for both understanding and working with the sexual addict in the same way that AA works with the alcoholic. He found the treatment to be effective. He has written a sequel, *Contrary to Love: Helping the Sexual Addict,* that is helpful for therapists.

The 1984 *New York Times* article quotes a number of others who are coming to this same conclusion. The findings of both Dr. Mark Schwartz from Tulane University in New Orleans and Dr. John Mahoney from Johns Hopkins Medical School are consistent with our own clinical experience, and confirm the addictive pattern of these sexual deviations.

The Pattern of Sexual Addictions

Sexual addiction is similar to an alcohol or drug addiction. Sexual addicts develop a dependence on the sexual gratification. The dependence becomes so powerful that it supersedes family, job, and even self-esteem; the sexual addict is "hooked." He or she leads a secret, double life—in many ways a distorted life. These addicts convince themselves that their behavior is justifiable.

The New York Times article summarizes the key criteria of a sexual addiction:

Having a sexual preoccupation that interferes with a normal sexual relationship with one's spouse.

Feeling compelled to have sexual relations again and again within a short period of time.

A compulsion to engage in sexual behavior that leaves one feeling anxious and depressed or guilty and ashamed.

Taking large amounts of time from family or work to engage in sex and to look for sexual adventure.

Being driven to sex as a means to hide from the troubles of one's life.

In the autumn 1982 issue of *Leadership* magazine, an anonymous pastor wrote an article entitled, "The War Within: An Anatomy of Lust." In the article the pastor outlined his struggle over a ten-year period with pornographic magazines, movies, videos, topless and bottomless bars, and peep shows. While he didn't use the word addiction, he described it similarly to others who outline the addictive process. The distorted thinking, the rationalizations, the blame on others, and the delusions that this pastor described as part of his painful pilgrimage all fit closely with Carnes's understanding of sexual addictions.

Sexual addicts go through a clear cycle. Carnes lists four stages in the cycle. First they talk about *preoccupation*. The individual begins to be obsessed with the desire for the addictive behavior, finding it difficult to think about anything else. One man told us that as he moved into his addictive pattern, he was carried along by a power over which he had no control. Totally possessed or engulfed by the preoccupation, he *had* to make the obscene phone call.

After this comes the *ritual* step. This step can help determine whether or not a behavior is an addiction. These rituals are predictable thought patterns and actions that precede or prepare for the actual behavior. The rationalizations are part of this ritualistic process.

The third step is the *behavior,* itself. The addicts are compelled through the behavior to the point where they are satiated. This may come after a certain level of arousal or after masturbation has taken place. One patient had a compulsion to have sex with several different women a day. He found that once a woman had her first orgasm he was looking for a way out of the situation even before he climaxed. It was the woman's orgasm that was his addiction. Once he had been able to give her an orgasm, he felt free of the drive to be with her.

Carnes's fourth step is *despair.* After the compulsive behavior is completed, relief is felt. Then the self-depreciating, bitter, hopeless despair comes raging through the addicts' total beings. They try to move back into normal life and responsibilities. There is great resolve never to do this again, prayer for forgiveness, plans for how it will be stopped the next time the temptation is present, and an avalanche of self-deprecating messages. There is renewed determination that this will never occur again. When the obsessive thoughts begin again the next day, a week later, or two months later, the addict feels caught in a trap from which he or she cannot escape. The anonymous pastor talks about the hundreds of prayers that he had said as a way of attempting to break the addictive cycle. None of them seemed to do any good.

No doubt you have noticed that we continually use the masculine pronoun in these descriptions. While there are women who get caught in the web of sexual addiction, men are the main ones who find themselves enmeshed in it. So to simplify the writing, we'll refer primarily to the male gender.

The Types of Sexual Addictions

As defined by Carnes, there are three levels of sexual addiction. The first level is those behaviors that do not go against another person's will, although at a deeper level they may violate someone. The second level is acts that violate another person's rights and have legal implications. On the third level are those addictions that include physical violation. Let's talk about each of these.

Level 1: Addictive Heterosexual Relationships

The habit of needing to conquer, possess, or subdue a man or a woman on a frequent basis is seen as an addiction. The person may be married and have a happy family, but be driven to be sexually involved with total strangers without any kind of relationship. This driven behavior will eat away at the addict's marriage, open him up to contracting sexually transmitted diseases, and set up incredible emotional turmoil. The stress heightens as his victims "fall in love" with him, and he seeks to find a way out.

A Christian leader, well-respected in his church community, was so driven by his compulsion for other women that he was unable to find the time to make the arrangements with his various women. So he corralled his secretary into setting up these appointments for him. This obsessive need to conquer sexually may be acted out within a marriage. The man limits himself to his wife, but makes excessive demands on her for a sexual experience three, four, even five times a day.

Involvement with prostitution is another first-level addiction. The excitement is often gained from the thrill of getting connected with the woman, negotiating where, what activity, and for how much, and paying the money. The risks are high—not only in terms of arrest and disease, but also to the addict's career and reputation. Yet for some, this is an outlet they are unable to control.

Homosexual contacts would be similar. Usually these are brief contacts that occur in public places with no development of a relationship. Again, there is a high risk of disease and discovery, as well as all the shame and guilt that accompanies the activity.

Preoccupation with *pornographic material* in either magazines, movies, videos, or live form is one of the most common forms of sexual addiction. The common rationalization is that the activity hurts no one. Yet the victims feel that gnawing sense of guilt inside themselves. The time taken away from their wives and children to indulge their addiction is engrossing. The money spent is also an issue. Most devastating are the lies and deceit necessary to carry on the habit. Many people occasionally look at a pornographic magazine and don't get hooked. They are not driven, controlled by, or secretive about it. Their interest in the material does not fit the addictive cycle.

Cross-dressing or transvestism, although often not thought of as similar to the addictive behaviors, does have the same cyclic addictive qualities. Transvestism is the habit of dressing in the clothes of the opposite sex. This is usually a man dressing in women's clothes for the purpose of sexual arousal, many times masturbation to ejaculation. The pattern generally begins by early adolescence, age twelve to fourteen. The young boy finds himself attracted to trying on female garments, especially panties, bras, girdles, nylons, slips, and shoes. Most boys go through a time of innocent curiosity about women's makeup, garments, and so on, but usually this is at an earlier age.

The addiction occurs when the secretive activity sets off arousal while the person is experimenting. He responds to the arousal with self-stimulation, which seals the habit. It is important to recognize that this is not a gender-identity problem; it does not mean that the person is homosexual. Yes, some homosexuals do dress in women's clothing to attract other men, but the transvestite dresses privately or with a woman partner solely for the purpose of genital arousal. These men are strongly attracted heterosexually. As the habit develops, the man is compelled to act out his obsession regularly. Some men keep a suitcase of clothes in the trunk of their cars, or at their offices, up in the attic, or in the garage so they can indulge the addiction as it grips them.

Some men desire their wives or other partners to participate in the sexual activity with them. They want to make love in the women's clothes or have the woman participate in dressing them. This habit may have developed as the addict was a little boy being dressed up as a girl by his older sisters. If arousal occurred in those experiences, it may have hooked him. For one man, this was a one-time event that occurred when he was twelve years old. His fifteen-year-old sister and her friends decided to dress him in their clothes. It was very arousing for him, but also embarrassing. This combination of the arousal with the uncomfortable feelings seemed to be the hook.

Even though these Level 1 addictions do not go against anyone's will, they certainly leave the victim with an internal battle as he attempts to reconcile his behavior with his Christian faith and view of himself. His exposure always brings trauma to his loved ones.

Level 2: Violation of Another Person's Rights, with Legal Implications

The Level 2 addicts, as Carnes points out, are violators of another person's rights; their behaviors have legal implications. The first of these behaviors is *exhibitionism*. The exhibitionist deliberately exposes his sexual organs with the intention of evoking a response from the observer. He may wear clothes that easily allow the genitals to be exhibited, flashing them from under a coat, exhibiting them through a window or at a public beach. It has been our finding that Christian people, especially the Christian leaders, involved in exhibitionism, have been raised in tightly restrictive homes. One would least expect them to be involved in this kind of activity. They are not violent, and in fact, they will shun violence. They experience themselves as inadequate sexually and are attempting to bolster their view of themselves by eliciting a shocked response from their female observers.

Voyeurism is the habit of obtaining gratification by observing others in the nude or engaged in sexual activity. It is natural for anyone to take a second look if he or she walks by a window and sees a provocative scene. This is not voyeurism. Voyeurism is the compulsion to get sexual gratification from peeping into windows. The purpose of voyeurism is to find some location where the sexual activity can be observed without the onlooker being detected, usually bringing sexual arousal, self-stimulation, and ejaculation for the Peeping Tom. One traveling evangelist told us that he would often spend three to four hours a night searching for window scenes in his home town. He would follow a ritual that had been established, but when he was traveling, he would have to establish a new ritual.

This habit may begin inadvertently. One man, now in his mid-thirties, told us that he had been walking home from school late one night after basketball practice and through a window observed two sisters changing clothes. As they continued their activity he became more engrossed and aroused. This began an almost-daily habit that has been most difficult to break. He had stopped the "peeping" for several years at a time, but then suddenly found himself back in the habit. The risks were great, the possibility of arrest and shame high. After a close shave with the law, the voyeurist may get control for a while. He is usually not considered dangerous or violent.

Indecent or *obscene phone calls* are illegal, inappropriate, and offensive sexual behavior. Occasionally adolescents will, on a lark, make offensive phone calls. We would not call that an addiction. But there are those adults who become habitual callers, getting their sexual arousal from making phone calls that become more and more sexually explicit. The caller may ask questions or describe sexual behavior while he stimulates himself. The hope is that the listener will not hang up the phone, and perhaps even talk to him. While this kind of call-in "service" is now available for a fee in many of the larger cities, it doesn't bring the same gratification as is found when the caller imposes himself on an unwilling victim.

A man in his late twenties came to us saying he was controlled by his drive to make obscene phone calls. He had done it so much during his seminary years that he had been discovered and arrested. He had stopped for a short time and then fallen back into the process again; he hated himself for it. He recognized how much it violated his beliefs and commitment, yet he was unable to stop himself. At one point he had gone to a healing meeting and had "the demon" cast out of him. This lasted for several months; then the habit returned. He was not able to get control until he faced the reality that this, indeed, was an addiction, and needed to be treated as such. He recognized that the desire, the impulse, would always be there but that he could gain control of the behavior.

The last form of Level 2 addictions is the *fetish*. A fetish is an attachment to an object for sexual arousal and release. For example, stealing may become part of a fetish. Or the fetish habit may remain an innocent activity that involves the use of some article of clothing, such as men's or women's shoes. The addiction will have developed in a similar way to cross-dressing. During childhood or early adolescence, the person developed a sexual attachment to an object as a source of sexual response. Now the desire for that connection controls the person.

Level 3: Behaviors That Violate Another Individual by Force and Violence

The third level of sexual addictions includes behaviors such as child molestation, incest, rape, and some forms of sado-masochistic behavior. The victim is a necessary part of the sexual arousal. Please refer to the previous chapter on abuse for details on these most painful addictions.

These addictions are not limited to the evil, wicked world. They are happening to Christians. Emotional trauma that is experienced later in life seriously affects the sexual adjustment of the addicts' victims. Many such stories were shared in the previous chapter.

The Sexual Addict

The sexual addict may be a successful businessman, popular pastor, caring father, attractive male, or the friendly neighbor next door. There is a tendency to label the addict as a sick pervert who needs to be locked up. But we meet them face to face in our everyday world. These people don't look different, but they come out of a world of deprivation and pain. As you hear their stories, their addictive behavior makes sense. This does not excuse them or rid them of the responsibility, but it helps us love them.

We think, for example, of the man who was continually told by his father how inadequate he was. He was not enough of a man. He would never amount to anything. It was too bad that he wasn't like his masculine brothers and cousins. As an adult, this person frequented homosexual video and peep shows where he would look for a homosexual to stimulate him to orgasm. He would leave, feeling that he had confirmed all the disgrace that had been heaped on him in his growing years.

This feeling of inadequacy is typical of almost all the addictions listed. There is an overwhelming sense of inadequacy. These men feel that they are not worthwhile people. They are despicable, not worthy of love, and not able to have their needs met. The hope behind this addictive drive is to at least get their sexual needs met. They experience sex as their most basic need and the only source of fulfillment in life. Carnes noted that these basic dimensions of the self-concept are foundational for each person who is addicted. He also points out that as the habit is continually practiced, a person may move from a Level 1 involvement to Level 2 and sometimes Level 3.

The Addict's Family

The addict's wife may not know about the habitual behavior, but there are often ways in which she participates in perpetuating it, just as the spouse may contribute to an alcoholic's uncontrolled drinking. In dealing with sexual addictions, both the husband and wife will probably need help in order for the addict to gain control. The family members are often victims of the frustration and irritation that the sexual addict expresses. This results from the loss of time, money, and involvement.

If a sexual addiction should be detected in your family, we encourage you to get help in facing the problem. Recognize the addiction as such and deal with it as a habit pattern. In acknowledging that it is an addictive habit, you gain the possibility of realistic control of the behavior.

Treating the Sexual Addict

The addict must face himself honestly if he is going to change. That is the starting point. He looks in the mirror and says, "I am out of control. I am devastating my life. I am hurting the people I love the most. I need to stop what I am doing and get control of this activity." An outside event may initiate the realization. Sometimes an arrest will force the reality. Other times it will be a more internal experience of the sexual addict "coming to himself." It is like the story of the prodigal son who was so hungry he wished he could eat out of a pig's trough. The Bible says, "And when he came to himself he said. . . ." The sexual addict must face himself for who he is. He must recognize how he has drifted down the path of pain and degradation, and accept his inability to help himself.

The person who is hooked on a sexual activity must be able to acknowledge out loud to himself and to at least one important other individual that he is a voyeurist, an exhibitionist, an abuser, or whatever his addiction may be. He must admit that he is helpless to do anything about his problem and that to gain control he needs outside help. He is forced to rely on God. This is demonstrated by Alcoholics Anonymous, which talks about the need to rely on a higher being from whom we can gain strength. Facing themselves and acknowledging their addiction and their need for outside help is necessary to help addicts gain control of their lives. At an AA meeting it is always striking for someone to get up to tell his story and say, "Hi. My name is Tom. I'm an alcoholic." As you listen to his story you may realize that he has not had a drink for the past twenty years, but he still calls himself an alcoholic in the present tense.

The sexual addict must speak about himself in the same way. If he were speaking at a Sexaholic Anonymous meeting, he should stand up and say, "Hi! My name is Tom. I'm an exhibitionist," even if he hasn't exposed himself for the last five years. The hardest thing for the sexual addict to accept is the lifelong compulsive nature of his addiction. Long after he gains control of the behavior, the impulses will come to the surface when he is emotionally or physically depleted, under heavy stress, relationally troubled, or spiritually dry.

It may be painful to think of yourself as a sexual addict for the rest of your life. Yet clinical experience confirms this perspective. As counselors, we work to uncover the circumstances that form the ritual around which the activity got started, identify that pattern or cycle of behaviors, and then cut into that pattern as decisively as possible. Your helper needs to be your ally—someone you can be open with and accountable to. It could be a spouse, friend, lay counselor, or professional. We deal with this extensively in *Counseling for Sexual Disorders*.

One man who for years had a habit of being involved with prostitution shared his problem with his Bible study and prayer group at his church. They became his allies. He became accountable to them for his behavior on a weekly basis. We have lost touch with this individual now, but for the first two years after he began this process he had complete victory over his habit of contacting prostitutes.

Groups are being formed to help individuals deal with their sexual addictions. These can be found through Alcoholics Anonymous, sexual-therapy centers, or sexual therapists. They may be called Sexual Addicts Anonymous or Sexaholics Anonymous. There may be other groups by different names. Do some research. Get an endorsement from someone you trust. It has been found that when people work with the same twelve steps that alcoholics use in the AA program, and have the group's support, they can get their addictions under control.

Finding the balance between the psychological and spiritual dimensions of sexual addictions really tests our capacity to integrate. For those who have a vital relationship with God, their relationship with Him will need to be dealt with. The anonymous writer of the "lust" article points out that in the Beatitudes the message is, "Blessed are the pure in heart for they shall know God." As people become more and more involved in their addiction, they also move farther and farther away from God. In the article, the anonymous pastor suggested the following ten steps that can help one fight the battle against addiction. We have added our comments in parentheses.

1. Recognize and name the problem. (This is difficult but necessary.)

2. Stop feeding lust. (Don't keep putting yourself in situations that trigger your patterns. For example, if your long walks in the evening are your opportunity to look in windows, walk in broad daylight. If you need your wife along on business trips to keep you from visiting prostitutes, then take her along.)

3. Demythologize it. (When someone is hooked on a sexual addiction, a myth will generally develop around that activity. Face the reality that the shock people experience when you expose yourself to them or make obscene calls to them is really disgust and surprise, not sexual arousal.)

4. Confess its real price. (Be realistic about the cost in terms of time, energy, money, relationships, anxiety, guilt, and worry, in relationship to yourself, your spouse, your family, your friends, and God.)

5. Trace its history. (Whenever we are dealing with a habit pattern that we are trying to break, it is important to understand how it got started. Become aware of all the little steps along the way that

led to this point. Write those out. Add to them as further thoughts come to mind.)

6. Study sex in perspective. (Keep in mind that the misuse of sex is an immoral, destructive, dirty activity but sex itself is a wholesome, God-ordained activity. The marriage bond is used throughout the Scriptures to symbolize God's relationship to His people. For a detailed account of this, see *The Gift of Sex.*)

7. Build fantasies on God's ideal. (As one of our friends put it, "Don't commit adultery in your mind, commit marriage." Guide your fantasies away from the obsession and in the direction of your spouse or hoped-for spouse.)

8. Work on some positive addictions. (As an addictive person, get yourself hooked on a constructive habit such as jogging, writing poetry—or feeding canaries! It really doesn't matter as long as it builds and enhances both you and your relationships.)

9. Recognize the humanity of your victims. (Whether these are the girls you are watching through the peep-shows or the girls you are violating, be aware that they have human needs and feelings. You are either invading their privacy or hurting their person.)

10. Obsession comes out of a legitimate set of anxieties; follow them to their authentic source. (Get a deep understanding of what is behind your obsession. It may be a need for affection, self-esteem, a father-figure, or a mother in your life. The better you understand what is behind your obsession, the more control you will gain. In addition, be accountable to someone for your addictive behavior.)

Conclusion

Sexual addictions are a serious dilemma in our society and in the church. They drain productive energy, distort reality, and destroy lives. Sexual addicts need our help and understanding just as much as schizophrenics or cancer patients do. We invite you to be open, loving, and understanding—but tough in your demands for control. We want to send a message of hope to those who struggle with these troublesome desires that rage so out of control.

For Further Study

Anonymous. "The War Within: An Anatomy of Lust." *Leadership*. Autumn 1982.

Carnes, Patrick, Ph.D. *Out of the Shadows*. Minneapolis: CompCare Publishers, 1985.

————. *Sexual Addiction Inventory*. Golden Valley, Minn.: Institute for Behavioral Medicine, 1988.

————. *Contrary to Love: Helping the Sexual Addict*. Minneapolis: CompCare Publishers, 1989.

————. *A Gentle Path Through the Twelve Steps*. Minneapolis: Compcare Publishers, 1989.

Hope and Recovery: A Twelve-Step Guide for Healing from Compulsive Sexual Behavior. Minneapolis: CompCare Publishers, 1987.

Hunter, Mic. *The First Step—For People in Relationships with Sex Addicts*. Minneapolis: CompCare Publishers, 1989.

Penner, Joyce J., and Clifford L. Penner. *Counseling for Sexual Disorders*. Dallas: Word, 1990.

Bibliography

Abramson, Paul R. *Sarah: A Sexual Biography*. Albany: State University of New York Press, 1984.

Allgeier, Elizabeth Rice, Ph.D. "Research Notes." Psychology Department, Bowling Green State University, Bowling Green, Ohio.

Alyson, Sasha, ed. *You Can Do Something About AIDS*. A public service project of the publishing industry, 1988.

Anderson, T. P., and T. M. Cole. "Sexual Counseling of the Physically Disabled." *Postgraduate Medicine,* 58 (1975): 117–23.

Andry, Andrew C., and Steve Schepp. *How Babies Are Made*. Boston: Little, Brown, and Co., 1984.

Anonymous. "The War Within: An Anatomy of Lust." *Leadership.* Autumn 1982.

Aral, Sevgi O., Ph.D., and Willard Cates, Jr., M.D. "The Increasing Concern with Fertility. Why Now?" *Journal of the American Medical Association,* 250, no. 17 (November 1983): 2327–31.

Barbach, Lonnie. *For Yourself: The Fulfillment of Female Sexuality.* New York: Anchor Books, 1979.

Bass, Ellen, and Laura Davis. *The Courage to Heal: A Guide for Women Survivors of Child Sexual Abuse.* New York: Harper and Row, 1988.

Bennett, Jo Anne. "AIDS: Epidemology Update." *American Journal of Nursing,* 85, no. 9 (September 1985): 968–72.

Berges, Emily, et al. *Children and Sex, The Parents Speak.* New York: Facts on File, 1983.

Bernstein, Judith, R.N., and John H. Matton, M.D. "An Overview of Infertility." *Journal of Obstetrical and Gynecological Nursing* (September/October 1982): 309–14.

Betancourt, Jeannie. *Am I Normal?* New York: Avon/Flare, 1983.

———. *Dear Diary*. New York: Avon/Flare, 1983. (Note: *Am I Normal?* was written for adolescent boys and is still available; *Dear Diary*, the companion book for adolescent girls, is out of print, but still available in many libraries.)

Bingham, Mindy, Judy Edmondson, and Sandy Stryker. *Choices: A Teen Woman's Journal for Self-Awareness and Personal Planning*. Santa Barbara, Calif.: Advocacy Press, a division of the Girls Club of Greater Santa Barbara, 1987. (This book is distributed by Ingram Book Co.—Bookpeople, LaVergne, Tennessee.)

———. *Challenges: A Young Man's Journal for Self-Awareness and Personal Planning*. Santa Barbara, Calif.: Advocacy Press, a division of the Girls Club of Greater Santa Barbara, 1984. (This book is distributed by Ingram Book Co.—Bookpeople, LaVergne, Tennessee.)

Bird, Joseph, and Lois Bird. "Reasons You May Never Have Considered for Staying Single." *New Woman* (January/February 1982): 102–3.

Brackett, James W. *Condom Info Guide*. Durant, Okla.: Essential Medical Information Systems, 1988.

Brecher, Edward M., and the editors of Consumer Reports. *Love, Sex, and Aging: A Consumer Union Report*. Boston: Little, Brown, and Co., 1986.

Buhler, Rich. *Pain and Pretending: You Can Be Free from the Hurts of the Past*. Nashville: Thomas Nelson Publishers, 1988.

Burns, Jim. *Handling Your Hormones*. Eugene, Oreg.: Harvest House Publishers, 1986. (We recommend both this text and its companion volume, *Handling Your Hormones, Growth Guide*.)

Calderone, Mary S., M.D., and Eric W. Johnson *The Family Book About Sexuality*. New York: Harper and Row, 1990. (This is a secular book in which moral values need to be differentiated.)

Cane, William. *The Art of Kissing*. New York: St. Martin's Press, 1991.

Carnes, Patrick, Ph.D. *Out of the Shadows*. Minneapolis: CompCare Publishers, 1985.

————. *Sexual Addiction Inventory*. Golden Valley, Minn.: Institute for Behavioral Medicine, 1988.

————. *Contrary to Love: Helping the Sexual Addict*. Minneapolis: CompCare Publishers, 1989.

————. *A Gentle Path Through the Twelve Steps*. Minneapolis: Compcare Publishers, 1989.

Christenson, Larry. *The Wonderful Way That Babies Are Made*. Minneapolis: Bethany House, 1982.

Clarkson, Margaret. "Singleness: His Share for Me." *Christianity Today* (16 February 1979): 14–15.

Close, Sylvia. *Sex During Pregnancy and After Childbirth*. San Bernardino, Calif.: Borgo Press, 1986.

Cole, Joanna. *Asking About Sex and Growing Up*. New York: Beech Tree Books, 1988.

Colgrove, Melba, Harold Bloomfield, and Peter Williams. *How to Survive the Loss of a Love*. New York: Bantam Books, 1984.

Comfort, Alex, and Jane Comfort. *The Facts of Love: Living, Loving, and Growing Up*. New York: Ballantine, 1986. (Parents need to add their values to the information in this book.)

*Cornelius, Debra, et al. *Who Cares? A Handbook on Sex Education and Counseling Services for Disabled People*. Baltimore: University Park Press, 1982.

Dickey, Richard P., M.D., Ph.D. *Managing Contraceptive Pill Patients*. 6th ed. Durant, Okla.: Essential Medical Information Systems, 1991.

————. *Oral Contraceptive User Guide*. Durant, Okla.: Creative Infomatics, 1987. 34–35.

Elstein, Max. "Effects of Infertility on Psychosexual Function." *British Medical Journal*, 2 (August 1975): 296–99.

*Elvenstar, Diane C. *Children: To Have or Not Have—A Guide to Making and Living with Your Decision*. San Francisco: Harbor Publishing, 1982.

Facts in Brief: Teenage Sexual and Reproductive Behavior in the United States. New York: Alan Guttmacher Institute, 1991.

Forbes, Cheryl. "Let's Not Shackle the Single Life." *Christianity Today* (16 February 1979): 16–19.

Forward, Susan, M.S.W., and Craig Buck. *Betrayal of Innocence: Incest and Its Devastation.* New York: Penguin Books, 1978.

*Foster, Richard J. *Money, Sex and Power.* San Francisco: Harper and Row, 1985.

Frank, Jan. *A Door of Hope.* San Bernardino, Calif.: Here's Life Publishers, 1987.

Gambrell, R. Don, Jr., M.D. *Estrogen Replacement Therapy.* Amityville, N.Y.: Essential Medical Information Systems, 1989.

"The Games Teenagers Play." *Newsweek* (1 September 1980): 48–53.

Gardner-Loulan, Jo Ann, Bonnie Lopez, and Marcia Quackenbush. *Period.* San Francisco: Volcano Press, 1990.

Gillespie, Larrian. *You Don't Have to Live with Cystitis.* New York: Avon Books, 1988.

Gordon, Sol, Ph.D. "Sexuality Education in the 1980s—No More Retreats." *The Journal of Sex Education and Therapy,* 8, no. 2 (Fall/Winter 1982).

Gordon, Sol, Ph.D., and Judith Gordon, M.S.W. *Raising a Child Conservatively in a Sexually Permissive World.* New York: Simon & Schuster, 1989. (This is a clearly secular approach to this topic.)

*Gow, Kathleen M. *Yes, Virginia, There Is a Right and Wrong.* Sun City: Fidelity House, 1985.

Greenwood, Sadja. *Menopause Naturally.* Volcano, Calif.: Volcano Press, 1989.

Grossman, Linda M., Ph.D., and Deborah Kowal, M.A. *Kids, Drugs, and Sex: Preventing Trouble.* Brandon, Vt.: Clinical Psychology Publishing Co., 1988.

"Guidelines for Effective School Health Education to Prevent the Spread of AIDS." *Morbidity and Mortality Weekly Report,* 37, no. S-2 (19 January 1988). Available from the U.S. Department of

Health and Human Services, Public Health Service, Centers for Disease Control, Atlanta, Ga. 30333.

Hancock, Maxine, and Karen Burton Mains. *Child Sexual Abuse: A Hope for Healing.* Wheaton, Ill.: Harold Shaw Publishers, 1987.

Hatcher, Robert A., M.D., et al. *Contraceptive Technology, 1990–1992.* 15th rev. ed. New York: Irvington Publishers, 1990.

Heiman, Julia, and Joseph LoPiccolo. *Becoming Orgasmic.* New York: Prentice Hall, 1988.

Herman, Judith Lewis. *Father-Daughter Incest.* Cambridge, Mass.: Harvard University Press, 1982.

Hock, Dean, and Nancy Hock. *The Sex Education Dictionary.* Pocatello, Idaho: Landmark Publishing, 1990.

Hope and Recovery: A Twelve-Step Guide for Healing from Compulsive Sexual Behavior. Minneapolis: CompCare Publishers, 1987.

Hummel, Ruth. *Where Do Babies Come From?* (Originally published in 1982 as *I Wonder Why?*) St. Louis: Concordia Publishing House, 1988.

Hunter, Mic. *The First Step—For People in Relationships with Sex Addicts.* Minneapolis: CompCare Publishers, 1989.

Jessner, L. "Pregnancy as a Stress in Marriage." In *Marital and Sexual Counseling in Medical Practice,* edited by D. F. Abse, E. M. Nash, and L. M. R. Louden. Hagerstown, Md.: Harper and Row, 1974.

Johnson, James R. "Toward a Biblical Approach to Masturbation." *Journal of Psychology and Theology,* 10, no. 2 (Summer 1982): 137–46.

Kaplan, Helen Singer, M.D., Ph.D. *The New Sex Therapy.* New York: Brunner-Mazel, 1974.

Kaplan, Helen Singer. *P.E.: How to Overcome Premature Ejaculation.* New York: Brunner-Mazel, 1989.

Keeling, Richard P., M.D. "AIDS on Campus: What You Should Know." *Reports, The Journal of the Association of Universities and Colleges,* 28, no. 2 (March/April 1986): 24–28.

*Keith, Louis G., ed. *The Safety of Fertility Control.* New York: Springer Publishing Co., 1980.

Ketterman, Grace H., M D. *How to Teach Your Children About Sex*. Old Tappan, N.J.: Fleming H. Revell Co., 1981. 7–76, 167–83.

*Kolodny, Robert C., et al. *Textbook of Human Sexuality for Nurses*. Boston: Little, Brown, and Co., 1979.

*Kolodny, Robert C., William H. Masters, and Virginia E. Johnson. *Textbook of Sexual Medicine*. Boston: Little, Brown, and Co., 1979.

Larson, David E., M.D., editor. *Mayo Clinic Family Health Book*. New York: William Morrow and Co., 1990. 1131–37.

Laury, G.V., M.D. "Myths About Masturbation Throughout the Ages." *Journal of Sex Education and Therapy,* 11, no. 5 (Summer 1979): 3–4.

Leman, Kevin. *Sex Begins in the Kitchen*. Ventura, Calif.: Regal Books, 1983.

Linton, Calvin D. "Dying to the God Who Is Me." *Christianity Today* (16 February 1979): 14–15.

London, Steve, and H. Jane Chihal. *Menopause: Clinical Concepts*. Amityville, N.Y.: Essential Medical Information Systems, 1989.

Mast, C. K. *Sex Respect: The Option of True Sexual Freedom*. Bradley, Ill.: Project Respect, 1986.

Masters, William H., and Virginia E. Johnson. *Human Sexual Inadequacy*. New York: Bantam, 1981.

Masters, William H., Virginia E. Johnson, and Robert C. Kolodny. *Masters and Johnson on Sex and Human Loving*. Boston: Little, Brown and Co., 1986.

*Mayle, Peter. *Where Did I Come From?* Secaucus, N.J.: Lyle Stuart, 1979.

———. *What's Happening to Me?* New York: Carol Publishing Group, 1979.

*Mayo, Mary Ann. *Parent's Guide to Sex Education*. Grand Rapids: Zondervan.

McCarthy, Barry. *Male Sexual Awareness*. New York: Carroll and Graf, 1988.

———, and Emily McCarthy. *Female Sexual Awareness*. New York: Carroll and Graf, 1989.

McDowell, Josh, and Dick Day. *Why Wait?* San Bernardino, Calif.: Here's Life Publishers, 1987.

McGinnis, Alan Loy. *The Romance Factor*. San Francisco: Harper and Row, 1990.

McIlhaney, Joe S., Jr., M.D. *1250 Health-Care Questions Women Ask*. Grand Rapids, Mich.: Baker Book House, 1988. Pages 505–53.

———. *Sexuality and Sexually Transmitted Diseases*. Grand Rapids: Baker Book House, 1990.

Menning, Barbara Eck. *Infertility: A Guide for the Childless Couple*. 2d. ed. New York: Prentice Hall, 1988.

Network Report. California Family Life Education. Fall 1981 to Summer 1991.

Nilsson, A. Lennart, Axel Ingelman-Sundberg, M.D., and Claes Wirsen, M.D. *A Child Is Born: The Drama of Life Before Birth*. Rev. ed. New York: Dell, 1989.

Nixon, Joan Lowery. *Before You Were Born*. Huntington, Ind.: Our Sunday Visitor, 1980.

O'Connor, Dagmar. *How to Make Love to the Same Person for the Rest of Your Life—and Still Love It*. New York: Bantam, 1986.

———. *How to Put the Love Back into Making Love*. New York: Doubleday, 1989.

*Oraker, James R., Ph.D. *Almost Grown: A Christian Guide for Parents of Teenagers*. New York: Harper and Row, 1980.

Penner, Clifford L., Ph.D. "A Reaction to Johnson's Biblical Approach to Masturbation." *Journal of Psychology and Theology,* 10, no. 2 (Summer 1982): 146–49.

Penner, Joyce J., and Clifford L. Penner. *Counseling for Sexual Disorders*. Dallas: Word, 1990.

———. *The Gift of Sex*. Waco, Tex.: Word, 1981.

———. *Premarital Video: The Gift of Sex*. Waco, Tex.: Word, 1981.

Penner, Julene M. *Childhood Sexual Abuse: A Risk Factor for Addictive Behavior in Adulthood*. Honors Thesis, Harvard University, 1990.

Prot, Viviane and Philippe Delorme, M.D. *The Story of Birth*. Ossining, N.Y.: Young Discovery Library, 1986.

Risk and Responsibility: Teaching Sex Education in American Schools Today. New York: Alan Guttmacher Institute, 1989.

Rosenfeld, David L., M.D., and Eileen Mitchell, B.S. "Treating the Emotional Aspects of Infertility: Counseling Services in an Infertility Clinic." *American Journal of Obstetrics and Gynecology,* 135, no. 2 (1979): 135, 177–80.

Schafly, Phyllis. "What's Wrong with Sex Education?" *The Phyllis Schafly Report,* 14, no. 7, section 1 (February 1981).

Seibel, Machelle M., M.D., and Melvin L. Taymor, M.D. "Emotional Aspects of Infertility." *Fertility and Sterility,* 37, no. 2 (February 1982): 137–45.

Shapiro, Constance Hoenk. *Infertility and Pregnancy Loss*. San Francisco: Jossey-Bass Publishers, 1988.

Shearer, Lloyd. "Teenage Sexuality." *Parade Magazine* (16 January 1983): 15.

Shedd, Charlie. *Letters to Karen*. Nashville: Abingdon, 1977.

———. *Letters to Phillip*. New York: Jove, 1985.

Sheffield, Margaret. *Where Do Babies Come From?* New York: Alfred Knopf, 1978.

Short, Ray E. *Sex, Love, or Infatuation: How Can I Really Know?* Minneapolis: Augsburg-Fortress Publishing House, 1990.

Smedes, Lewis B. *Sex for Christians*. Grand Rapids: William B. Eerdmans Publishing Co., 1976.

———. *Forgive and Forget: Healing the Hurt We Don't Deserve*. San Francisco: Harper and Row, 1984.

Smith, Harold Ivan. "Sex and Singleness the Second Time Around." *Christianity Today* (23 May 1979): 16–22.

Sowby, Sherman K. Sowby. "Problems of New Morality." A Home Study for Continuing Education for Registered Nurses.

Stoop, David A. "Moral Development." *Theology News and Notes* (March 1978).

Swindoll, Luci. *Wide My World; Narrow My Bed*. Portland, Oreg.: Multnomah Press, 1982.

Tseng, C. Howard, M.D., Ph.D., T. Guilas Villanueva, M.D., and Alvin Powell, M.D. *Sexually Transmitted Diseases*. Saratoga: R&E Publishers, 1987.

Values and Public Policy. Edited by Gerald P. Regier. Washington, D.C.: Family Research Council of America, 1988.

Wabbes, Marie. *How I Was Born*. New York: Tambourine Books, 1990.

Walker, Herbert E., "Sexual Problems and Infertility." *Psychosomatics,* 19, no. 8 (August 1978): 477–84.

Warren, Neil C. *Make Anger Your Ally*. Brentwood, Tenn.: Wolgemuth and Hyatt, 1990.

Whelan, Elizabeth M. *A Baby? Maybe: A Guide to the Most Fateful Decision in Your Life*. New York: Macmillan, 1980.

Whitman, Frederick L. "Childhood Predictors of Adult Homosexuality." *Journal of Sex Education and Therapy,* 6, no. 2 (Fall/ Winter 1980).

Wilder, E. James. *Just Between Father and Son*. Downers Grove, Ill.: InterVarsity Press, 1990.

Wilger, Thomas, M.D. *The Ovulation Method of Natural Family Planning* 2d ed. Omaha: Pope Paul VI Institute for the Study of Human Reproduction, 1983.

Williams, Warwick. *Rekindling Desire: Bringing Your Sexual Relationship to Life*. Oakland, Calif.: New Harbinger Publications, 1988.

Wood, Barry. *Questions Teenagers Ask about Dating and Sex*. Old Tappan, N.J.: Fleming H. Revell Co., 1981.

*This book is no longer in print but is still available in many public or medical libraries.

Subject Index

abdomen, protruding, 248
abnormalities, anatomical, 75
abortion, 20, 28, 33, 57, 67, 71, 72, 139, 161
  spontaneous, 73–75
abstinence, 21, 22, 34, 138, 140, 148, 170, 187, 192, 194, 195, 254, 294
  following childbirth, 78
abuse,
  child, 266–85, 302
  consequences of, 272
  evidence of, 283
  physical, 178, 185, 220, 268
  sexual, 123–25, 168, 178, 265–85, 302, 312
  statistics of, 266
accidents, sexual, 143
acne, 31, 176
adaptation, 62, 219
addiction, 313
  drug, 140
  sexual, 301–14
adolescence, 3, 53, 108, 109, 133, 138, 146, 164, 170, 277, 307
adolescents, 135, 141–53, 160, 161, 170, 171, 176
adoption, 3, 4, 53, 58, 60–63, 139
adultery, 269, 314
adulthood, transition to, 68
affection, 100, 102, 123, 135, 151, 189
affirmation, 135, 143, 150, 153, 195, 228, 231

AIDS, 23, 139, 140, 166, 168, 171–73, 177–79, 187, 287, 295–99
alcohol, 40, 150, 198, 249, 254, 268, 277
Alcoholics Anonymous, 312, 313
alcoholism, 234, 256, 303
allergic reactions to spermicide, 24
anatomy and physiology, sexual, 171
androgen, 250, 251
anemia, 75, 234, 248
anger, 54–58, 86, 102, 229, 230, 268, 275, 282, 283
anus, 83, 288, 292, 294
anxiety, 54, 75, 79, 81, 88, 151, 212, 215, 238, 247, 313
arousal, 45, 49, 59, 171, 189, 193, 214, 252, 253
  sexual, 80, 85, 89, 103, ·141, 144, 198, 201, 207–9, 212, 215, 227, 228, 233, 237–39, 259, 304, 307–10
artificial insemination, 42, 45
assisted decision making, 135, 149–51
atherosclerosis, 250
awareness, sexual, 197, 208, 256
awkwardness, 129, 132, 142, 210
  during pregnancy, 70

babies, 4, 5
  "Where do babies come from?", 119–21
bacteria, 291–96
barrier method of birth control, 23, 27

DR. CLIFFORD PENNER is a clinical psychologist with Associated Pyschological Services in Pasadena, California. He holds an M.A. degree in theology and a Ph.D. in psychology from Fuller Theological Seminary. **JOYCE PENNER** holds an M.N. in nursing from the University of California-Los Angeles and an R.N. from Mounds Midway School of Nursing, St. Paul, Minnesota. The Penners conduct sexual-enhancement seminars and work together in sexual therapy. They also teach sex education in public and private school settings. They are the authors of the best-selling *The Gift of Sex, A Couples Guide to Sexual Fulfillment,* and *Counseling for Sexual Disorders.*